HERDING THE MOO
As told by Joe Smith

Order this book online at www.trafford.com/06-0269
or email orders@trafford.com

Most Trafford titles are also available at major online book retailers.

© Copyright 2007 Joe Smith.

All rights reserved. No part of this publication may be reproduced, stored in a retrieval system, or transmitted, in any form or by any means, electronic, mechanical, photocopying, recording, or otherwise, without the written prior permission of the author.

Note for Librarians: A cataloguing record for this book is available from Library and Archives Canada at www.collectionscanada.ca/amicus/index-e.html

Printed in Victoria, BC, Canada.

ISBN: 978-1-4120-8514-4

We at Trafford believe that it is the responsibility of us all, as both individuals and corporations, to make choices that are environmentally and socially sound. You, in turn, are supporting this responsible conduct each time you purchase a Trafford book, or make use of our publishing services. To find out how you are helping, please visit www.trafford.com/responsiblepublishing.html

Our mission is to efficiently provide the world's finest, most comprehensive book publishing service, enabling every author to experience success. To find out how to publish your book, your way, and have it available worldwide, visit us online at www.trafford.com/10510

www.trafford.com

North America & international
toll-free: 1 888 232 4444 (USA & Canada)
phone: 250 383 6864 ♦ fax: 250 383 6804
email: info@trafford.com

The United Kingdom & Europe
phone: +44 (0)1865 722 113 ♦ local rate: 0845 230 9601
facsimile: +44 (0)1865 722 868 ♦ email: info.uk@trafford.com

10 9 8 7 6 5

Praise for Herding the Moo

New Book Exposes Martial Arts Cult

When I was publishing Martial Arts Professional Magazine, I did a three part story called *Cult of the Quan* that provided an inside story to the Chung Moo Quan cult. The story generated a lot of buzz and concern. About the same time, the Reverend Moon held a huge event for martial arts with the expressed goal of "taking over martial arts."

With its myths and mystical background, the very nature of Master, Grand Master, Supreme Grand Master and Divine Grand Master titles and followers seems to invite eccentric leaders and organizations.

Herding the Moo is the title of a new book by Joe Smith. While it seems pretty clear Joe Smith is a pen name, the story he tells is one every school owner could benefit from learning about. It's a story of influence, abuse and classic cult-like tactics designed to break down the student's resistance while gaining control of all of his or her personal wealth. The organization was created by John "Iron" Kim in the mid-70s as the Chung Moo Doe school. The name has changed a few times and is now Oom Yung Doe — http://www.oomyungdoe.com.

This story is amazing and scary. This is a must read for a school owner.

John Graden, Martial Arts Teachers Association

Review of Herding the Moo

Every once in awhile an experience comes along in the form of something we read or see or even smell, that produces vivid recollections of one's past to the point that a person can forget who they are now, and only recall what they were like during that time. Almost against one's will, a person thinks the same thoughts, acts in the same ways, and feels the same fears, as they did during that time. When the memories evoked are of one's time in a destructive cult, the recollections can be that much more powerful, even overwhelming. This was akin to what I felt as I read Joe Smith's book *Herding the Moo*

Exploits of a Martial Arts Cult, about his experiences in a destructive cult thinly disguised as a legitimate martial art, the same cult that I was involved in for six years while a teenager.

This was the group headed by John C. Kim, a.k.a. Jack Park, a.k.a. Chong Su Nim "Iron" Kim, the self-proclaimed top martial arts master in the world, even claiming to hold the championship title for a martial arts tournament which so far as anyone can tell, has never taken place. The martial art, the front used to draw people in, has gone by various names during its existence, many of which had *Moo* in the name, hence the title of the book. Names like Chung Moo Quan, Chung Moo Doe and Oom Yung Doe are those the organization has used in its commercial side; also more innocuous sounding and general names like 8 Martial Arts for Health.

The other part of the title, *Herding*, is an excellent description of the true aims of this organization; which were to use mind control tactics and intimidation on its members until they truly became like cattle, following blindly to each edict and directive issued by Kim the organization's leader; filtered down to the "herd" by equally intimidated and controlled senior-level members, who were the so-called instructors.

As a former member of the group Mr. Smith writes about, it struck an especially powerful chord with me. I recognize the book's intense focus on mind control solely as it was practiced within the Moo organization. People not familiar with how the Moo worked and the level of fear that the group's management instilled in the individual will be puzzled at Mr. Smith's descriptions of various Moo-centric practices, such as the organization's unique loaded language come to be known as Moo-speak. Though destructive cults share many common characteristics and practices, as explained in Steve Hassan's B.I.T.E. model, how each organization goes about manipulating and exploiting people has a unique signature. Related link: http://www.freedomofmind.com. People are typically far more ready to believe that a cult is disguised as a religion or pseudo New Age movement, rather than a popular form of exercise.

This book will strongly resonate with those who were at one time involved with the Moo, or who knew people who were. The process by which an innocent person becomes involved in the Moo will cause a lot of nodding of the head of a reader who has experience within the group, as well as descriptions of how the nightmare expanded and deepened with the passing years and Mr. Smith's greater level of involvement. As one who went through it, to see the martial arts movement names from the Moo, the odd rituals described in so much detail, the senior instructors (many of whom I recognize) laid out bare in a way I couldn't have imagined when I was a member and they seemed like gods — it's a chilling experience; even these many, many years later.

Those who weren't involved in the Moo directly but who had friends or loved ones who were; will be uncomfortable at the thought of what their friends or loved ones actually experienced. Even those who weren't involved at all with the Moo, but in other destructive groups, will recognize many of the same patterns if not the exact techniques.

Such a profound experience resonates throughout one's life, whether consciously acknowledged or not. In my case, I left the group in 1988, but didn't discover its true nature, that it was a nationwide cult and fraud that ruined thousands of people's lives, financially and emotionally, and its leaders had been arrested on tax charges; until almost exactly seven years later. When I made that discovery, by chance on an Internet search engine, emotions that I didn't even know I'd had came rushing to the surface. A less intense version of this emotional experience was felt by me upon reading Mr. Smith's words. Not everyone has easy access to the Internet, but a book can go with you anywhere, and is of a permanent type of media, a tactile memoir of one's time in a horrible experience beyond what many people can imagine.

I recommend this book for anyone who was involved in the Moo, and for anyone with an interest in how a cult can subtly work its way into a person's life before that person vanishes, and a cult droid, in Mr. Smith's words, takes their place. Hopefully this book will convince others to rethink their involvement in the Moo organization, which still exists, and bring peace to others whose lives were turned upside down by the greed of a megalomaniac.

Ex-Cult Member, November 2006

DEDICATED

To all former and current members in the cults of Chung Moo Quan, Chung Moo Doe and the more current version, Oom Yung Doe, even if you don't believe it is a cult. To the hundreds still trapped we can only hope you find your way out.

I want to offer a special mention of personal thanks to: Angry White Ghost, Ben Mooed, Blucraft, Compassetic, Frozen Su Chung, Henri Tomasi, Hephaestus, Info-Seeker, KC Elbows, Nick D., Royal Dragon, Kim Rieser, Bill Simpson, Sally Smith, Sciuropterus, and Wujji; and to John Graden, Steve Hassan, Marc MacYoung, Rick Ross and Matt Thornton, for helping me to finally break free of the Moo cult and for persevering over the years to fight the cult's dogma, discover the truth and share genuine martial arts knowledge.

Joe Smith

How It All Started

A field near Naperville Illinois circa 1975; Kim in black, showing a poorly staged and executed vault with one of his first participating dupes in the background. Notice the size of the feet in relation to the defender, the positioning on the hill, the Z-axis distance between the two men.

Tryouts such as these led to the rooftop jump staged picture, once the techniques of Kyong Gong Sul Bope illusion were crafted to look more realistic with a bit more practice and junior league trick photography. From this meager beginning, a sizeable cult was formed.

MOVING FORWARD, LOOKING BACK

Reflecting some twenty years after involvement with Grand Master Kim's martial arts cult, we can view the fraud with improved perspective. John C. a.k.a. Chull or Steel Kim, later changed to Iron Kim, was released on parole in 2001 after serving most of a five-year sentence for leading a multi-state conspiracy to evade federal income taxes.

Many of the guys we trained with in Kim's organization testified against him at the federal and state trials. The authors here were excommunicated a few years before television news reports brought the focus to his operations that resulted in the IRS, FBI and State Attorney Generals' investigations.

Hundreds of friends and colleagues were caught up in the mayhem Kim created. A dozen we knew fairly well and had spent years with in training became felons as a result of falling into Kim's deception. They lost homes, families, businesses; respect for themselves and decades from their lives.

They are a decent lot generally. Like most they sought self improvement, the means to learn effective self-defense and most importantly, shared the willingness to attempt to raise themselves up, to earn a better life, to be around the right type of people. To believe in Chung Moo Quan, Chung Moo Doe, or Oom Yung Doe, and to blindly put faith in a fake martial arts master was the critical error we all made.

It started out reasonably innocent like most who become soldiers for cult leaders. The eliteness, the hard work, the camaraderie, the common energy, the accomplishments of rank; these are the hooks. But this organization was and is sinister. It takes control of people's lives in Manchurian Candidate fashion until the only thing that matters is serving Kim. It begins with the rigid environment of a pseudo-martial arts school, and cash payments. The Moo is all about the cash.

The self-styled John C. Kim schools only exist to funnel money upward. They have skillfully adjusted the operation's silhouette over the years to reduce visibility to local authorities. This gathering is to tell but one story of the thousands misled and lied to by Kim, or perhaps his name really is Park, according to his arrest warrant.

My involvement lasted nearly eight years. Generally here, three aspects of the cult will be presented. Parts of this book are stories of martial art training in a retail store front dojo; other stories are about the exploits of a group of young warrior wanna-bees growing up together, other parts are of a more serious kind; the re-telling of the methods of indoctrination, manipulation, and retention techniques employed by the cult as observed and participated in firsthand while progressing though the ranks.

Some of these stories are remarkably funny, some are insane; however the desired outcome for any action in The Moo was consistent, it had to benefit Kim. (The Moo was a term coined by detractors in the Chung Moo Quan era circa 1979 to 1990, still used today, e.g. Chung Moonies, to describe members of the latter Chung Moo Doe schools or the current marketed name of Oom Yung Doe).

Luckily for most of my generation we saw our way clear eventually. The lies stopped holding up, enough of our friends had left, the money we worked so hard for, wasted. A few key individuals have helped hundreds rebuild their lives. They started discussion boards, wrote essays and manifested their convictions against the Moo. They researched martial arts history, lineages and documented teachers of authentic styles.

The vanguard of Anti-Moo, they sought out real teachers and learned true martial arts, sharing with those who also sought a way out of this cult; and passed along their learning, rekindling our original pursuit of the arts.

Others like them performed research into cults, manipulation techniques and behavioral control practices. This group asked experts for help and publicized their accounts with the media; they used the courts to seek redress against Kim and his legions.

To all these folks and to anyone who was or might be seduced by The Moo, this is for us all.

Joe Smith

TIME LINE

Feb	1980	Joe Smith signs up
July	1982	Joe reaches black Moo belt
Nov	1987	Joe leaves the cult of Moo
Nov	1989	CBS news reports in Chicago "The Cult and the Con"
Aug	1990	First raids on schools in Chicago
April	1992	Illinois Attorney General sues to force sale of the Farm
April	1995	Feds arrest Kim and disciples
Sep	1996	Federal Tax trial starts in Chicago
Dec	1996	Kim and crew found guilty
July	1997	Kim begins prison
April	2001	Kim paroled
Jan	2002	The Cult is back in business
May	2006	First edition of *Herding the Moo*
June	2007	*Herding the Moo* at Book Expo America, New York City
Aug	2007	Second revised edition of *Herding the Moo*

MOO RANK INSIGNIAS

First Section
One section black on belt end, sign for private lessons.

Second Section
Both ends of belt are black, hanging in front, sign for black belt training.

Third Section
One side of belt to the waist is dyed black, sign up for more courses.

Fourth Section
Both sides of belt are now black to the waist, black trim around the collar added. Bowing procedure more formalized, sign, sign, everywhere a sign.

Fifth Section
More of the belt is dyed black, additional uniform trim is black. Pay off early what signed for or be left behind.

Sixth Section
The belt has only one white section now, uniform top completely trimmed in black. Pant cuffs are trimmed in black.

First Dan (Degree)
One black stripe on pant leg, bow changes to fist covered by hand, with an even greater signing opportunity.

Second Degree
Two black stripes on pant leg, special patches showing your loyalty available for purchase. Do you qualify for owning your own school?

Third Degree
Three black stripes, more patches to buy, your financial servitude is just beginning. Time to sell the house and explain to the wife this is for the long haul.

Fourth Degree
Gee, it's only been five years, more debt than you can imagine. It's not a cult, it's not a cult, it's not a cult… is it?

TABLE OF CONTENTS

Part I	Signed Up	1
Part II	When to Bow, When Not to	21
Part III	Middle Belt.	53
Part IV	I Want to Believe	91
Part V	Black Moo Belt	117
Part VI	Living on a Prayer	155
Part VII	Revelations	207
Part VIII	Anti Moo	265
Epilogue	. . . .	291
Glossary	. . . .	299

PART I

SIGNED UP

"I am always ready to learn, although I do not always like being taught"

—Winston Churchill

PART I—SIGNED UP

INFORMATION

It was early morning on the way home from Joe's factory job in the western suburbs of Chicago. He moved there from Wisconsin a few months earlier and was looking to start training again in martial arts, having taken Shotokan Karate during his brief time in college. Joe liked what he had learned and hoped the guys with whom he shared a house would also be interested.

He noticed a new strip mall on the edge of the sprawl with a big hand painted wooden sign that read Champion of All Asia with a conventional Karate jump kick image and lots of pictures in the front window. What appeared to be the master was pointing, seemingly leading the small group of rugged looking scraggily bearded dudes with multiple stripes on their legs through stance training in a field somewhere.

What Joe did not notice or think was peculiar at the time was the master had his back turned towards the camera and no caption or mention of any students' or instructors' names were used. Apparently the leader, he looked splendid in his dark purple jump suit with Chung Moo Quan in large letters across the back. The place looked authentic. It had bamboo curtains, swords on the wall and even an official looking ornate flag. Besides, who would make a claim of being a champion if they were not so? Joe's limited knowledge of martial arts and small business enterprise would be his undoing. He decided to stop back when they were open. It was a convenient location to learn from the best.

On his next day off Joe parked out front with a new Cutlass, which was a mistake. This showed he had money or at least the means by which to obtain it for loan. Opening the door to inquire if classes were available, the string of bells alerted them to informations, as walk-ins off the street were called.

"Uh, waiting there a minute, have a seat," remarked what was apparently a black belt instructor in the office. His language sounded strange but soon this would be common, expected amongst the members. The instructor didn't know it then of course, but in fifteen years he would also be sentenced along with Kim for his role in the tax evasion scheme, implicated for a lot of other shenanigans over the years but never formally charged.

The walls were framed with wood beams, stained dark and the bamboo curtains had real looking Chinese-like characters on them. Joe read a pamphlet they had on the table in the waiting room. And read it and read it. Learn the 1500 year-old art of Chung Moo Quan, it said. The large white poster on the wall had some of the same pictures from the front windows with cities like Pusan, Sydney, Manila, Hong Kong, and Guam listed along the bottom.

After leaving the cult this became obvious nonsense. There never were schools outside the United States, or at the time, outside of two metropolitan areas. This was merely a deceptive ploy used to con people as to the credibility and authenticity of Chung Moo Quan. Make up whatever you can, and if people believe it, then it becomes true.

Not many students were in the school that day; one walked though and said someone would be with Joe in a minute. An instructor was in the back giving a private lesson. Even on day one they put that lure out there, private lessons. Joe had no idea he'd end up spending tens of thousands of dollars over the next few years with these guys. The guy doing the walk through was a fourth section, about half way to Moo black belt, he was eighteen years old. By the time he reached forty he'd also be a convicted felon with nowhere else to go when released from prison but back into the waiting arms of the cult. It would be under a different name, but still designed, built and operated by Kim.

After about ten minutes the instructor in the front office, John, motioned Joe inside and asked what he wanted. Making potential students wait was a preliminary test, Joe thought.

"I want to learn martial arts, this place looks pretty cool," Joe explained.

"Uh huh," John flatly replied. "You ever take martial arts before?"

"Yes, I took Shotokan Karate in Wisconsin for about a year while in college, I liked it and want to continue with training," Joe added.

"Oh, yeah? Well this is chung…" and he slams his locked forearm into Joe's chest just above the solar plexus, sending him backwards out into the waiting room, spilling onto the couch. It knocked the wind out of him. What a dirty trick. Joe got up and pulled the parts of the beaded curtain from the office off of him.

"Why did you do that?" Joe asked rather loudly. Another black belt, also with striped legs and gold lettered thick black belt, joined in from the practice room. He stepped onto the couch, walked around Joe and stood next to John. The second guy glared at Joe, trying to intimidate him.

Joe said, "I came here to learn, why are you afraid of me?" They were older than Joe; each outweighed him and no doubt knew how to fight. Or so he believed. Joe sought acceptance and a chance to learn. Over the years his involvement would end up costing a lot more than mere dollars.

The second guy, with scraggly beard and fierce stare bowed to his partner and went back into the training room. The first guy asked Joe back in, stating that was just a minor demonstration of what he could learn.

"Bet you never felt anything like that before, I was shocked when I first got touched a little bit, how'd you like to learn how to harness that?"

"Well, maybe I would, can I ask a few questions? Are you registered?" Joe queried.

"Yes, I am registered to Asian governments, so is Paul, the other instructor. Here are our certificates," he motioned towards the wall behind him, "and these are Master's certificates."

This was the first introduction of the importance, in their minds, to "Master." He was revered it seemed, but in an eerie sense. His pictures were everywhere. He was the focus of everything we did for as long we were in the cult of Moo.

The Moo-structor moved on saying, "Grab my arm." Joe obliged and John reversed the grip and held Joe in a take-down move.

"I guess you know what you are doing," acknowledged Joe, the information. These were new, strange tactics in the close confines of the little office, with the royal looking flags, the swords and spears on the walls, the certificates hanging up, mounted above. When Joe began to explore beyond the world of Moo it was quickly seen the moves demonstrated were not that strong or skillful. It was how it was sold to make it appear that way. All things in Moo were to be a set up, a façade, an illusion of whatever reality you wanted it to be.

"Do you guys teach Kung Fu and Tai Chi here?" Joe inquired. It's what the sign said.

"Yes, we teach all eight martial arts, including weapons form. The big difference as you shop around is our style is not watered down, it comes direct from Master who is eighth generation," explained the Moo-structor.

"What if someone holds a knife to your throat?" Joe thought this was extremely difficult even for an accomplished martial artist to defeat. A recent skyjacking had a well known Kung Fu champion on an aircraft where a deranged passenger took a flight attendant hostage with a knife to the throat. The media reported there was nothing even the champion could do without risking her life.

John began to breathe heavily; he held Joe's fingers up to his own throat, "Like this?" he asked, hesitating for a second before knocking the hand away and holding Joe's forearm in another take-down grip. Easily impressed, Joe fell into the trap.

"What does it cost?" This was his biggest mistake.

"Forty-five dollars for the first month, a uniform is an additional forty dollars, there is no contract to sign (yet) and you can come in as much as you want." This of course was the hook to get you to submit to their rules; they would spring the private contract and other accessory charges on us later.

"Do you have anything you can put down?" Joe was asked. But he did not. Truth was Joe had ten bucks on him. Promising to return that day and pay for a month to try it out, Joe returned home explaining to his friends about the experience.

"Dude, they knocked you down, wanted money and called you weak because you didn't sign up right away and now you're going back?" Stubborn as ever, thinking if he did something no one else would; making Joe better off somehow, he returned to the storefront school.

The instructors wanted personal contact information, where he worked but also Joe's bank account numbers, in case of payment by check they said. When Joe was being groomed as an instructor, this was explained as to see how open minded and trusting was the potential student. Essentially, it was to see how far they could manipulate anyone who walked in the door. The more they could get from you now, the more they would try to get from you in the future.

The first lesson was overall, positive. Joe wasn't much of an athlete in high school. And now at twenty-three was in fair shape, better than most I guess because of his factory job and outside activities, such as hunting; but not in a refined, honed condition. This was one reason he signed up. A few calisthenics, their version of deep breathing and ordinary stretches similar to what Joe had experienced in Shotokan Karate, with a couple of obscure posture holdings not seen before were the high points of the lesson.

T-position (twisted horse in Kung Fu, the Moo way has long term detrimental effects) was heavily emphasized in all early lessons and throughout the curriculum for Moo. A difficult posture, it serves more to break down new recruits or keep nonconforming members to tow the line rather than develop martial skills from the way the Moo teaches it.

Feet shoulder width apart, then rotate one foot 180 degrees, stand on the ball of the opposite foot, extending the arch, heel points up. Bring the opposite knee inside the heel of the rotated foot to within a few inches off the floor, keep the upper back and shoulders straight up, lower back and butt arched, while extending both arms out in a line with the feet; pushing out with the palms, looking through the thumb and first finger, pulling the wrists back hard. Twist the hips to align between both feet. The shoulders and upper body should sit mid-way between both feet, equally weighted. Again, this is Moo and it's all wrong. Find a text on Louhan or better yet a qualified Louhan teacher for the authentic practice. For now, let's get back to Moo.

If you began by rotating the right foot 180 degrees you would look over your right shoulder, through your right palm which was now in a vertical plane over your left foot. This over torqueing was quite strenuous and we would hold it every day, sometimes in sets for effect. You'd start out with a thirty second hold on both sides, and by first degree be expected to do at least ten minutes each side, without coming up. You would pivot around on the balls of the feet. Today, few if any current Moo black belts can do this.

The problem is over time the forced postures wear down the body, instead of building it up. The alignments contradict authentic Kung Fu, the joints become brittle with the Moo way of practice as opposed to more pliable. But we had no way of knowing until after we spent years Mooing, saw the flaws in the system, its leaders and training methods and started over in authentic systems with real teachers in place of salespeople.

Nonetheless, the first lesson was impressive. Joe's small group that afternoon on a cold February day learned basic horse and punch (also taught wrong in the Moo, wrists should be flat, not bent), two basic kicks, front and knee break, plus two self-defense tactics against a punch.

The assistant instructor, Earl, a newly minted black belt showed forms available to learn in a few months, even the cool looking sticks and poles, weapons forms, if the students signed up on private lessons. They provided a 'we are getting our moneys worth feeling' yet like all things they taught, even the supposed higher forms and advanced techniques we practiced for years are largely useless against a determined attacker or skilled fighter. Moo teaches you how to Moo.

We can say this because in considering Moo training objectively, the fundamentals are flawed. The stances leave one vulnerable and unable to move effectively, the weighting is not designed for self-defense, instead designed to look cool. The forms are showy; the weapons movements are flashy but useless. The body does not develop as promised, the only thing continued practice brings is the chance to gain more rank with all its privileges and perhaps the next level of uniform. That was another big hook, getting a uniform.

The lesson ended as it began, a deep breathing sequence then bowing to the flags and to the main instructors who opened the door and stepped briefly into the practice room. Each time they would do this they stared at the flags as if to connect to something. What was learned many, many years later was that when Kim set up a new school; on the sly he would place his personal prayer seeking wealth and money behind the flags. Having everyone bowing and putting their mind towards school by concentrating on the flags several times a day, it was his intent to manifest this wish.

To conclude the lesson Chung Moo! was shouted loudly with clapping several times. Eight was the prescribed number. The details of why eight, for eighth generation master, would be explained once the full indoctrination was rolling. But you had to have a uniform and some color on the belt for that to take effect. Whoever reaches any kind of rank within a cult tries very heard to earn it, which is why anyone stays on, even today. It's very difficult to walk away from what you think you earned.

As the students put on their shoes and socks in the waiting area; the assistant, Earl, was ordered by the ranking instructors to go retrieve the mail. He bowed to them, bowed again upon leaving the office, and again while at the door before stepping outside. He ran to the end of the row of stores less than fifty yards away, but in full sweaty uniform and bare feet. He held the mail inside his uniform and repeated the bowing upon return. We were being groomed right then in the proper ways of the Moo. Earl let on about how now was a good time to be starting, schools were poised for growth and Master was releasing a lot of new forms never before seen in the United States.

It all seemed so genuine, the framed words on the blue and white painted walls with wood trimmed borders and places to hang student's uniforms. Terms like Courage, Belief, Volition, Try Hard, Pain is Gone and Pleasure is Come, Ultimate, Valor, and Persistence; each with the supposed proper Chinese inscription above them. There was a brief essay with the signature of Master John C. Kim framed on the waiting room wall titled *Persistence*.

—*Nothing in the world can take the place of persistence. Talent will not; nothing is more common than unsuccessful men with talent. Genius will not; unrewarded genius is almost a proverb. Education will not; the world is full of educated derelicts. Persistence and determination alone are omnipotent. Calvin Coolidge, 30th U.S. President, 1932*

Fast forward a moment twenty years ahead. Here's what we learned about *Persistence*. A friend and former regional instructor Moo wrote the following note as I began my rediscovery:

Back in the early eighties these words were on a nice plaque, prominently displayed in the Minnesota schools. The plaques were a source of inspiration, and helped me and many others get through tougher lessons and a lot of the nonsense that came with the training. Each time I entered the office seeing the plaque inspired me to press on. The problem with it was when Kim came to town and decided the plaque was unfit to be in schools because John C. Kim did not say it or write it. This is not the Calvin Coolidge school of Chung Moo

Quan. The plaques were taken down from the schools. This saddened me greatly, none of the writings of Kim (Match for One Thousand, Determination) none of that motivated me as much as this plaque. But don't think that it's a cult or anything.

I wrote back: The words on Persistence were included in the early Moo literature. We used to pass this along to informations and folks we'd meet while out passing flyers drumming up business for the cult. We were led to believe it was Kim's words. In our schools, in Illinois, the quote had his signature at the end. Yes, it inspired me too. It did for a long time after, thinking there were at least a few things he got right, there was some truth to the scam. But now we learn he stole material such as this as well and used it as his own. Many of us were convinced Kim, or is it really Park and is he really also a doctor as he claimed, wrote it. They included it directly in with their schpeel, plagiarized it without quoting the source. At least yous guys had a nice plaque.

We learned a lot it seemed these first lessons. After a couple weeks Joe was in noticeably better shape. The warm-up exercises and practicing the basic down-blocks, out-blocks, and in-blocks in the controlled settings had brought back his timing and speed developed earlier in Shotokan. Joe's kicks and punches came back too and he enjoyed learning a couple new moves or improving what he had each time he went.

Joe attended the afternoon group everyday. It was a good schedule with the night job, time to recoup, eat and do well in Chung Moo and at work. Joe started thinking he was on the right track and was looking at attending college again part time. He was spending time wisely and spending less money on entertainment. The USA Hockey team had just defeated the USSR in the Olympics. Everything was going well. Joe was considering going to the night time group, just to check it out, to see all the higher belted students and perhaps see a glimpse of what it would be like to have a couple years of training in.

This one afternoon as Joe pulled into the lot there was another car close by with the trunk open and some dude rummaging through it. He and friends, two of which were standing on the front sidewalk right by the front door to the school, were deciding which weapons they should use.

Cool, another demonstration, except these guys weren't from Joe's school. The steel framed glass front door at our place had a big hand-painted tiger face covering it. It was said Master Kim himself drew the outline and instructors painted it in. It was then approved by Kim. The tiger emblem was so big it was difficult to see in or out. The dingys, the label given out for members of any other school, were peering into the school and Joe's two main Moo instructors were peering out. Seeing Joe, they cracked the door open, telling him tersely to step in. Ah, okay, he thought. As soon as he did they indicated to change quickly and stay in the back. Cool, get to use the back room, all riiight.

There was some shouting from the parking lot; it was quickly realized these were not friendlys, something about a letter from the other schools. Wanting to see what was up Joe and a few other students walked through the main room to near the front curtain separating the practice room from the waiting room. Apparently from the sidewalk, it looked like they were about to be overrun, so the visitors left with their weapons du jour and chain letter in hand.

The instructors explain this can happen occasionally and not to worry. Master John C. Kim came to the United States to smash down wrong way teachings, so of course, they are jealous. Don't worry; even by second section you have more form than they have at black belt, you just have to practice hard and remember Chung Moo is 70% mental, 30% physical; what they have is 70% physical 30% mental. They jump and kick all day; they can never reach what you can reach. This is because Master came to the United States to teach those who earn his knowledge. Besides, all their so-called training is watered down. Chung Moo Quan is 1500 years exact line teaching generation to generation. We were sent here to bust out a new district, there are already five schools in Chicago, this is the newest with over twenty nation-wide. Master mentioned (cult-speak was used heavily in the early years) there was room in the USA for over one thousand schools. Someday you might all have a chance. You could see the chests swelling in everyone there. We smiled and watched the dingys drive away.

SPECIAL PRIVATE COURSE

Our favorite assistant, Earl, had been transferred to another school and a new guy, Eric, brought in. He was constantly on edge and ran strenuous workouts. He didn't explain as much or work with us on techniques, just drilled us back and forth on the basic sparring patterns we had learned thus far. And he was a lot less forgiving on any improvising. This was a huge no-no in Moo. As a student you could not try any 'what if's' or work on street-like situations.

In Moo the only allowable practice was the scripted patterns and telegraphed punches and kicks. After awhile some started to doubt if the techniques would work effectively in real life. It would probably lead to greater injury as you'd step into a confrontation thinking you could handle a situation when unless they were going to bow first, wait for you to punch politely then return the favor, they'd knock your lights out.

Near the end of class Joe was invited into the office. So pumped up from the workout high, he nearly opened the direct door to the office as a substitute to going by way of the practice room curtain and through the waiting room. But, the Moo belts cut him some slack; they had other priorities in mind. Joe entered through the beads and bowed.

"Sit down," the light-haired instructor said. "How do you like school so far?" he asked.

"Yeah, so far it's good," said Joe.

"Don't say yeah, say yes, it's more correct," said his handler.

"Okay," Joe responded.

"What do you want to really learn, what is your goal?" the instructor continued.

"I want to see if I can make black belt, given enough time, I know it takes awhile but I want to see how it goes and hopefully someday I'll make it," Joe stated.

"What if I told you there was a way you could move like a black belt in Karate, like that stuff you used to learn, you could be like that only better in just nine months instead of three years?"

"Yeah…, I mean yes… that would be great."

"Then you need to get on special private course. We teach privately here too, you've had a chance to see the back room, that's where we work with students on their particular needs to help them develop faster."

"Does it cost more?" Joe asked straight up.

The instructor frowned, saying, "It does a little bit, but let me explain; you can drive your car in rush hour traffic and get to where you want to go, eventually. Or, you can take the fast lane and go as fast as you want and get there a lot sooner."

"Well, I'd like to continue on where I'm at and keep learning the basics to make sure I have them down correctly," Joe countered, skeptical of the sales pitch.

"Don't say down, never put yourself down," corrected the handler.

"How much is it?" Joe asked a second time.

"$900 dollars for nine months of special private instruction. You get a private lesson every time you come in plus regular group as much as you want and complete use of all facilities."

"I can not afford that, I have car payments, and rent and want to go back to college. No thanks, maybe later, I like what I'm learning now just fine." Joe hoped that would end it.

"Listen," the sales-structor said, turning up the pitch, "you want to be a black belt, this is the way to do it…"

This went back and forth for a few more minutes until the group lesson formally ended. Joe was allowed to stand at attention and bow in the office. They stopped pressuring him for that day to sign up on course, as it was known. The other instructor had stepped in; he was listening from outside the office. They suggested at least Joe should get into a uniform to be more a part of the school if he was serious about training. His next time in Joe brought a check to pay for his personal symbol of cult membership. It would be the last time he ever paid in non-cash terms.

Another week goes by and the afternoon group noticeably changes. The new guy Eric spends most of his time flirting with two girls who regularly attended. They had advanced rank on their belts. One was a second section with both ends of the belt dyed black, the other a third section with an additional section dyed to the waist. They had been in school a little over eight months and had a good repertoire of movements. They practiced a lot together. Years forward one would testify against Kim and the cult. They both currently dated instructors.

During these next few days, the instructors or an assistant, most likely a sixth section, with uniform all trimmed in black just like the instructors but without the full black belt and stripes on the legs; would pull select students aside and work with them on what seemed to be advanced forms. They would block and kick the length of the room, about twenty feet, trade attacker and defender roles, then move back along the same line. This was special private form. Those not on courses, like Joe, were left to work on what they had for the remainder of group lesson.

Every now and then, those on course would move to the back room where the Judo or in Moo-speak, the Udo mat, was built onto the floor. Of course we could not see what was going on, but the sounds were intense. The instructors calling out step in harsh staccato tones, the sharp exhales and sounds of quickly executed movements were intriguing.

After about three weeks, and a couple more conversations about higher course, out of the five or so who were the bulk of the afternoon group only two were left, Ed and Joe. Ed also worked a factory job, was about the same age and had a troubled home life growing up. Joe recognized they were of the same kind, street kids looking to construct something better for themselves.

Ed too had been talked up about special private course. They discussed it one time after class and were immediately told in no uncertain terms to keep all cross-talk to a minimum in the waiting room. In general, students were not allowed to speak amongst themselves unless it was in the practice room and only then when under the direct supervision of an instructor-droid. You spoke when spoken to. In later years this loosened slightly as Kim adjusted the rules somewhat attempting to defray the cult label.

Ed said he was going to do it, it was only nine months and besides they'd credit what he had paid in thus far, about a hundred dollars, so for the extra cost per month we'll get twice the instruction, and besides, it would make passing the tests easier… ah that was the hook. Getting that belt dyed in and the measure of accomplishment with it was very alluring. This was another critical miscalculation. Believing that a belt somehow confers rank, believing that a rank somehow automatically equates to a measure of knowledge and/or skill.

The next day Joe was again pulled into the office and questioned about special private course. This time they switched roles, the lead guy had waited outside last time. He tried a different approach, more pointed. He made fun of Joe's new car, said he was spending money in the wrong places, on things when it should be for Joe's training. "You can have a high performance car or you can have a high performance body, it's up to you."

But he had already decided. Joe wanted to progress faster, to learn more. Even more importantly, Joe did not want to be excluded. He asked to review the terms. It was agreed that he could bring in $100 each week for three weeks and that would be the down payment of $300, leaving monthly payments of $100 each for the rest of the contract. In Joe's case, five months as they would credit the monies already paid leaving eight hundred due for the course and since he was in effect paying off the course faster, they said they would teach faster. Joe was happy, accepted by those who had been sharp with him up until now; not able to see their overriding goal was to collect cash, funnel it to Kim and keep students under control for future cash collection.

Joe began reading the fine print of the contract. The instructor grabbed it from him and said, "Here, here's what this says, this paragraph means if we move you have the right to cancel, we're not going anywhere... this says we promise to teach you as agreed..." and so on.

Joe asked for a copy, the sales-structor grimaced. "What, you don't trust?" he nearly yelled.

"No, it's just that it's normal to obtain a copy, isn't it?"

"Look, you're not buying one of your silly new cars here, understand?"

"Well alright, thanks for taking me on as a private student," Joe said, and offered his hand to shake as he stood up. The other instructor in the room looked as if Joe had erred in diplomacy again. The one behind the desk begrudgingly shook Joe's hand and frowned.

Special private course began the next day, pay day and Joe had one hundred in cash. They asked him for it as soon as he came in. They had him follow them into the office and bowed to the flags. We would also learn they were bowing to the certificates on the wall, these were believed to have near magical powers, like an oracle to mentally connect to Kim. Joe bowed still just following along, thinking it was mere custom to show respect to the flag. The instructor turned and offered his hand for the money, smiling. Joe reached back, pulled out his wallet and opened it in front of his handler, producing five twenties and gave up the hundred dollars.

"Hmmm," grunted the black belt, "better to hand over with two hands," he said.

"Excuse me?"

"Use two hands when handing anything to higher belt, especially lesson payment. Higher belt does not have to accept your offer, we do so only because it is better for you."

Joe clumsily put his wallet away with his new uniform tied and hanging on the arm in approved manner, and using two hands again offered the payment.

"Not over the corner of the desk," it was said pointedly. "Here, over here," almost impatiently the instructor waved Joe to step directly in front of him, across the desk. Under the glass were dozens of cut out pictures of Kim, showing an assortment of poses, weapons and mode of dress.

Joe handed over the money. The droid purposefully counted it again even though it was only five twenties and had seen it counted out.

He grunted again, "Hmmm, you're holding more aren't you? You got paid, why not put more towards your future?"

Joe explained he had other bills to pay. Carefully pushing and probing as far as they could, the droid said, "Step out, go change, private lesson will start right away."

Ed and Joe were the only ones in that day. They learned the beginning sequence of a new stance training form named Short Form or Tong Hoo. This name would change over the years as instructors left, went crazy or lost their mind as Kim would tell the remaining followers. The form designations would change so anyone who split could not possibly be teaching authentic Chung Moo Quan if they couldn't even use the right label. The branding of the organization itself would change, several times, to Chung Moo Doe in the late 1980's to Oom Yung Doe in the late 1990's. There were a few short-lived experiments such as Ying Yang Doe which were used to defer attention. They were soon folded back into the main organization.

Tong Hoo had seven steps total, it was to develop the body, strengthening and adding flexibility to apply the self-defense moves they would soon be learning. The method was by holding each position for thirty seconds, as far as you had through it, about five times then run though at slow speed holding each position briefly then five times though at medium speed, trying to make each move exact. This procedure was called five, five and five. Five times hold, five times each position exact, five times fast (or medium).

The goal was to build up to holding for two minutes at each position. The instructors were to check and improve the student's posture as he or she developed, making each position more exact as the student progressed. This practice so it turns out is derived from authentic time-honored Shaolin training methods. However, the Moo method places too much pressure and stress on critical areas of the knees, hips and back and much more importantly, ignores the internal. They do not understand correct alignment, how energy and breath should be used to build from the inside. But they say they do, in carefully structured presentations and stories.

This is the critical flaw in all things Moo. Instead of living up to what they said they were sent to the suburbs to do, help you develop; they help you bring in more cash by giving out a few movements, recheck the point of sale marketing and manage the relationship until the student is ready for the next buy-up to a higher course. No one ever works their way through an entire course, learns all the moves, techniques and achieves well-rounded proficiency.

The instructors become instructors by their ability to look like, to the uninitiated, they have something worthy of becoming; to hold a respect line and act correct and can sell the courses, to make the precious cash come in. You also have to be able to generate interest by having students bring in additional cash at select times. Like at Christmas, or near April 1st, Kim's supposed birthday; funny how it's Fool's day, or when it was time for lunch. For now, let's get back to practice.

When young, it seems like you are learning a lot and the body will build up quickly. But it is short-term, it does not last. The tendons and ligaments become less pliable, the strength goes away, it becomes difficult to recapture the spirit and energy you once had in learning what you thought was real martial arts. This was and is the design all along.

As you progress through the ranks of the Moo cult by learning steps and forms and being able to parrot Moo history to the underlings; you become expert at signing up students on course and making the cash come in. You practice less and less and the practice you do get in can not fully deliver all the promises you were told it would because the system is flawed by design, Kim's design.

Twenty years after leaving the cult we find those who have been around Kim the longest have severe body problems, bad backs and joints, and are in poor general physical condition. Kim himself uses a heating pad and Asian Tiger Balm patches to alleviate his problems.

Back then however, that special private lesson was a good one for two young true warrior wanna-bees. They twisted and posed, postured and held, and their kicks and punches flew from their bodies as they tried hard to make something of themselves, high on practice and being allowed deeper into the school regimens. Advanced students, those with some sections on their belts, nodded acknowledgement, accepting them.

FIRST SECTION TEST

Soon afterward Joe and Ed were told they were ready to test first section. The fee was fifteen dollars; bring that in as soon as possible. By the time many of us reached first degree, after about two and a half years of cult dedication, we'd bring in one thousand just for the opportunity to test. First section test took place one week after getting on special private course. Candidates were ordered to set up a chair under the flags in the main room, change into uniform and await instructions. The other students were ordered to use the rear practice room. After changing and about a five minute chance to loosen up, the dark-haired instructor strode out of the office, stopping to bow to the flags in the main room and then to those testing. They lined up and bowed again, this time adding in the other instructor in the office, and again to each other.

The test lasted about twenty minutes and covered horse and punch, five basic kicks, Kata number one, a few punch defenses done on each other, a couple of self-defense grabbing techniques such as breaking a shoulder hold and cross-hand grab. The Moo calls this Hapkido or Aikido but it is nothing like these real arts. The Moo teaches only bits and pieces without the real knowledge of the applications. Persons properly trained have little difficulty defeating

Moo. The testing concluded with a couple of kick defenses. One was a side kick defense.

Ed kicked towards Joe and he stepped out, hooked his arm under Ed's leg and held him up, not wanting to dump him on the hard floor in the main room. In the back, on the comfy old carpet-stuffed home built Judo mat, they had dumped each other a few dozen times in the past week.

"If you don't knock him down, you don't pass," growled the droid leading the test. Joe dropped Ed and when the roles were reversed he dropped Joe, both of them smarting from the falls. Their lengthy Judo training until now had not prepared them for the shock. Joe felt that drop intermittently for years and it was not until he started Tai Chi training was he able to permanently remove the feeling. Ed quit in a couple weeks after more pressure for the next level of membership, black belt course.

The test ended, they again lined up, bowed, shouted the cult name in unison and clapped. Their innocence disappeared when the testing droid said, "Way I look, you both passed, John C. Kim style School of Chung Moo Quan."

They received the same score, twenty points out of twenty-five possible. They were presented with the clipboard to sign then told to turn around, take off their belts and hand them back. The long thick bands of cotton polyester, stiff with newness would be dyed one section black, and the test scores presented to head instructors for review.

PART II

WHEN TO BOW, WHEN NOT TO

"Easily impressed is easily enslaved"
—(as said by) Head Instructor Forrest Troutner

PART II—WHEN TO BOW, WHEN NOT TO

MEETING MASTER KIM FOR THE FIRST TIME

Joe's first time was as a white belt after less than a month in Moo when he received a call at home. Joe worked nights and took lessons in the afternoon. He drove over on the way into work that night, told it was unusual for beginners to meet him, but in this case the hustle had begun.

Joe parked next door at the neighboring Pizza Hut; the lot was full in front of old school number Seven. We soon figured out anyone with a decent car did not park near school as it would gather dents, mysteriously.

Full of trepidation, remembering the introductory shoving around, Joe exited his vehicle and saw Kim sitting on the couch with his back to the door, being introduced to higher ranking students and instructors. It looked like he stood up each time to shake their hand. Joe's uniform snared on the car door and fell to the ground, in a puddle.

He tried to re-assemble but chickened out. It was hard enough walking through the door in the daytime; there were all those higher ranks there now. Joe looked over his shoulder and left. No one saw him. He should have been listening to what he was sensing, as that is his nature. He worked nights in a good paying job and just wanted to get there on time. Years passed before realizing given all the made up form, the legends, the history that folks like Joe were an easy mark.

After a couple days Joe got a call on why he didn't show up for this tremendous opportunity. He explained what happened and was told it was alright. Up until third section the Moos had what they called the regular summit to get Joe to come in. He'd practice for a few weeks, they'd knock him around in trying out what they had learned, yell and scream and hustle him for cash "…Go pick up coffee and a beef sandwich, what's wrong with you?" So Joe would not go there.

Then they'd call and lay the 'you can be something' scam on him. Joe did feel good after he practiced, but didn't know any better. He looks back at it now as just the big hustle it clearly was.

Joe kept going though, taking lessons during the afternoon. About one month later Kim returned. Everyone showed for seven o'clock night time group lesson, the tension was palatable. Kim arrives, the instructors freak and scramble towards the front door. There's this Korean dude with a tall white guy introduced almost in passing it seemed, as Head Instructor Forrest, tagging along. As they enter the school the main droids again yell like drill sergeants, "Stah-Hand Up!" Everyone immediately goes to attention.

Kim pokes his head into the main practice room as the curtain is held up by the two main droids who look like they are ready to jump out of their skin. He bows towards the flags intensely for a few moments, glances around the room and murmurs in a very low tone, "Begin." The curtain drops and he moves to the office. The beads are spread apart and held up in loud dramatic fashion as he steps in.

Warm-ups were about thirty minutes, much longer than before, run by two sixth section assistants from other schools. It's an intense workout. This is a big deal. Joe counts over twenty students, the room is filled and space scarce. His rank, first section, is safely packed towards the rear. At each holding position everyone counts loudly. The highest student rank was fourth section. Everyone was very tense, second and third sections were over-stressing due to the build up.

Kim jiggles the office door handle and Forrest growls in a commanding way, "Stand Up!" from the office. Kim comes out dressed in a dark red training outfit. He bows intensely again towards the flags and quickly at all of us. He motions for the others in the front room to step into the practice area; Forrest, a head instructor at third degree black belt, and the two second degree instructors at the school. They step in, bow to flags, then to Kim, then to us. They step off to the side, waiting and watching.

Kim briefly checks the groups' warm-up movements, he had been observing from the office, the window shade had been moving. Remember feet apart, arms at side then raise arms overhead in a swinging motion, elbows straight, then as arms are brought back down knees are bent and arms continue to circle behind keeping the upper body straight… count 1, 2, 3…

Well, the feet were supposed to be together and we were all doing it with feet apart. The instructors looked like they'd been caught shooting the Pope their eyes were so wide. Kim orders the mean dark-haired instructor to demo that exercise in front of everyone; who starts, then Kim yells No! and corrects it, explaining feet together. There were a couple of other mistakes pointed out. The atmosphere was very rigid, which is found in most but not all hard-style schools. Everything with Kim was always over-acted; the hype, the stories of accomplishments, the legacy in over one hundred countries.

We then paired off for self-defense and Kim walked around, checking our movements with instructors following by rank after each group he checked. We were working on hand grabs when he bellows, "Boy! What doing!" and tells Joe to grab his forearm. He wanted us to be more serious without any nervous chatter. Like several layers of rubber wrapped around a pipe, the guy's arm seemed very strong. He does the move, grabbing Joe's hand with his opposite, peels Joe's grip off, and then lightly slaps both sides of his head so he can feel the weight of the master's hand and twists Joe's arm outward and away to the point he's off balance, but does not drop him. Joe understands the concept. Kim does the same to Joe's partner, also a firstie but closer to second section rank.

Except now Joe's uniform is out of order so while Kim is demonstrating on his other half, Joe steps aside, turns so as not to face Kim as required to show respect and adjusts his gi. The main instructor moans, Joe missed his chance to see the movement and Kim again turns his attention to Joe, who smiling stupidly, gets into a staring contest. Kim's eyes were a dark brown putrid color and bloodshot, no doubt from no sleep, a higher mental form so we would find out. Joe looks at the main droid, the guy who signed him on course, like what did I do? Kim growls, "Boy, grab." This is the real deal Joe thought.

Kim shows Joe the technique again this time with a little more emphasis. His friend gets a chung during his additional turn. Joe asked him if he's okay and the instructors glare at him, "He (Kim) knows just how to touch." They practice back and forth some more, reviewing what they learned.

After a few minutes, the class is ordered to sit around in a circle against the walls. Kim calls out the dark-haired instructor and says, "Cross hand grab." The second degree looks absolutely terrified. Here's this guy who terrifies us, getting his.

Kim does the cross-hand defense and instantly drops the instructor. Next he reverses the move, Kim grabs the instructor, who tries to defend and flips the second dan backward in slow motion. When the two-striper tried the same technique Kim used, Kim had this almost amused look on his face as his student struggled to cope. We could see the strain on Paul's arm until it looked like it would break but he rolled ever backward, did a back flip and landed in backward knock-bone (flat on back) position slapping the hard practice area soundly. There were three layers of used carpet covering concrete. The same spot where Joe had to dump the opponent during his first test.

The instructor lands hard but springs back up almost instantly, shuffling forward in bow position, saying, "Yes, Master." Kim looked very much in control. A few days later we asked politely about that move, the instructor said it was spontaneous, reflexive and never done prior. It looked different, but not wholly superior to what Joe had seen before in Karate demonstrations.

Next, the master picked up a komb, a miss-nomer it turns out for a machete with red tassels or cloth tied on the handle end, and flashed it around with quick sudden moves. It looked impressive; however he did not explain what he was doing. He did some body positioning with the weapon and some related movements; bits and pieces of what we'd soon learn as form. He was certainly flexible. We wanted to move like him but not be as cocky.

Kim then talked at length, a story about how he didn't learn English because he didn't like the teacher, but don't be so stubborn in your learning, keep an open mind. He was setting us up to accept whatever story was told. He also said briefly as the class attention started to wander, "There was one point didn't want to talk too much about," but he heard instructors had brought it up, that Bruce Lee, he handled with one finger.

"His case I have to stop," Kim said, "too much wrong ways he got into." Kim would use the broken English to his advantage, talking in circles to wear you down. As the months passed, one day after a lengthy afternoon practice the instructors would tell us, almost like they were letting us in on undisclosed information, that Kim had used his mental powers against Lee. The psychic hit. Supposedly, few people in the world were capable of such a feat.

Lesson ends with the required bowing and thanking, he walks

slowly into the office. A little while later he leaves the school after more bowing and thanking; and the tension level drops noticeably, for a few minutes. Next thing we know, as we're changing in the back room, Kim is entering the rear door. Forrest has keys and Kim is there again lecturing about something. Part of it was, "You have two Chung Moo Quan instructors, you can ask them which way." We felt like we were learning from the best available.

He kept looking at us in a strange way Joe thought. He noticed the master was now wearing what looked like an expensive gold watch and a gold chain around his neck, very 80's. Were we expected to notice and by our reaction he'd gauge our worth as students, if we were 'moved by money?' Anyway he leaves; almost smugly it seemed, with Forrest as chauffeur, the mint condition silver 1976 Lincoln Mark IV running with lights on, waiting as well for Kim's command.

During the next few days there was the customary follow-up. What did we think of Master? We all thought it was great, indeed. We had no idea how un-great it really was since we had near-zero experience with anyone with a truly advanced knowledge of martial arts. Kim doesn't have that. What he does have is high-end charisma and the skill and ability to work a crowd, or a cult.

We quickly learned what to do in case Master comes into town and we are entrusted to handle certain part, Moo-speak for running errands. Mind you we were very new to the organization, yet we're being told that in order to be correct, we need to make sure that new sheets and pillowcases are obtained then washed and make sure to use softener, then dry and fold carefully before placing back in the original bag. That was the lecture one afternoon.

Others were dramatic. Like how Kim could move very quickly when needed. We were told that one day, by an instructor doing his best to emulate Kim's odd vernacular, "Master had certain part needed to handle downtown but he put too much concentration towards school and teaching so no choice, he have to move, he decided to use form and walked more faster ways, to Chicago in under twenty minutes." So the story goes, Kim can walk at high speed so much so that it looks like the wind. Walk on water, can do that too, so long as you know where the rocks are.

Sam Shi Mu Gae form where he starts to move so fast there looks to be more than one person is another accomplishment of the Kim.

No one has ever said they have ever seen it, aside from the "One instructor I showed one time, his mind could not handle, he went crazy, so I never show anymore," as explained by Kim.

When all the higher belts, these guys who can move around in what you think is martial arts are standing and bowing and saying yeeess, in hushed drawn out monotone to the next highest belt in the room, if you want to progress towards black belt you believe as well to some extent. Repeating without knowing for sure is the bigger failure.

His actual name was never used in describing any of these feats or legendary accomplishments. The protocol was Master, or Main Part or simply M.K. in reference to Kim. When he promoted himself selfishly to Grand Master he announced he should only be addressed as Chong Su Nim or roughly translated supreme grand master. I say roughly because the use of the term Su Nim is yet another bastardization of recognized Korean parlance for a high ranking accomplished martial artist. It is taboo for any Moo to use the English name of their master in any type of utterance. Over the telephone any reference is kept to an absolute minimum and then only by code.

SUMMERTIME IN MOO-BURG

Joe liked afternoon group. There was plenty of room and they received more instruction time. An hour and a half to two hours every other day was beneficial and a good balance. One day, just as he was stepping into school, an instructor shouts loudly, "The Koreans are here! Quick, get inside and stay in the back," he said to Joe and the other students. Something was up, Head Instructor Forrest was also set to arrive shortly, it was to be a special lesson today.

Soon there were two middle aged Korean guys out on the sidewalk, the same ones Joe saw hanging around nearby when he stepped in, pointing to the pictures in the front window. Forrest arrives and starts yelling at these guys on the sidewalk.

"What do you want? Huh? What do you want!" he bellows.

The two main instructors immediately run to the door, but Forrest raises his hand to keep them restrained inside the doorway. You could almost hear them growling, like pit bulls straining on a leash. Forrest repeated his shouts. At about six-foot five, lean and tough and a former Marine, he could use his voice effectively.

"Get out of here!" he yelled again. The Koreans back up slowly and leave. What we did not know then was the Koreans were of course, martial arts guys and they wanted to meet this new fellow in the area claiming to be Champion of All Asia.

After the lesson that day, Joe politely asked what was up with the visitors. Forrest responded by calling them mosquitoes, they were merely an annoyance. "They want to learn from Master too, just like you, but they never have opportunity," he said, "because they teach wrong way exercise, that's all that other stuff is; it's junk." Thus more new terms were learned, junk dealer and junk shop to describe other types of martial arts.

It was common practice back in the day, Joe recalls, that if a student from another system did decide to sign up and start Mooing, they would make the new student turn in his former belt as a condition of gaining Moo rank. Sometimes it was right away by first section but always before fourth section, depending on how far they thought they could push the student and how much cash they could get out of him.

The student's previous belt, the symbol of that hard work, would be cut up in school, in four pieces and thrown in the trash for everyone to see. It was just another way of demoralizing people to get them to bow to Moo.

Forrest went on to promise he will tell us about learning directly from the one true master, John C. Kim, but right now he has to go check other schools. He bows towards the flags and the certificates in the office and steps out to the Lincoln Continental which had already been pulled up to the curb by one of the main droids. The other, waiting testily as Forrest spoke to us, accompanies him outside. Forrest drives off giving one final bow from behind the wheel to the waiting troops. As the main droids step back in a fourth section says loudly, "Stah-Hand Up!"

In the following weeks we got into T-Kick form and some sparring techniques called Daze movements. These were awkward at first but the principals seemed sound, if, your partner stood there and waited for you to do the move, it was effective. What were really effective were the stories of the forms. Stories to entice you to want to learn them, stories to reinforce what we were being taught was the best anywhere in the world.

T-KICK FORM

It was said that in Asia, more Asia ways, as we'd see and hear on television in a few years; whichever province had the strongest martial knowledge or form, could then rule until defeated or overthrown by another group with superior skills. Sounds probable; T-Kick form was purportedly developed in one province, don't ask which one that is not important nor is how long ago. Just remember the knights or king's army if you will could not be defeated or conquered for hundreds of years as they could attack with impunity via their specially developed T-Kick.

From equal weight sparring position, the front foot remains turned in while the rear foot is brought forward over the front knee and by using the hips, thrust forward turning the attacking rear foot to knife edge to strike the opponent. The hands and forearms remain in sparring defensive position during the kick. It's like front snap kick but turn the foot to the outside knife edge. The hips turn inwards to each other. Practicing low, back straight, butt out; build those legs.

For beginners it's tricky and encourages this must be real. The form is: Left foot forward sparring position. You could practice blocking a punch with your left forearm as you step back. T-Kick with the right leg, thrust forward but bring back to cover. Then, right step forward, pivot the body 180 degrees into a low reverse sparring position; left foot rear kick, turn forward into a side horse position. Now with the rear foot (the right one), use a fan kick towards the opponent's head in the direction of the attack and drop into a horse stance on the opposite side. Slide-side or step-behind side kick; and finish with a side-horse punch. We could practice back and forth on both sides once we understood what we trying to do. The defender mostly slid backwards and practiced blocks.

It's not bad straight line movement except the T-Kick is rarely developed enough to be effective. How to use it was not explained thoroughly, you had to ask and get kicked a few times. The way it was taught it would be difficult to use especially from that stance. A front or side kick from a cat stance, with slight weight on the front foot, is a lot faster and has penetration if the hips are tucked in and not stuck out to the rear like a duck as in Moo.

The back and forth repetition becomes constraining and sparring plateaus. You could mix it up with different partners but if you deviated one iota from the script there was hell to pay. Putting your own mind in was a mistake in Moo.

This hurts individual development as it's difficult to practice combos you may like. You are not allowed to fully explore how to use what you have learned. That was one of the hidden aspects of the program you weren't supposed to figure out.

You'd sweat up a storm when you got the chance to practice then get called in to stew in the office to be talked up for the next course. We got in more practice when main instructors were busy then when they were watching us. Very little teaching went on; it was more of 30% practice, 70% lecture on history or development or some other crap no one wanted to hear except the Moo-droids standing in formation in the waiting room.

Most of us practiced this form for beginning coordination and timing. It looked impressive to informations with no experience to see first sections moving a little. "You'll be able to learn this in just a few weeks, but you have to be on private course," they'd be told.

The silly history was a big hook, we thought it was real in the beginning. It would have been interesting to look back after a few months and question ourselves as to whether or not we really thought T-Kick form was the once-sacred holdings of elite forces defending their sovereign territory. If we had done this, more ponderings would have opened up sooner. We would have thought more about what we were in fact learning after a short time in the cult. I think we would have shaken our heads and said, naw, it's something someone with some hard-form knowledge put together to sell in the U.S. market. Comparably there was nothing available at the time. It wasn't like car dealers in a row. All the best known martial arts were downtown, far removed from the source of true royal ways in the suburbs.

BA GUA

There was a special group lesson to be held at night. All first and second section students were encouraged to attend, adjust personal schedules as needed. Two head instructors, Forrest and Tom, both now fourth degrees, the highest ranking Moo belts in the U.S. under Kim, would lead the lesson.

Upon arrival the parking lot and the waiting room were filled half an hour before the scheduled seven p.m. lesson time. There are more students than when Kim was here, Joe thought. Forrest and Tom were already inside the school. Each student was motioned up to the beads by the office to say hello. Those of higher section rank were asked a few questions by Forrest in his gravelly low voice. Tom, a large dude with protruding teeth, stayed quiet except for a few unintelligible remarks only Forrest could hear. Clearly Forrest was the senior; he sat behind the desk while Tom sat across from him in the seats used for students undergoing conversations. One main instructor was in the office, standing nervously. The other handled the waiting room. "Step inside and start to move around," Forrest told a group of us.

About half an hour later the lesson began. The warm-up was exhausting; there were new strength challenging holding postures introduced, the freakishly warm weather was taxing the ventilation system. We were ordered to deep breathe. In Moo deep breathing the upper back and shoulders are straight of course but the spine is allowed to curve with the butt sticking out. In fact, assistant instructors would walk the ranks putting their knees into student's backs and pull the outreached arms back to properly align the position. The hands were to be level with the temples, the palms relaxed. The most noticeable aspect was the forceful breathing; the diaphragm was worked very hard.

"Breathe In!" Forrest would command, then "Out!" Becoming an instructor droid himself, Joe learned to effectively mimic this style. It is impressive and inspiring to have thirty or so dedicated folks in uniform move or take action on command just because you said so. Zeik Heil!

Joe did finally learn the correct way to breathe, after he left Moo. Breathing should be natural, relaxed and in a seated position is not necessarily the best way. Standing meditation is very powerful. The Moo way does build up the lower diaphragm and general breathing in a short amount of time. But the gains leave quickly unless practiced regularly, like all Moo forms. Tai Chi or Yogic breathing develops more slowly, the techniques are more profound and take longer to fully learn, however the achievements stay with you longer, in this author's opinion.

The rest of the lesson was basic kick and punch techniques. We worked on kick defenses and Forrest, along with Tom showed our rank of students a few new ones. They were effective against round house and side kicks. This was cool beans, getting taught readily usable methods by such a high rank. Then Forrest demonstrated correct sliding side kick. Where from horse (side stance) position; one slides the rear foot up to the front foot which is raised up to execute a side kick. To do this he selected a larger student who was enthusiastically practicing throughout the night. A third section, he looked proficient and wasn't as exhausted as us newbies.

Forrest had the sofa cushions from the waiting room brought in and told the target student to hold them as a measure of defense. Next, Head Instructor Forrest explained in slow motion, the body positioning and timing required to execute the kick effectively. He then moved fluidly, propelling the student across the width of the room; the cushions did their job in protecting vital areas. Afterward, the trainee of nine months exclaimed he had never felt anything like it.

We were then paired off to practice the slide kick and the defense. The group ended about two hours after it had started by a furious one hundred-count punch-out. From low horse position, fists clenched at our sides, it was the main droids turn to use their voice energy and yell, Punch! We executed singles, then doubles, then combinations at the solar plexus and the point between the upper lip and nose. The group energy generated during punch-out was a long standing favorite by all Moos.

The final ten were the most intense. Extend the right hand! shouted the instructor.

Kee-Hah! thundered the group. The ceiling tiles rattled as the count progressed. Forrest seemed pleased. The group ended with the customary bowing to the flags, then for the first time, Forrest said, "Bow towards Master's certificates… then higher belts, lower belts and each other."

Cheee Yung Moo! We screamed with shrill pointed emphasis and clapped along with Forrest eight times. We bowed again towards the flags and thanked head instructors, instructors and assistant instructors in unison. This bowing and thanking would be repeated almost daily, sometimes several times a day, for the remainder of our years in the cult.

We were about to move into the back room and change into street clothes when Forrest started to point to certain students while asking the main droids, "What about this one?" The instructors would mock a decision process then answer, "Yes, be alright." Five first and second sections were picked out. At first section and only on special private course, Joe was clearly the junior member. The main instructors seemed shocked as did the assistants. To get into Ba Gua at such a low rank was unprecedented.

"Only about fifteen minutes and not too low, you understand," Head Instructor Forrest said to the instructor who led us into the back room, after bowing and thanking of course.

"Alright, make a circle," the second degree began. "What you're about to get into must never be explained or showed to anyone who has not been given this form, understand? If you do, it's shhiiick." He made a cutting motion across his neck, "And I'll be the one to gladly do it."

We got into a low sparring position, with one hand bent at the elbow, the wrist pulled back at eye level, out in front and extending into the center of the circle. Our backs were straight, butt thrust out with our lower hand in a similar manner, in front of the solar plexus but under the opposite elbow. We began to walk in a counter clockwise circle and breathe heavily, rhythmically in step as we walked. In, out, in, out, breathing hard and stepping for a few minutes then we were ordered to switch sides and direction. The form now went the other way with the hands reversed, the details of how to switch were explained many lessons into the future, for tonight the main emphasis was on the timing of the heavy breathing and the stepping.

After about fifteen minutes we were allowed to stand up. What a head rush! We were then shown to jump up in the air pulling our knees to our chest and land hard punching toward the ground bending at the waist and exhaling. We did this ten times. We lined up, bowed and Forrest stuck his head in the room, the beads held up out of the way by the instructors.

"How do you feel?" he asked, somewhat gently, but with that underlying growl still present. We didn't know what to say, we were in a euphoric state. Our arms and legs were feeling the effects; we were wrung out, tired and happy. All the higher belts listening in laughed when Forrest started to chuckle. "Alright," he said, "go ahead and change."

The reason for light headedness Forrest explained as we more faster ways, in cult-speak, put on our shoes and socks, was that Ba Gua sets the body and makes it balanced, so you feel near euphoric. Make sure to practice Ba Gua as the last form to end the day at least until you become accustomed to the effects. No hard physical movement for at least eight hours. Great, Joe thought as he headed off to work in a factory, loading trucks, great.

Joe started scheduled vacation the next week from his full time gig and picked up a part time delivery job in the afternoons. Because he had gotten in the highest most classified form of the Moo at such a low rank, he was ordered to be in school by 11:00 a.m. every day for half an hour of Ba Gua. Joe was expected to also get in another half-hour of the form on his own at night for the next two weeks while he was on vacation. That way his body would build up enough to accept the form in its true version.

Well, the truth is Pa Kua, pronounced ba-gwa, is not all that hard to find. It is documented as hundreds of years old but not thousands like the Moo says and it is a system unto its own. At least it can be, more than a few schools of martial art training have different methods of Pa Kua in their repertoire and it is an exceptionally legitimate practice. The Moogwa way, however is not. Kim bastardized a little known, at the time, form of exercise and pawned it off as his own. A well-respected book on this subject was written in the 1960s by Robert W. Smith and put back into publication recently. I read it twenty years after my first indoctrination sessions with the Moo. It was one more piece of the truth revealing the fraud now called Oom Yung Doe.

There are many different ways to practice Pa Kua, some are down low; others have distinctive changes or switches and different actions in stepping. Since the form developed over centuries and my discovery of the authentic varieties is new to me, I am not qualified to explain the intricacies. What is readily apparent is real Pa Kua does not have the forceful, strained breathing. Nor does it have the ludicrous legend and history the Moo fabricated.

BA GUA (MOOGWA) HISTORY

Over the next few weeks and on into the years that followed, the legend of master Ba Gua, the first Chung Moo master, would be told and re-told, modified and expanded. It wasn't called Chung Moo of course back then 1500 years ago. We were never told what it was called then, that wasn't important. What was important was that you handled (paid for) your course and believed what they told you. What follows is the abridged version.

Master Ba Gua was a hermit that lived in the mountains, in Asia. The assumption was China but no one ever questioned it. One day he came into a village where he was befriended. When the village was about to be attacked by an invading horde, Ba Gua organized the defenses. Every one he taught, trained hundreds of soldiers who trained even more (thousands, depends on who is telling the story) and the attackers were defeated. The king offered his throne and the village in return. Ba Gua refused, slowly walking away back into the mountains, the shuffling sound of his feet and the intense breathing making a sound like: ba gwa, ba gwa, ba gwa. Isn't that a great story? The reason for the upside down king marks you see in school is from that tradition. Kim would place marks in the corners of the schools, and on all the weapons during the approval process (described in detail ahead) and in the cars and certain artifacts he controlled. It looked like a simple Chinese glyph, inverted. But because Kim hand-scribed it, it held special reverence and power.

The Moo sold a lot of people on their version of Pa Kua simply because we didn't know any different. And more importantly, Kim knew that in the suburbs a bunch of stupid 'Mericans would likely be easy targets to learn the 1500 year-old art of Chung Moo Quan just like the literature said. Look, they even have schools in Hong Kong and Pusan and Guam; it's got to be real. Our friends outside of school, while we had them, were impressed; especially with the stories of higher belts in other states who can make light, then wind come out of the palms, if your mind is true.

TRANSITION TO CULT MENTALITY

Further along that summer, it was another weekend night and the hommies were looking to go out. Joe wanted to practice his ancient form of Ba Gua. Joe's housemates, guys he knew for several years were miffed. They went out without him. He had succeeded in alienating them, now Joe had to re-align energies with his new cult and all its requirements.

After loosening up with the special warm-up stretches and other proprietary elements of preparing to practice Moo; Joe got in a good twenty minutes of the down low, breathing hard muscles straining exertion that is Moogwa. During his practice, concentrating on the requirements of this strange procedure was difficult. All sorts of thoughts kept entering his mind; the stories of Kim and his out of this world natural ability, the legends of the Chung Moo Quan, Joe's friends turning away from him. It seemed to build up until the finish of the form. Using all his strength he jumped as high as he could pulling knees to chest and landed hard; punching downward ten times total before bowing east then west and shouting Chung Moo!; making sure to clap eight times.

The ground shook, the windows in the rear utility room of the house began vibrating and the front door to the house was being pelted with what, Joe wasn't sure. Wow, this bonding with nature stuff really does work. A huge thunderstorm had rolled up and was lashing the neighborhood. He was convinced there was a connection.

MINISTRY OF SILLY FORMS

Here's a quick run down of the background and teachings employed by Moo to sell their brand of goods. There were two hundred and eighty-nine hard-form or Kong Su Kata in Chung Moo Quan. Two-man Kata is number one thirty-two. Horse position throughout in an H-pattern, it uses both sides; arms and fists moving each step, back-knuckle attack each time. It was said the highest movements in Shotokan Karate were the beginning block of Kata twenty, a double fist circle out-block while stepping forward at a forty-five degree angle, right fist over head with the left in front; at the same time the right side shifts back to a sparring stance with no weight on the front, both feet are at forty-five degrees.

It used to be up to Kata nineteen was taught plus one thirty-two, the two-man. And that was it, even for black Moo belts. A few years went by then Kata twenty, twenty-one and twenty-two were passed but they were no big deal. They have a Buddha palm-esque block as the second move, wonder if Kim saw that on a magazine cover too, with other different combos of basic Kong Su thrown in. Repeat, pay cash, Moo.

It was said that even with fifteen years of Tae Kwon Do or Karate, and only if someone learned from a very high hard-style belt, that's what they'd have in form; all Kata moves and none of the supposed higher form that even second or third section Moos were learning. What happened to the in-between specifics of Kata? Why were they never taught or further mentioned? Simple, they were not yet invented.

It was also said that the very first movement of Ta Bouk Chung, a form to develop breathing and power, but just another Kata made up to look like something, was higher than any Kata due to the release at the end of each movement. Approximately thirty steps were given out. We did enjoy that form and felt it helped endurance, timing and application of differing attacks. The idea of it being a higher form never stuck as I happen to believe it depends more on the person and what they do with their practice, as to what develops.

It could also be said that the way or method of instruction is also key, and agree heartily. But to insist this style is better than any other coming from someone who continuously re-invents forms, legends and names of his school, convinced only he knows best, throws away any substance of such a claim.

Sudo form or was it pseudo-form, also termed seven-step sudo Kata, was fun but rigorous. A first section movement, it was used as a review lesson even at second degree weekly groups for main instructors when the cash shortfalls started to impact Kim's lifestyle and he wanted to reinforce through physical lessons we weren't trying hard enough.

Chung Yu, or wooden arms, defense and attack against two or more. Allegedly this was beginning training for soldiers in ancient times along with the seven-step above.

Kong Su sparring form, not given out until near sixth section for some reason, was a straight-line block and attack script that got one used to harder contact. No deviation from the plan was allowed and variations in timing were frowned upon lest you get the 'what are you doing, putting in your own mind again' verbal correction. Under this scripted training, it was difficult to develop ourselves but we tried our best. A few bruises made us think we were doing something.

Ho Sam Ka Chume Bope, nine cats climbing three stairs or some such nonsense, was not given out until second degree and never taught again. This is a weird one to describe; it is supposed to be one of the highest Moo hard-forms practiced in the mountains on steep slopes and uneven terrain, thus explaining the odd first step. Jump to the side landing one foot then the other in horse position with double-sided down-blocks following with the timing of the feet. It is just another odd kata Kim put together to keep you busy.

The Side Kick Story: For the first three hundred years of all martial arts there was no side kick in any style because Chung Moo had not yet invented it. Every method of training, knowledge and understanding comes from Moo. The most powerful kick at that time was front kick. Any kicks developed since were by Chung Moo or Moo Doe masters. One day centuries ago a higher belt is traveling along and here comes a bear. The higher Moo prepares to defend himself with the strongest weapon in his arsenal, a front kick. The bear charges and claws the top leg muscles of the Moo, who turns his body sideways in a moment of divine intervention; miraculously channeling all remaining energy through his damaged appendage and kicks the attacking beast from the side position in the culmination of the life or death struggle as it unfolded. The bear goes down with one kick. This is what we were told, this is what we believed for we wanted to advance and have our belts colored in. So we nodded and said yes and thanked for opportunity.

And you paid how much for this? We could go into bad posture, poor structure, misalignment and the misuse of joints and all the resulting problems as a result of practicing the Moo Doe way. Students are forced too low in many cases. The upper thigh should not be driven into a level-with-the-ground position all the time. The knee should not be pushed forward well past the ankle and the foot should be straight ahead, not turned in. Moos turn the front foot and knee in because they were told they'd be open to an attack, so they use too narrow a stance and their hips suffer as a result. They end up leaning forward, further stressing the knee. But they thank and bow every day, seeking value for what they paid.

MORE LEARNING IN THE CLASS OF MOO

Early on, one of the subtle techniques Moo and other cults use to solidify their hold on cash contributing members is to say they have potential, could really be something. Another sleight of mind is to point out what's really important in life. Like... friends. What are friends? Define them. Nah, those aren't friends in a real sense, those are acquaintances. You talk, share ideas, go out, whatever, but they're not really friends. Friendship goes much deeper. Americans don't understand this but in Asia they do, because the culture is so much more developed.

A friend is someone who will help you, even when it may be the best thing for you but you can't see it and don't want to hear what he is trying to tell you. Because your friend truly, deeply cares for you though, he will keep helping you until you become better. Like instructors do to get you on course. Instructors are your friends, but you don't want to sign up, so they keep explaining, keep trying to pull you up. But you don't listen, so your friends, your real friends know you simply do not recognize the value so they keep trying to work with you so you can benefit. A real friend has more knowledge than you and only wants to help you.

At this point you might offer examples of how your outside friends have helped you in tough situations, stood beside you. But the Moos are ready for this, explaining that once fully accepted into the cult you'll have ten times the number of true friends you do now. You'll have friends throughout the country even though you have just met, your position will be so recognized and theirs by you likewise. The bond is that strong as it has been for centuries. You should sign up.

The Moo salesperson will continue: Look at all the benefits you've experienced so far, and you are just on beginning course. Once you get on higher course and start to learn higher form, to feel what that's like, you'll see what we mean. Those outside ones, the ones that don't have true Moo, they are (in Moo-speak) missing. But don't feel bad for them and don't try too much to explain, they wouldn't understand what you're trying to accomplish for them; just as sometimes it is hard now for you to understand what instructors are trying to explain to you, to help you, to make your life better.

Your mind should be on handling your course and practicing hard. Put full concentration on what we are sharing with you and you will see the difference. Your outside friends, acquaintances really, will start to see you differently; even your family and your boss at work may seem shocked by the changes.

It may seem more difficult for you. That's where you'll start to want to be around the school more, to seek out others who want to improve themselves. It's like you're in a car merging onto the freeway, you want to keep up with other students so you hit passing gear and suddenly the people you were around are left behind.

That's up to them and you should not think too much about it. In your case, keep looking forward until you also reach the point of instructor and can help those ones. You should think about maybe moving in with those who are like you, on course, trying hard, making higher belt is mentally very comfortable.

Understand? Now, how much you brought in today, huh? Almost every conversation was about "reaching a higher point" and the best way to get there was via school and the courses they offered.

BLACK BELT COURSE

After about two months involvement with the mini-mall McDojo it was spring time at last. Joe's skiing has improved the remainder of this past season. More flexibility, more energy; being twenty-three and starting a regular exercise program does that to people. But the Moo tries to make you believe it's because of their magic form. Every time entering the place it was asked, how do you feel? The best possible answer was "good." Not better or stronger because then you'd be drilled as in "better than what?" or "stronger than who?" Joe formulated a patented escape with "better than I was."

Of the dozen or so people starting out within a few weeks of when Joe began taking group lessons only a handful regularly attended. The afternoon group was failing, students were encouraged to attend night time group, or to bring friends in for free introductory lessons. Joe brought one friend in, a first-year law student. He saw his way clear and Joe saw little of him after that. Every time they'd meet, Joe would launch into stories of the greatness of the Quan, of all the great things Kim was said to be capable of, of the great organization that is Moo. His friend would wish Joe well, knowing he was too determined, too stubborn, and too gullible to understand what was really going on.

One dude of stocky build in his early thirties and apparently successful by his dress and car, stopped by one afternoon then stopped coming. He was a second section. There was a discussion in the front waiting room with one of the main instructdroids. It quickly became elevated with the student yelling, "All you want is more money… talk to my lawyer," over his shoulder as he stomped out, the bell chimes ringing angrily as he flung the door open, still in uniform. We noticed when our practice session finished he had left his shoes behind.

This was our first time hearing the "no-mind" term. The instructor strode back into the practice room and after the requisite bows and thank-you-instructor scripts were chanted, he announced the now ex-student was in fact told to leave. This same technique would be used over the years repeatedly for anyone who left the cult.

Unqualified, missing, confused, walking dead, selfish; the effect was to condition and continuously reinforce that anyone who left was bad as they were against us. The primary control mechanism used in all cults is building a mental wall to any outside influence detrimental to the cult's weak protective membrane of entrapment. It left us nice and secure in thought within our cult microcosm. It was all ours.

Soon after being exposed to Moogwa and attending a few night lessons when the head instructors were teaching, Joe got on black belt course. He paid two hundred dollars a week for two months, in 1980 terms, to qualify for the down payment. The entire course was ten thousand dollars. The pitch was it was equivalent to college tuition or a fancy car. But it was worth so much more. We were told the story of the Indian prince who was under the tutelage of two Chung Moo instructors Kim personally selected. Just like it said in the flyers, it was a royal style.

There were more new forms to learn. Pal Gae and Du Do Gi were critical in further development. History, application and how the Moo forms build the body internally were stressed. In fact, Pal Gae is yet another bastardization of other authentic forms, jumbled up to look like something. Over time, it wears the joints down. None of the highest belts still in the organization will even attempt Du Do Gi anymore. It's great for kids to build their legs as a game, but not for building effective self-defense.

Instead, we are told stories of Kim's greatness. How the first time he held T-position he held it for twenty-four hours before switching sides, or how he did Du Do Gi for eight hours because no one told him to stop. After a time you begin to believe, at least partially, the stories you are told. You want to be part of what they say they can do.

It all seems so real.

Another fable was how after starting to make progress towards higher belt, the points on your body begin to change. For example, the nerve endings on the forearm, wrist and hand begin to toughen up from exposure to the varying self-defense grabs and counter maneuvers. This is true, the sensitivity decreases. And it's conceivable a sort of immunity would develop at the most vulnerable areas such as the point in between the web of the hand or even, so we were told, the solar plexus.

Is that possible? Why yes it is, lower belt. Once reach fifth degree these points are shielded. The body adapts thanks to the higher form you are learning. Here's a minor example. Several of us stood in a row. The main instructor went up to each of us with his index finger cocked behind his thumb and like shooting a marble, plunked our Adams apple inside our throats. Everyone swallowed hard on the new cud, gulping reflexively when it was our turn.

After a day or so we took turns cautiously tapping each other in the throat to feel the effects of our newly granted immunity. Shazaam! I don't feel a thing! For some reason Joe found himself gazing outside, watching the traffic flow by for a moment. We were evolving into higher beings, and all those white belts outside, they did not understand. No-minds.

Joe passed second section with flying colors, testing in late afternoon with a student from night time group testing for third, who had come in early. They became friends and hung around together for the next month or so and were planning to share rent. They'd make good roommates, both wanting to be black belts, and practiced together a lot. But then a funny thing happened. Joe kept bringing down as much cash as he could to pay off course. His new friend, Jim, stopped attending classes then returning phone calls. Joe kept practicing wondering what had happened to all the folks that signed up only to leave shortly thereafter. When he met any former students on the street they acted weird when Joe said he was still in, trying to make black belt. He felt strangely alone. He asked about Jim. He moved, the instructors told Joe. What really happened was Jim was pressured for more money, to buy the next course and he moved alright, so the instructors would stop calling him.

After awhile Joe started to drift away from the school too. He was transferred at work and making the hour-plus drive one way was a strain. They wanted you in there every day, to control you because they had taught you secret forms. If you took a couple days to relax, they made comments like "look what the wind blew in" and ignore you in the practice room. They played a good game. They kept using the hook "you could really be something if you'd just try... we're here to help pull you up, that's what higher belts do."

Joe went to Chicago Fest in lieu of attending a night time group when the head instructors were coming around. The next time in Joe was scolded for missing such a great opportunity. "Look at all you learned last time, and now you're throwing it away," they chided.

He rarely got out to large events like sports games, concerts and such. Learning martial arts was helping him climb out of a personality shell and these guys were trying to put Joe back in it via micro-controlling and manipulation. Joe floundered for a few more weeks then cast everything aside and plunged ahead full bore Moo. He would soon sell his car, deciding to put all energy and concentration on making black belt. Nothing else mattered. Obtaining any trappings of comfort could wait.

TEN MILE WALK TO MAKE THIRD SECTION

His car, less than a year old had more than the allotted amount of mileage on it for warranty repairs. It also had a front main seal oil leak. Naturally the Moos were sympathetic to this as they wanted the cash value of the car, so they suggested turning back the speedometer. They had been trying to get Joe to sell the thing and bring in the proceeds for course. They had also tried to convince him to obtain a personal loan at the bank, but he balked, having no other collateral.

One of the few remaining outside friends Joe had left was a mechanic. He provided details on how to turn back the dial since, as higher belts mentioned, all the car companies were thieves anyway and he was just helping to even the score. They'd spin back a few miles and GM would correct their obvious manufacturing defect. Joe and colleague spent most of a day he should have been sleeping to be ready for work dismantling the dash and beginning the mind-boggling slow process of winding back eighteen thousand miles to an appropriate digit under the magic twelve thousand with a variable speed drill stuck in the back of the odometer.

Several hours later the windings were sprawled on the kitchen floor, the drill still plugged in and spinning away. He had touched the drill to the side wall and spun it too fast; the car instrument was now complete junk. No choice but to find another instrument cluster. It took a couple days but Joe located a source on the far south side.

He went there with a co-worker, a beefy guy who for the cost of a case of beer was up for most anything. They met with the parts dealer in a run down alley and headed back to the suburbs via his buddy's vehicle. The new dash fit in well, the car would be fixed.

Joe dropped off the former idol of his hard work at the dealership and walked ten miles that day to practice for the final run thru before third section test. He started to walk back to the car but had to call a cab, his legs so sore they were locking up and time was running out to make it to work. Dehydration plagued many of us during our time in Moo. No one in the school had any idea about leg and internal muscle cramps although they claimed to know everything.

Third section was accomplished without much difficulty, Joe again testing with just one other student who had also brought in his fee of sixty dollars. Third section exam lasted about forty-five minutes, mostly consisting of drilling the forms and steps learned in the past month. The self-defense aspects were more thorough, we had to execute multiple techniques for different types of situations, demonstrate proficiency in knowing more than one kind of shoulder grab, more than one cross-grab take-down; be able to move in more than one or two ways against a combination punch attack, have more than one defense against a round kick, and so on.

Joe bowed and thanked and paid homage to the flags, Kim's school and the instructors. After a couple days the belts were handed back in another bowing and thanking ritual. They were newly dyed in black, three sections out of the seven of the length of the belt. When worn on the uniform, the two sections hanging down in front plus one section outwardly visible to the waist would show black.

The reward was a two hour lesson, non-stop, of a legendary form named Tong Nong. Said to be Bruce Lee's highest and he only had the first three movements. Which Joe and two other third sections got because they were handling course; that is bringing in every dime they had. Ocean form, as Tong Nong was said to represent, theoretically lasted over eight hours with no moves repeating. We were told it took several generations of Moo to develop and we were oh so lucky to be taught, let alone even see it. Years later this very same proprietary to Moo asset was said to be twelve hours long then at another time, fourteen. Eventually we figured out the form we so revered was merely a contrived choreography along with its legend and history of development.

In summary, the movement was supposedly taken from the action of ocean waves on an island. The wave crashes in, runs back out, comes in again then spreads out on the beach. The pattern takes on the characteristics of a group of waves eroding the shore. As it progresses, in theory, the waves have moved up onto the plains then the foot hills and finally the mountains where the series of steps takes on the characteristics of a hard-style martial art.

If this seems like a way to sell existing Kong Su or Tae Kwon Do exercise as a repackaged new and improved product, well then you're ahead of the game. Nonetheless several thousand people, perhaps as many as ten thousand over the past thirty years, have been conned into believing it's some kind of ultimate martial arts practice.

We didn't know any better. We Tong Nonged every day, sometimes for hours non-stop as that was the way we were taught to practice to obtain the full effects. Here, believe this; now go do it for hours, for years on end until you think you got your money's worth. It seemed to make more sense as more movements were taught. However, for developing fighting ability it lacks real value, the steps too impractical to apply effectively. It is fair aerobics though.

After about six months you had about thirty steps. And yes they did repeat but don't mind the fact we said earlier it is eight, no twelve hours long; you are only beginning to train so you should be doing, not asking, understand? Thus we Mooed. Joe and I practiced those first few Tong Nong moves for composite days within the first month we learned it. All we wanted to do was practice; get more form and the next belt rank.

We also learned another form said to be shown by Bruce Lee in the movie Enter the Dragon. Kim even said Lee's name spelled in Chinese meant Little Dragon. See how clever Kim is? He worked in a subordinate term and the minions accepted it. Thus we took in Eel e Kick or spinning fan kick form as another authentic training method. It mimics certain aspects of kick training but to say this is another hush-hush formula handed down throughout the centuries to only a chosen few and the reason Bruce Lee isn't around anymore is because he showed this and other secrets to Westerners well, that's a bit of a tall tale, don't ya think? Still, we Mooed on. We wanted that next black section on our belts.

NOTED LOCAL EVENTS

During Joe's first summer as a Chung Moonie, a couple things happened that would shape the coming training. One night a car pulls up in the front lot; backs in and flashes the high beams into the windows of our strip mall gathering place. The group was in full swing, we had paired off for kick defenses when the front door whips open, the bell chimes slap around on their string. "Hello!" yells a loud voice. The two black belt instructors immediately move out of the office and confront the stranger.

"What do you want?" one yells back loudly. It is a Korean man, mid-twenties and he says he is a black belt, wants to see our style. Having witnessed this greeting before, we all knew the new guy was in for a rough time. We are herded into the backroom by the fifth and sixth section assistant instructors to start kicks at high volume, to demonstrate the ferocity of our place of worship.

Being about the lowest belt there, Joe is last to make it through the bead curtain into the back room. He sees one instructor, a future felon; execute an unprovoked standing forward sweep towards the visitor, who stumbles back against the wall, hard. Both second degree interns then push him onto the couch and yell at him viscously. Joe considered it appalling to see this happen. It is not true martial arts, we had no idea our mentors were so crude. What Joe could recognize was the lack of control and confidence exuded by the highest belts in the school. This was explained to us as this guy was looking for trouble and needed to be thumped.

Other events which were not fully explained at the time which repeated every so often were the scuffles occurring as a result of passing flyers about Chung Moo Quan in other nearby shopping centers. We'd hear things like assistant instructor so and so knocked one down, or used knee break and elbow to hit a dingy.

The truth was more often than not the fledgling Moo was knocked around by someone from a real lineage or sent packing with his precious flyers and told not to come back by the local merchants or store owners who didn't like trouble on their sidewalks and had little interest in supporting the Champion of All Asia as the literature advertised. This was the beginning of seeing how the school controlled and manipulated all information about the students and their lives. Need to know, what to know, was determined by how much you could pay.

LEGEND OF RETURNING FROM THE MOUNTAINS

In some schools, pictures of Kim showed him looking quite fierce with what seemed to be sunburn or wind exposure, wearing a cape or royal looking shawl draped over his shoulders as he faces the camera holding a large Chinese-type sword. His hair looks ragged and uneven, said to be from using a rock to cut it down to shoulder length after being in the wild for so long. It was out of the question to use the sword he carried with him in the rugged mountains as the weapon meant survival and life. It was said he would practice for several days without stopping, developing unmatched ability and precision with the weapon. If he dropped the sword, he would stop for the day, as it meant his mind was not right for practice.

The intricate looking drape appeared hand-sewn with the elaborate stitching and deeply vibrant colors reserved for royalty, of dark red fabric and bright gold thread. The background to the photo is undefined, there is only Kim staring at the lens, holding the broadsword with the exquisite tapestry flowing over him like a king. We were told this picture was taken soon after he emerged from the mountains for the third and final time; he had survived the ordeals put before him and was thus officially, master.

The story of the cape was that an old man awaited the chosen one who would one day emerge from the mountains. The elder man's role in life, his purpose, was to await he who would become the man in the picture. According to the legend, the way the old-timer understood, it was his destiny to make the artifact, and then wait for a traveler to come out of the mountains at a certain time of a certain year as foretold in prophecy; and hand to him his life's work. The wearing of the robe would confirm the final steps of Kim's ascendancy to greatness.

During the winter in the mountains, the temperature would go to fifty or more below zero, so cold that even Kim could not risk falling asleep. He spoke once, of long ago people had immunity to cold, but newer generations had lost this earlier natural defense. In the mountains, on those extremely cold nights he had to stay awake and could not allow himself to dose off completely lest he perish. This greatly developed his already talented senses to be able to detect approaching wild animals and to be keenly aware of his surroundings. This defensive posture was said to make him invincible. If somebody tried to shoot, he could move out of the way before the trigger was fully pulled. Many higher belts would attest that during large gatherings of instructors, Kim said he knew who was in what part of the house or even in the driveway as a result of his mountain training.

WAR TALES AND OTHER STORIES

During the Korean War, Kim was said to have practiced Tong Bong (short staff) and other forms for hours amongst the dead after the battlefields were deserted. One version said Kim was a major general; other versions had him as simply a major. Captured briefly by two enemy soldiers after a battle, he is alleged to have back-knuckled and killed the one behind him as they marched him to the enemy camp even though they knew he was the legendary Kim. He then escaped. No other details or proof of military service was ever offered or put forth. Born in 1933 he would have been about age twenty at the end of the war, a very high rank for such a young officer. As an expert, Kim often commented on the current military forces of the world. Republic of Korea Marines were of course highly favored, followed by U.S. Marines then British Special Forces in their fighting capability and discipline.

This last excerpt is notable because every time he had an audience, Kim would comment on just about any aspect of life; giving constant direction, subtly or openly to the clan on what was best, Chung Moo, or not as good, everything else. He always had the ultimate explanation. Any one leaving the collective would miss out, but those staying in continued with their acceptance of his views and never developed their own identity. The Quan evidently had knowledge kept hidden for centuries of: desalination of water; protection from nuclear radiation with roasted barely tea called por-re-cha; certain exercises if performed only minutes per day would maintain health indefinitely; and knowledge once sought by Mohammed Ali for another comeback to extend his boxing career for ten years, but Kim refused as Ali would use for the wrong reasons.

Kim also spoke out about sparing; he didn't like the competitive nature of Tae Kwon Do and other sorts as it was potentially injurious and developed the wrong qualities in students. They learn to score points or just show off. If students were ever seen engaging in such activities as free-sparring within a school, they were disciplined harshly.

Self-defense in Moo was to be practiced seriously and with no intent of showing up or hurting another, but was expected to be diligently pursued, as much as you could take. As long as the respect line was held up and proper care for each other exercised, vigorous self-defense was encouraged. Apparently, in later years the schools became even more lax in these vital areas, producing higher ranks with belts gained by purchased testing.

FURTHERING THE TRANSITION TO FULL CULT MEMBERSHIP

Joe wanted that next rank. School became all consuming, he would make black belt. It took a couple days of scouring the local news papers for a suitable commuter car. Something clean, dependable, may be in need of some minor repairs he could work on over the next few months. Joe found a ten year-old two door Mopar, dark blue with relatively low mileage. A gem he thought, at only five hundred dollars clear, and the seller was throwing in an old CB radio.

Joe sold the Cutlass to another dealer to pay off the loan and of course, walked about ten miles to hitch a ride from a co-worker back to his new vehicle. All was well. The next week, the loan from the Supreme was cleared, everything settled out. Buying a reasonable set of tries and some minor brake work for the Mopar, Joe proudly brought in an extra fifty dollars towards course and was laughed at.

After lesson that afternoon the instructors asked where is that fancy car. They said they had noticed Joe was parking in the lot next door, but where is it now, in the shop again? Why not sell it? Joe mentioned in the correct bow and stooping mannerisms of the school that he had in fact sold it and picked up another vehicle. They immediately asked where is the cash from the car sale? Joe explained he had to pay off the loan. At first they seemed outraged, but then asked about any money left over. He produced the fifty dollars. They grabbed it, saying, "That's it? We need to talk."

The next hour was spent in the office in the spot called the cooker. Anytime your handlers suspected confusion or a moving away from the cult's plans, you were brought in for a conversation and placed in the far seat in the corner of the office. One instructor salesperson was sitting next to you, the other one behind the desk in command position. The lectures would range from your family and your upbringing, the mistakes that were made unto you but it's not your fault and how school is now your real family; how higher belts care deeply for you and how all you need to do is bring in cash to cement that relationship, to show you too care. That you have a bright future, school is growing, you could be one of the elite in a short amount of time with several schools of your own; to how Master came to this country solely for the purpose of developing the United States into the martial arts powerhouse it was destined to be.

Joe left that day like many of us had several times before, exhausted mentally and physically, just wanting to grab a few hours sleep before work. But this time at least, he hadn't signed on for any new courses. He still had black belt course to pay off. At least he was fifty dollars closer, only seven thousand more to go.

During the next month or so his attendance was sporadic. The droids continued to call Joe at the factory, saying they were friends or a landlord needing to get in touch with him so his boss would get Joe to the phone. They kept asking when he was coming back, not to give up. Joe retorted by saying he would keep practicing and come in to school when he could. They still seemed genuine or perhaps Joe was still too susceptible.

He didn't practice as much away from the school as he had before. Everyone Joe came up with had quit, he guessed. Plus he was broke, and the guys he lived with previously were not as open towards him. They said he had changed; all Joe talked about was school. He was at a crossroads; figuring, wrongly, to press on and at least complete the black belt training. Joe dropped out of college from lack of funds, looked at the military but decided at the time it was too much of a commitment, at least he should get this accomplished.

PART III

MIDDLE BELT

"Greatness does not need to be talked up; it stands on its own"
—Rush Limbaugh

PART III—MIDDLE BELT

INSTRUCTOID COURSE

Going to school during the day and working at night was the issue he reasoned. If he could obtain a decent day job and attend night group, the real group, consistently, Joe could train alongside the others he had heard so much about and, hopefully, blend more into the main crowd and be less subject to the lectures.

It took a few weeks of persistent attack but in due course he scored a union job as a driver's helper on a major brand soft drink delivery truck. With great money, benefits and the chance to be out and about, perfect deal for a young guy; this would be his ticket. The future looked bright, finally.

Joe asked for a private audience with the sales instructors after a good revitalizing afternoon practice session. Starting a new gig in a few days and given the factory enough of a notice, he was dwelling in a brief comfort zone of eat, practice, sleep... eat, practice...

They made him wait for about an hour before sitting him down in the office. They asked what's up. Joe announced he had obtained a different job. What, you changed jobs without asking, they exclaimed. They were about to start a lecture, when he blurted out it was a day job so he could make it to night time group. Oh, well that would be alright, how much does this one pay, they wanted to know. Forever calculating the cash worth, they were.

Joe fudged a little bit, sensing they'd want him to bring in something every pay day like before and not just monthly. With no furniture to speak of, nice clothes were a luxury; Joe didn't even own a sports jacket. They made their play about instructor course. The cost was eighteen thousand dollars. Although having no money for down payment, because Joe was true, they would credit everything he had brought in to date, about thirty-five hundred thus far, towards instructor course. The last course you'll ever need they said. But, you'll be required to handle all testing fees as they come up.

Joe agreed. Another contract was written up right there; he was familiar with the process and the blanks to be filled in by now. Joe had no idea these documents were not legal instruments, merely two pages of finely printed garbage to induce trainees as to the legitimacy of the courses.

During this last process, the main instructor telephoned Head Instructor Forrest and proclaimed Joe's enrollment in the elite cadre of budding instructors. As the phone was being handed across the desk into nervously sweaty hands, Forrest's gravel-voiced utterances were about the future and trying hard is just now beginning. The instructor took the phone back and loudly thanked into it, then hung up the receiver.

About one week after starting his new job, just before Thanksgiving, Joe tested for fourth section, a real milestone in Moo. There was no advance notice or hint about what was taking place that Wednesday night. Joe had been attending the night time group lesson for nearly two weeks. There were more students around of all ranks now, about twenty almost every evening. Joe estimated there were probably fifty full time students in the school; it seemed to be going well. He made new friends. Scott, Mark, Jim, Ron and Larry had been on instructor course already for some months and could move proficiently on command. They were taught separately from the others, a lot more Pal Gae and more Daze movements and fancier punch defenses. By this time their take-downs and moves, although still a little awkward, had improved markedly by having each other to practice on.

Looking forward to the holiday break, upon entering school Joe found Scott and the others were in the waiting room with strange looks. Another head instructor, not Forrest was here tonight unexpectedly, the dumb looking one who spoke in mumbles.

He said to Joe, "You're testing fourth section tonight, are you ready? Did you bring down test fee?"

Joe said, "I don't think I'm ready and I did not know about the test or the fee, I don't have it." The main instructdroid was standing next to the bigger, head droid. They both smirked.

"Test fee is two hundred-fifty, bring it in when you can, why don't you think you're ready?" retorted the bigger droid.

The others in the waiting room were ordered inside. Joe was asked again what he felt were his deficiencies. He explained he only had nine Kata and had been in during night group for just a short while. He might pass but wanted to do better on the test.

"Fourth section is more mental, that's why no warning about the test," explained the head instructor, Tom, labeled a hillbilly behind his back when he fell out of favor from time to time with his master. Kim would chastise one so-called higher belt in front of the others to make sure everyone towed the line or did what he wanted. For tonight, Tom's mission was to keep students' mind in school and keep the cash coming in. Even a master has upscale mall shopping to think about during the holidays.

"Main thing," Tom explained, stuttering quietly so as not to be overheard, "is that you pass test, form we can catch you up on anytime, go inside and try best you can." Acknowledged and shoes off, Joe changed quickly to prepare for the mental challenge. The outcome of which had already been decided.

The test took place in the main room. Both fourth section and fifth sections, about seven students total took part under the supervision of a fourth degree head instructor and the two second degree main instructors. They put the plebes through combinations regimens this time, which was a twist not experienced in practice. Starting out with five moves of one form, and then switching back to five movements of another, then back to where they stopped previously in the first form. All made it through the imaginary obstacle course without too much problem.

Then came combination jump kicks, rolls and follow-on attacks. So this is why we did this in lesson two nights ago. It was enjoyable to go full all-out, the entire length of the room, knowing you were testing. Joe mistaked in moving past the invisible line drawn in front of where the higher belts administering the proceedings were seated. Although several feet away to their side, in order to complete the ordered movement restricted airspace was used. The offender was immediately screamed at. If did it again, he would fail. Joe bowed apologetically, excusing himself and returned to the far end of the room to repeat the required sequence abridged; putting all accomplishments he had made over the past nine months at risk.

The self-defense was fairly comprehensive. It covered every grab, attack and throw learned from when we were white belts. Moves came out not practiced in months, but they worked. We were amazed, this must be real we were thinking, each of us could see it in the other's eyes.

Those testing for fifth section had more weapons training than those testing for fourth. We repeated what we had, three of us confided after the test we were looking forward to having that much short staff, long staff and sword routines, hopefully in about a year from now. The test ended with a furious combination kick and punch-out. The soon-to-be fifth sections were noticeably better at the kicks; we also looked up to them in this regard.

A little more than an hour and fifteen minutes after we bowed in, we were shouting Chung Moo! and clapping, then bowing and thanking, signing our test sheets and shaking hands with the proctors. We all passed, but off to the side were told by the second degrees to be quiet while changing, to save the jubilation for outside school. The results were announced to the other students, but it was said congratulations and the related bowings would be afforded at some other time. There were mostly only a couple of sixth sections and earlier-promoted fifth sections still in the back by then. Most of the lower belts had been hustled though when they wished to leave during the test, giving us a few seconds of rest in between commands.

This of course, was all for show. To build in the minds of the lower belts the importance and value of the testing ceremony, and that of rank. To allude to the magic and make the underlings curious enough to want it, carefully crafted marketing was the strength of the Moo cult in its heyday. Even when the head instructoid and slave to Kim bowed out and stepped into the office after the test, he did so purposefully to show his differentiation of rank and to call Kim and let him know the cash would soon be on its way.

During the following days Joe and the rest of us had to complete the final mental aspects of fourth section test. We had to sew our own black trim on our uniform front collars and we had to obtain both American and Korean flag patches for the shoulders without going to a junk shop, a Karate or Tae Kwon Do place.

The local fabric store, a kind none of us frequented in the past, was completely devoid of the simple black cotton cloth we wanted. The newly minted fifth sections were walking out of the huge shopping center millenary boutique tucked away on the third floor of the mall as us newbie fourth sections we walking in. In a mock hazing effort they tried to keep us from entering the store but we appealed to their senses and the rank architecture of the cult and they let us pass.

Obtaining the flags was much trickier. No flags, no belt handed back was the deal. We had until the next time in school after the holiday. Monday near the end of work Joe is on the South Side of the city assisting with a delivery and right next door is one of those flag and insignias places. He bought the merchant's last three Korean flags along with three U.S. patches, figuring he'd lose one somewhere or a fellow student would need it. We sewed the patches on our uniforms while in the car down the street from school that night before stepping in for group. We had our black trim and patches; our belts were ready, dyed now to fourth section. We had passed the halfway point to black belt.

The next few months were spent learning more of the school's code of behavior, along with a few more steps of the ultra-special forms; Tong Nong, Pal Gae, plus more weapons movement. We bowed differently now. Right closed fist covered by left open palm, fingers straight, the elbows bent and hanging down so the hands were about one foot in front of the solar plexus. Up until this point we bowed as all beginning through third sections do; feet together, arms at side, fists down, the upper body bends, the head nods down depending on the extent and emphasis desired of the bow. We could now stride head up and bow like Homo Moo-erectus. During group lessons we stood ever closer to the front of the line.

Additional requirements were to uphold all other codes of behavior in the school, to set an example for lower belts. Make sure to say Stand Up! and Thank You Instructor (whoever) in a loud clear voice on queue. This was your position, your role in the cult, you had worked hard for it, don't let up now.

MOO-ON FLUX

For a brief phase of time all seemed well. Joe's new job required lots of overtime which helped to pay down the remaining fourteen thousand plus or minus, in 1980 dollars, he had promised to bring in for learning how to be an instructor and if qualified, handle his own school. He wasn't fully convinced that would ever be his future, yet he Mooed on. The instructors said if he tried hard and practiced,

Joe had nothing to worry about. All the extra time spent handling towards course, as they put it, would pay off by extra lessons and special attention when he could make it into class.

Shortly before Christmas that year Joe came home late from work and the phone was ringing off the hook. No one was on the line so he hung up. A few minutes later it rang again. "Uh, you have chance to be around Master, head down to school right now or be left behind," the instructor grumbled then hung up.

Joe packed up his uniform, grabbed a few extra dollars in case he was asked to fetch a sandwich or coffee for higher belts and headed towards school, fully utilizing the Mopar's potential, making record time and breaking a few laws of physics along the way.

We assembled in the parking lot; Joe was assigned to transport several of us to the Naperville, the de facto headquarters. This in itself was a big deal, this was school number One. Joe's companions were higher belts by one section; guys he had met at the picnic and tried to make friends with. They were still aloof; he didn't have the chance to practice with them much, due to conflicting schedules. This was by design. Joe made a lot more money than they did and if students were allowed too much time together to compare notes, and contract prices, well that could cause some problems. It would be a long time after leaving the Moo cult when these and numerous other subtle details of the manipulation would surface when those of us in this same vehicle that night would discuss stories of back in the day.

We arrive and the parking lot is jammed. There is a line of students waiting to bow and get inside. It's very cold and the windows are heavily frosted. We could almost smell the tradition, if that's what it was, from fifty feet away as we hustled out of the car and up to the front walk.

It's ten o'clock p.m. The scene didn't look completely out of line with the holiday shoppers still out and about. School One had few neighbors and they were closed, the parking lot and the donut shop with its back to our headquarters were all ours.

"Faster ways shoes off, get in back and change into uniform!" orders the junior rank head instructor. "Higher belts will be here any minute."

We sped through, quickly changed then tried to find space to warm up, not knowing what to expect. There was about thirty of us total. About ten minutes later the front door flies open and Stand Up! is yelled into the building from the outside as the gold Lincoln pulls in. The main curtain is not held up this time as Master Kim strides to the office; then steps out from the office to perform his flag-staring expose. He greets all of us with a smile and a quick bow, the tension lessons somewhat.

While he speaks to head instructors in the office, we are put through the paces of Pal Gae at a good clip for about half an hour. Several second and third degrees walk around checking movements and catching up those of us who were a little short of where we should be. We were taught a few moves of Pal Gae set two. As rumor had it there were like eighteen different Pal Gaes but in Asia it would take decades to learn them all.

Kim jiggles the door handle and before walking out in a new dark red jump suit, Stand-Up! is commanded by Forrest from the office. The ex-marine had a distinctive flair for using voice commands effectively. In a micro-second, everyone instantly stands at attention in bow position, slapping their fists into their hands, the black trim on our uniforms gathered shoulder to shoulder in a dynamic example of herd crispness and mentality.

Kim begins to talk, mostly about the organization, how it's growing and how we all may have opportunity, but it's up to us to earn. He then checks Pal Gae by looking on from up in front, the head instructors saying step, at moderate speed. The room was too crowded for him to check students closely. Kim mentions a few pointers but none of it sinks in. It wasn't supposed to. This lesson, like any of the lessons he gave, was about us accepting him as something he is not. Continually seeking approval and our energy, the position of 'Master' was created in our minds.

We are brought into the back room in two groups, highest belts first. One third of the students below first degree would be gone in a year. Attrition was high but never talked about, considered bad luck. While waiting our turn in the main room, we practice punch defenses using kicks as the responding attack, those Kung Fu looking sequences no other martial art possesses. A few new ones are given out; higher ranks are shown more complicated types with additional strikes so as to keep the lower belts seemingly deficient. We diligently repeat our learning for another half an hour and then it's our turn to be the group in the back.

Once settled and standing in formation, Kim explains about kicking. It should be loose, relaxed he says, and has a student, one of the guys who rode with Joe in the car, step forward.

"Punch," says the master. The student steps forward politely and sticks his arm out with a fist at the end. Kim's body seems to compress then extends with the leading edge foot turned over so the instep just brushes past the students face. It looks impressive. Kim goes on to talk for awhile, about schools in Asia and how students don't have the opportunity we do. One student nervously calls him head instructor. Kim laughs and says, "Who you fooling?"

However it's no great offense, this time. Kim explains the student is just jittery, "But if at second degree make that mistake, then take a stripe," he says, indicating it will lead to loss of rank. This is probably the biggest weapon to ensure behaviors or to fight against insubordination the Moo and other cults have; loss of rank or position to keep the faithful in line, never speaking out, questioning form, behaviors, or activities of the group.

Lesson ends and we are dismissed en masse, Kim says he has certain thing to handle and leaves school magnificently, accompanied by the head instructors who place an expensive cowhide coat over his shoulders before entering the Lincoln. We all change and are hustled out of the school, the thanking and bowing abbreviated by several head instructors whacking our bodies in brotherly fashion to move faster. It's now well after one a.m. Saturday morning, enough time to sleep in before being at school in another twelve hours.

HANDS OF STEEL AND WIRE

Chull Sa Chung as the Moo-term was said, was another of the highest and, most surreptitious of rites in Moo. Often times as a lower belt we could detect the lingering effects of this practice on the hands and bodies of our teachers as they staggered into school at eleven a.m. opening time, walking stiffly, apparently worn out from a lengthy practice the evening before. These sessions were rumored to be very difficult. The instructors' hands and uniforms smelled of vinegar and what would soon be recognized as "herb."

Chull Sa Chung, or hands of steel and wire, was a training method whereby applying a special mixture of herbs and seasonings to the hands then hitting specially prepared bags of two different textures, beans and small stones, were engineered to toughen and strengthen the hands. It was sermonized at length how the greatest effect of this conditioning was internal

It was also stressed how in Asia, instructors and higher belts have to wait many years before they have a chance to earn the opportunity to take part in Chull Sa Chung practice. It has been kept behind closed doors for centuries. Disreputable orders in martial arts have stolen bits and pieces of the knowledge so it is only trusted to certain ones most loyal to Chung Moo.

In the United States, it was also explained that Master wanted to "faster ways" build up the instructors so he decided to pass on this training. It is truly a historical occurrence. Years from now, once Chung Moo Quan is established across the country, then it will be very difficult to get in Chull Sa Chung. If you all try hard, all of you on instructor course, you may have a chance. This is why we pushed you so hard to reach where you are at now, was the lecture one evening as school was winding down after group lesson.

It was starting to warm up, the seasons changing again towards spring and about once a week most of us wanted to do something else besides Moo every night plus Saturdays, consequently night attendance would vary. We were required to call from work on the way in to pick something up, such as coffee or a sandwich for our Moo managers. School was becoming like an extra job with slowly diminishing payback.

During the required après day job telethon on the Friday evening before Easter Sunday, a stern admonishment was given over the phone, do not miss tonight's lesson and be sharp. Usually this meant a visit by a head instructor or perhaps even by Master. We made extra sure to stop and eat beforehand. A few extra minutes of warm-up time would be sacrificed for a hot meal.

It was different this night. Several of those who were on instructor course were milling around in the small waiting room at the front of school. As soon as Joe went in, the third degree poked his head out of the office and said, "Head to School Three we'll be there in a little bit, when you get there, make sure you ask head instructors if they need anything, understand?" Cool, Joe thought, School Three, where is that?

We piled into one car and headed south to Downers Grove. This was another landmark establishment, handled by a head instructor with a background in bouncing on Rush Street prior to his Moo career. Numerous tales of dingy thrashing originated from these historic walls.

The school was the same as the others in many respects. Same curtains and partitions, same shingles and simulated temple roofs, matching blue painted walls with wooden borders and pegs to hang uniforms. The framed words seen elsewhere, the pictures of Kim in the waiting room and office, the flag and weapons array were there, in nearly identical places. The difference was the main practice room was long and narrow, with a superb high ceiling which still had swipe marks from swords, and the back room even smaller than ours.

There were many fourth section and up students, most of whom we had not seen before, but a couple of the fifth and sixth sections in our group seemed to know some of the others. They nodded and bowed politely, and spoke a few words, although very quietly. All of Chicago was there from the seven schools in existence at the time. Some were so new they did not have any fourth section or higher to send, only main instructors.

All three head instructors were present as were the main belts and assistants from each school. When we lined up to bow, the line extended to the back wall and across, then started up the other side, it was impressive. It felt elite and intimidating, standing as nearly the last one in that line Joe related. The walls reverberated with Stand Up! as we snapped to. We bowed in to the flags, the certificates, and higher belts, nodding along as if it were natural.

"Alright," began Forrest with his unmistakable low-tenor voice, "let's get started, and make lines…" The second and third degrees quickly herded us into formation, five across and seven deep. We began a long series of basic warm-ups but at high repetition. A new series of speed forms was also introduced in preparation for the main event yet to come.

From a comfortable long sparring position or fugal walk stance with front knee bent almost to where the front thigh is level with ground, the back leg straight. The back leg is brought up, knee to chest as both hands are raised above the head, relaxed with elbows bent. The hands and leg are then thrust down alongside the body, snapping back into fugal walk, letting gravity accelerate the fall. Timing of the foot, landing when the hands snap down is critical. The arms and hands remain open and loose, the back in line with the body, turned to the side. The result is to open up the circulation and make blood flow to the hands.

It does, the fingers begin to plump up from the forced circulation, but it's easy to pull a muscle or strain a joint which happened to many of us. We counted through twenty-five then switched sides, another twenty-five then switched until one hundred and fifty each side was reached. Our heads collectively spun as one. We had no idea what this lesson was about, why it was ordered or anything else. We were being tested, in a different way. No one seemed to know the reason, we were told be here, here we are, as one mind, just like it says on the walls. Thus, we Mooed.

After forty-five minutes of warm-up we deep breathed, again at length. As a rule for a general group lesson it was ten times slow, followed by ten times fast with holding at the end. On our own we often did twenty or twenty-five to build up an extra charge and to replenish. This night we did fifty. Deep breathing in the Moo is close to hyper ventilating. It is a rigorous diaphragm intensive workout that does circulate a good deal of air but it also strains the lower back and promotes a pot belly from the billowing out, then rolling in, of the stomach. It is not the ideal method of breathing deep as compared to authentic Chinese or other methods of practice. But we were there to follow instructions, to Moo.

Next came a half-hour of Pal Gae, nonstop. We began at a slow pace, stopping for a few seconds in each position to get in, Moo-speak meaning to open the joints and twist the tendons and ligaments into the prescribed posture. The pace picked up and soon we marched along in place, keeping up with the step, step, step cadence droned out by third degrees who switched off in lead. The room was very crowded and as Joe turned on command during one set he inadvertently knocked into a second degree making the rounds checking the lower belts. The second dan quickly slapped Joe in the nuts, helping him stoop lower as required by the next posture.

After Pal Gae we deep breathed again. Forrest and the other head instructors then divided the room into roughly two groups. The first group comprised of higher than median rank headed into the back room, barely fitting. The rest of us stood in line waiting… then a senior third degree instructor came from out of the office, through the front curtain, held high by second degrees; with a big cooking pot like the kind used for pot roasts and such, the big round purple ovenware things. It seemed heavy and he wore gloves, the pot had been simmering on a hotplate concealed in the office. He was heading straight for the back room, the curtain there was already up. He bowed and was ushered through without setting the sacred pot down. Ah, the smell, like vinegar and…herb.

Those in the back room were about to get in Chull Sa Chung, whereas we were about to get in Ba Gua for over an hour. It was one gigantic circle with fifteen players shuffling around, staying as low as possible, with several second and third degrees screaming at us, "Stay low, get down!" They used tong bongs, short wooden staffs about an inch and a half in diameter to encourage us to keep our legs bent, not come up and to keep the pace. Forrest used a practice Samurai sword made of split bamboo. It had a greater effect on the circle walkers, who would ebb and flow like a school of fish evading a predator, the circle bending reflexively as he thwacked a lower belt if it seemed they were not pushing as hard as possible. Strange noises were emanating from the back room, the chung box seemed to be in use, but our focus was on the circle.

We switched sides every ten minutes, and there was no mercy from our overlords during this, they kept us low with staffs in hand. This was a lot longer than we had tried Ba Gua previously and it was a test to make it through. When we ended, in time with the group in the backroom completing Chull Sa; we finished with hands widely spread and circled for a couple minutes instead of jumping up and punching toward the floor. This we were told was the higher form way to finish Ba Gua. In reality, just as Moo bastardized an authentic form, so too it is with this exercise, stolen from an accredited style of walking and changing as it is correctly described. Details are readily available from practitioners of the art or in texts written about Pa Kua. Again, at best, the cult has Moogwa.

Nonetheless on this night we felt exhilarated and tired. When the other group moved into the main room they appeared as exhausted as we were. What ever they had done back there we were about to find out. We exchanged rooms. Chull Sa Chung was now being explained to us by the senior instructor who had carried in the large covered pot. The other group was now getting in their Moogwa in the main room.

We rolled up our sleeves as ordered while he spoke using replicated broken English, emulating the master's speech out of respect, we thought. He was high enough belt he was pretty good at it.

"The herbs in this pot come from all over the world, some from the bottom of the ocean, others from mountains and lands far away, from various continents. The exact mixture, the quantity and quality is a top secret and you should not ever consider stealing this or…" He makes a cutting motion across his neck. "And for now, don't talk too much outside of school about this since they would not understand."

The third degree, whom before tonight we had never seen and was not introduced, continues saying the reason to heat this up with a hot plate is so that it gets in. By now, after over a year in Moo we had heard "get in" so frequently it was associated as a positive and the students from our school who had traveled with us seemed to know what was going on. A few had participated in this ordeal previously, so it was like a rite of passage to Joe.

When it came your turn, the hands were stuck in the pot, the mixture very, very hot. Years hence it was explained it did not need to be near scalding to be effective; this was done so on purpose to be memorable in the student's mind. Was it ever! The mixture had twigs and bark and a mash of foul but wonderful smelling mud we generously applied, squeezing the formula into every digit and segment under the direction of another third degree.

"Press hard seven times on each finger then on each palm, get in the front and the backs and put extra on every joint. This is like medicine to protect your hands and to take the bad blood out of your system."

One student would be washing, as it was dubbed, and when finished he waited his turn to hit the bags. Another student who had just finished his turn at the chung box would then wash again a second time to complete his or her turn. There was one female in the entire group and she hit as hard on the bags as any of us initially. The real test of manhood was to keep pounding all the way through without letting up.

On the edge of the mat was positioned the box, a plywood contraption slightly lower than waist high, sturdily built with two-by-four frame and wide enough to accommodate two large denim bags, each about the size of a large sack of potatoes. Inside one was filled with mung beans and the other small dried peas. This detail wasn't revealed for a long time. The idea was two different textures each being hit by both sides of the hands in conjunction with the fantastic herbal blend would over time build the body into "hands of steel and wire." Where the palm feels like a piece of steel and the fingers feel like a wire brush. The CMQ symbol showed an open palm in the center.

After washing and soaking up the herbal mixture, the student stands in a high horse stance, feet about shoulder width apart, facing the box; holding the arms outspread in front but relaxed palms facing down towards the bags. On command, the body drops by compressing the knees, back stays straight and the palms are slammed down onto the bags; using emphasis to make full contact with the bags and feel the shock wave travel along the length of each finger simultaneously.

The student then rises up to starting position, trying to let the intense stinging in the hands dissipate, back still straight and turns his hands over, palms face up and on command slams his back hand onto the bags, again protected by the magic herb; led on by the screaming cadence One! Two! Three! plus the presence of your fellow Moos. The palms are turned over repeatedly; it takes focus to avoid merely flailing away. The technique is to let the whole body drop with your full weight driving into the bags each time, back and front, Blam! Blam! Blam! …the hollow box absorbing the blows transmitted through the bean bags.

This introduction was fifty hits, then switch bags. It was exhausting and made one pee heavily. We were allowed to use the bathroom immediately if needed. As several of us became higher belts, we would build up to one thousand hits and occasionally pee blood, sometimes uncontrollably. But it never stopped us from wanting to hit the bags. Afterward, practice is difficult but hypothetically multiples the effects many times over. Our group finishes and we are ready to step out, the higher belts have finished their Moogwa. We line up in the front room.

Joe is the lowest belt in the room, and along with those standing in front of him, is promoted to the title of assistant instructor. His roommate who was higher rank than Joe, having tested earlier by a few weeks would have undoubtedly been promoted as well, but he skipped out this night since he didn't call in like he should have. This was another stealthy ploy of the Moo to keep everyone motivated to the fullest extent possible. Play each other off the other, keep them together yet at the same time separate to defray critical evaluation and make sure to point to the internal competition; while emphasizing the oneness in the parallel Moo-ideal mindset. And most importantly, absolute reverence for the respect line, The Line.

Everyone changes quickly. It's approaching two o'clock in the morning and we put on shoes and grab coats quickly; the formalities in the front room, the bowing and thanking are kept to a minimum as the second and third degrees want to get in their turn with the bags. As we departed, a few had already started, the ceiling tiles in the back room jumping in response.

The night ends with Forrest laughingly saying to us in the last group to leave, "Make sure to go find that bigger bunny this weekend, and cook him up." Joe stayed awake the rest of the night then slept most of that weekend, as did the others, waking up very hungry and sore early Monday morning, just in time for work.

LEGENDS OF THE BELT SYSTEM

Legend has it that in Asia, there are five steps to black belt. Thus fifth section equals black belt. But in the U.S. the system was for seven steps as Asian students had more patience and would not become bored, they were more dedicated, and understood the value of practice. So the seven step process was designed to keep U.S. students motivated since true martial art was new here. In the future it would be different. We were very lucky to be getting in on the ground floor, what with the thousand school forecast.

Around the fire one night over the July 4th expedition to camp alongside a freeway in southern Michigan, a student asked Head Instructor Forrest about a story told of Kung Fu in China. That beginning students wore white uniforms and over time, from the practice in dirt-floored places and contact with the ground; the blacker the uniform, the more experienced was the practitioner.

Higher belts could be recognized by the darkness of their uniform. The story also held that as more and more sweat and grime was expelled from practice, the belt became darker.

Forrest replied, "I don't know how, seeing as your acquaintance comes from another style, how he knows this, but it's true. The idea of a black belt comes from the body cleansing itself; the bad stuff comes out after years of practice." He went on to explain, "Look at your own uniforms, see how there're yellow from all the crap you put in your body; later on the body is cleaner, it becomes more difficult to get the bad stuff out."

Other higher belts there that night pointed out the waist or belt line was where the bad stuff is collected, at the mid-point of the body, several main organs are there. Over time the perspiration predictions proved out, we still sweated massively but didn't reek in the nearly the same way.

Most of us as beginning students had no idea it was shoe polish used by the Moo. When it came time as instructors to process their belts after testing students, many of us sought out real leather dye. It was more costly but worked better. It penetrated more, didn't rub off, and looked darker. There were rules for handling students' belts. The area had to be clean, you could not face north, no women around and the drying area had to be secure from same and never ever tell a student it is shoe polish or their mind will drop. No kidding. That's why we used leather dye.

We checked with another higher belt that we trusted, one of the few level headed main Moos who remained that way even after seven or eight years in. He said leather dye was fine, besides it comes in nearly the same bottle from the store, so if ever questioned on it, there you go. The idea of the sections being darkened in and additional trim being added to the uniform was drawn from the old legends, but distorted by Kim to control his followers.

After that first campout, may of us felt were we in an exclusive club, a strange sort of extended family with its own little oddities nobody talked much about, and went along with the program. We began to accept things as facts; the cult had filled a void in many of our lives.

In a month or so a new location would be opening up a few miles from Joe's first indoctrination center. It was a Saturday afternoon and things were winding down. Joe was the only fourth section left in the practice room; the others were working or handling certain parts as it goes in Moo-speak. One of the head instructors visiting our school said it would be alright for Joe and me to go to the new location, meaning Kim had not yet approved it as an official school, and lend a hand.

When we got there, two newly detailed Lincoln Continentals were under guard, parked by the front doors. We identified ourselves to the overseers and asked if we could step inside per our orders. They motioned us in. Inside were all the guys that would stand by Kim and go to prison for him along with several of those that would testify against Kim and the organization. But for tonight, we were joined as one in efforts to make our future happen.

Boards of differing widths and lengths were cut, and stained a dark brown. This was the trim. The wood had already been erratically beaten with hammers to give it that authentic look. The ceiling was painted over to seal in the dust from the fiber tiles. The shingles over the front waiting room façade were in place and being varnished. The walls had been painted that afternoon, and the desk with the cut glass top and pictures was in place; with the carpet and padding stacked in the corners, the new facility would be open to the public in a few days. It was coming together quickly with nearly two dozen seasoned Moo workers and a few newbies to haul trash and bring in more supplies.

This would be the ninth John C. Kim style of Chung Moo Quan in the Chicago area. Number Two had burned down, the number never re-designated and of course there was no number four in Chung Moo. The story being the fourth master of Moo left centuries ago and the direct line tradition thing suffered as a result. In Asian customs life is described as birth and youth, middle age, old age, then the fourth step, death. Or spring, summer, fall, and then winter. Accordingly in the world of Moo there is no Kata number four, no student number four, nor any multiple thereof. We had even been told the story of how once at 4:44 in the afternoon, Master Kim fell unconscious and was transported to the next life where he saw Grand Master. This was before Grand Master was given a name, which occurred after my tenure in the cult. After a brief discussion reviewing Kim's purpose and mission as master of Moo, he travels astrally back to

Earth and then has to use acupuncture to revive his circulation. The story concludes that as proof of his journey, Kim shook hands with those present and they said his hands were still cold.

But here we are on this fine summer evening finishing out yet another school for Master Kim. One of the higher belts in the room would be given a chance to run it, just who was not yet known. That determination would be meted out by Kim during the following week or so. Key requirements were: enough hucksterism skill to sell the stories and make students bring in cash, get them to sign on the dotted line; absolute loyalty to Kim no matter what; and the ability to make Moo seem like something, to masquerade the forms with flash.

You would think the order should be loyalty, form competence then cash generation, but cash is king and loyalty can be bought. Lots of uniformed clowns could move well enough to sell form. We were often told that over one thousand schools were possible in the United States; Master has set his mind towards ensuring our future. Our work tonight then was just one small step in this prophetic legacy.

As midnight approached, we cleared the floor and found buckets, and chairs for the highest belts, to sit on. Three higher belt instructors brought in a dozen or so pizzas and after the required dispersion rituals we feasted mighty, thanking first, however. Before eating it is customary in Moo to throw out a piece of food, preferably meat so as to appease any bad spirits or chopki, that is ghouls, which might be around. The idea is they will go after that and not what's on your plate. We ate well knowing all requirements and offerings had been satisfied, besides, who's gonna mess with this group?

Forrest did say one dingy came in a couple days ago and was roughed up by a pointed-to head instructor, notorious for his street fighting in a previous life.

"You were just making sure nobody got hurt, isn't that what you told the cops?" said Forrest.

The curly haired two hundred-fifty pound-plus head instructor, Dave, answered sheepishly, "Yes, if that would be alright."

All the other instructors began to laugh like Klingons. Slowly at first but building to a crescendo. The verbal submission, acceptance and reward of cult behavior at the higher levels were put forth, examined and nodded to by anyone who wanted acceptance, everyone there.

Even us low belts could chuckle and join in, a little. Although we hadn't pulled the information's hair out, tossed him on the sidewalk and then lied to the police, we were there in spirit, or better said, our imagination. This is what it was all about, eating boxed pizza while sitting on the floor of the next fabricated champion of Asia cash collection facility and patting each other on the back for being true, right, and correct. The feeling of camaraderie was the greatest hook, nearly as great as the demanding workouts.

THE NEXT STEPS

Several main instructors across the organization had been promoted to head instructor and the former head instructors promoted to the newly invented title of regional instructors with a one stripe addition in rank. There were also now assistant regional instructors, so it became sort of confusing when it was expected to thank several higher belts of differing position when they were standing in a line. Each correct title had to be said exactly at the appropriate time or the lower belt committing the offense could face loss to his own rank. After a few weeks of chanting the new monikers several times a day, everyone absorbed the expanded structure. It was explained as this is the way it is in Asia, but the U.S. has never had these positions or rank before. Again, suburban Moo was history in the making.

Fifth section test was nearly a year after fourth section for Joe, and this felt genuinely good. Between fourth and fifth there was time to practice all the new forms learned and expected to someday pass to others as instructors. There was more Tong Nong (ocean form) and more Ta Bouk Chung (volcano form) and Yuk Tong which was described as being able to move in six different directions. Funny it did not have a cool sounding name like the others. Funnier still is these forms, cobbled together bits and pieces of authentic training, have been re-arranged over the years so that anyone who left would not be teaching the true brand, merely riding on the glory of the ex-champion's illustrious coat tails.

Joe also learned extensions of the weapon movements we already had. Unsurprisingly there were the same beginning steps re-worked and grouped as a series. Add series one plus series two... and presto here's an uber-killer mechanism practiced by royalty for thousands of years; and because you brought in enough cash we will teach you these ancient mysteries right here in this tiny suburban enclave. Don't explain too much to friends and co-workers, for they would not understand. Let us do that, your role is to bring them in for an introductory lesson. Think of how much better it would be if someone had done that for you.

Joe was taught about handling school and passing flyers. The first was about the basics of the envelope system and how to report verbally over the telephone how many students had come in that day, how many were in now and how to take attendance. The intricacies of the cash recording and transportation methods would be taught later. Another aspect was cleaning school.

Special attention to detail was mandated in the office; bowing to the flags and the certificates of Kim, then carefully wiping all finger prints off the glass top on the desk and never from over a corner. Clean the phone, empty the garbage and make sure nothing is left in the desk drawer such as over-looked cash payments the main droids spaced out. This happened only a few times in Joe's Moo career as the penalty was a loss of rank and no self-respecting cult member ever wants that. Your position even if regained is never the same and you are treated differently, like a rejected part, remanufactured and sold at a discount.

During the week, the cleaning of a school could take hours depending on the available droid power. Vacuuming, if you had one, the alternative was picking up crap by hand; dusting, cleaning the rest room, wiping the mirrors; there was a process and procedure for each aspect of the chores. The instructor factor where the effectiveness of the group is diminished by an order of magnitude for each additional member added, was certainly in effect. We made a pact at our location that we'd bow once to start it off. We all knew each other and we'd clean school better that way without having to stop and bow every time somebody walked through a room. We were our own little sub-cult, paying our dues and earning as they had undoubtedly for centuries in Asia.

It was also mentioned we should concentrate on passing flyers to build up school since this was our future. Every Saturday morning about eight o'clock there would be a gathering at a pre-determined point, away from our house of training so as not to attract attention, and plan the day. A 7-Eleven parking lot was choice locale as the coffee was the quasi-official drink of Moo. It was considered a status symbol to have the rear floor of your MUV (Moo utility vehicle) overflowing with discarded coffee cups and beefy been burrito wrappers until they flowed up onto the rear seat, then it was time to dump out. The bigger the mess in the back seat, the tougher your week must have been, thus the perceived level of trying hard recognized by your close personal herd. It was like a fight club badge of honor, and no one would ever want to borrow your car. They'd grab the new guy's nicer, cleaner, vehicle if he was dumb enough to park it near school.

At other times the initial meet was at the main instructor's leased residence, called Master's (name of the town) house or apartment since everything came or was handed to us, from Master. The idea being you give everything up; then as you earn, certain things are handed back to you. Like a place to stay, clothes, furniture, a car and later even a wife.

There was a strict protocol when going over by higher belt's living quarters. The sub-highest belt of the group would call ahead. When there, we'd bow and step in, by rank and be mentally checked by the sleepy-eyed full instructors. The flyers of school with pictures of staged events and listing the bogus international locations would be handed over with reverence. Never hand over the corners of a table, never rolled up so as to fray any edges and never ever casually thrown about in a car or when carried by a person.

Once dismissed, we would split up into groups of two or three and descend upon the targeted area. Flyer passing was banned from most of the larger indoor consumer mega malls, so roadside plazas, gas stations and downtown areas of older suburbs were favorites. The owner or manager would be politely asked if the flyer could be put up. Some were favorable, some not. We brought our own tape and removed older flyers that had been there awhile and needed to be turned back in to Moo HQ. These soiled artifacts were to be burned, but only on certain days of the month, termed nail days. Flyers could not be taped across the corners as it symbolized a cut in the direct line to Master. We followed all these instructions with due diligence.

A good count for a few hours work was between ten to twenty flyers up in suitable areas. We were back in school by noon so as to get some practice in before opening.

Some times we'd be ordered out to pass flyers all day on a Saturday. It depended on what was going on at school. If they wanted to work a crowd of beginners then we'd be recovered early and on the flight deck to perform steps and jumps and form while we practiced in front of the new dupes. This of course was to get them to bring in their cash. "See how much form they have, see how they move, plus their self-defense is unbelievable," the main droids would inform the first sections, just like we had been informed the previous year.

But, if larger down payments or course offerings were scheduled, well, then we were told to call back. Which of course we would, to report our increased propaganda tallies. After a day long flyer blitz throughout half the county, you really wanted to practice for awhile. If one of your groups had been nominated as sufficiently mentally clear to hold a key to the front door, it was often that you would start practice on a Saturday long after everyone had left, but were still finished and out so it would not look suspicious to passersby or next door occupants.

Rumors and suspicion of cult activities were a growing concern as the neighboring areas became more aware of the schools. If main instructors or selected higher belts were going to a lesson at another school or going to see Master; fourth sections and up were required to start up the car, make sure it had gas which often times it did not so you'd have to go fill the tank at personal expense, in uniform with maybe a coat or shoes on. The car would be brought up front, cleaned of course or at least wiped down.

The higher order would promenade from school with every instructor course student outside waiting in line by rank. The instructors would bow in the office, bow again by the front door then be escorted the few feet to the waiting junk. They would bow to us from in the car as they chugged away. The nearby fast food workers would be watching in amusement for this as it occurred several nights per week. Young female employees there had declined any attempts to go out with future instructors despite the rich tradition and legacy that we held. Seems dating a cult member wasn't too high on the list for those well-adjusted to society.

One cold late autumn night, Joe was ordered to bring up the car used by his roommate, this gigantic whale of a Chrysler. Vehicles were termed the "car you drive" since you were not born with it, it was not part of you, thus "your car" was not in Moo vocabulary. "The Lincoln" was used for higher belts, or it might be said, "Take the red car," for example. This time it was, "Bring up the whale." His roommate, a fifth section, had already serviced the vehicle Joe was informed. He would ride home with Joe, the whale to be recovered on the way to work the next morning.

It thundered up and Joe taxied the bulbous four-door into position in front of school. Tonight attendance was light; everyone was off handling something so the departure contingent standing on the front sidewalk in bare feet would be minimal, two or three at most. Something else was not right, though. What was that, dust on the dash? Joe wiped his hand. Holy crap it was dope! Somebody had rolled a doobie and they were still there! Two fat ones sitting under the speedo! This can't be! Larry said he stopped this long ago.

He must have fallen off the wagon and forgot he had this set up and to let higher belts use the car...the consequences would be extreme or so Joe thought. Grabbing the two personalized cigarettes Joe stashed them in his uniform just as the door was opened for the newly promoted head instructor who jumped in smokey the whale and sped off. He had a strange look on his face as he turned for the departing bow, almost as if he were expecting something and not finding it.

SEX ON THE WAY TO MEET THE GRANDHAMSTER

There was this head instructor who was on the chosen path to making regional. Not that well liked, couldn't move real well, but was skilled at ordering people around and explaining about the grandhamster and what an unbelievable experience it was "to be around." He was in charge, so to hold the line we did as ordered. Most of his passing of form was verbal, and never showed the movements in detail, but he was a good mimic of the Kim, emulating the broken speech and quirky gestures.

He was clandestinely dating a female student. A dedicated instructoid wanna-be Moo was dating her roommate. The head droid would consistently give the under-droid a difficult time, pointing fun at him during groups, labeling with derogatory terms, putting him down and generally not fulfilling the role of a higher belt. This went on for several years. We put up with this garbage because we hoped we'd move past it eventually. We looked for the good and disregarded the substantial amount of crap trickling down from the top. This is why we can say we made whatever good might have been in Moo, not the Kim.

One Saturday after a round of early morning flyer passing, feeding and changing the bib of the head droid and getting a couple hours form and sparring in; the under-droids are released for the long awaited weekend. A full day of not having to call, answer or pick anything up, at least until maybe Sunday night. The way around that is all the under-droids would call at once and for most, the phone was busy. Oh well, we tried, couldn't get through. We'd rotate who would call first. A full day of freedom and moderate relaxation was in store.

Even the head droid seemed jubilant that Saturday for he would be going to see the grandhamster and for this he lived. It was his chance to outshine all the other head droids who wanted the hamster's attention. As soon as he received word he was selected to join the elite ranks for a weekend gathering, he would announce with strained exasperation, "Maaaster is in town." This meant we were not supposed to get in (have sex) and to be available if something should come up. In reality Kim never left town and lived like a spoiled brat in the southwest suburbs, he just used the ruse of traveling and coming back to enhance the image and importance of serving him.

So this day, this one particular under-droid, after departing the cash collection station in the 'burbs where the concentration and care of the eighth generation grandhamster was kept in focus; decided to swing by the females under-droids' place to make plans for going out. He discovered his girlfriend wasn't home from work yet, but her partner in rent, the friend of the head instructor was; waiting and willing to discount her failed attempt at controlling her very own droid.

Competition sets in and soon enough the friend is performing her interpretation of effective communication in carnal oratory terms. As the substantial gulping proceeds, a larger type junk car is heard outside, attempting to bump and park along the curb. It's the head droid also stopping by before the weekend gets rolling. Not wanting to be caught of course, the under-droid takes refuge in the closet, the kind with serrated and not solid doors. He has clear view and hearing of the demonstration about to occur.

Making his way upstairs, the head droid wastes no time. He begins his instruction, "Hurry, hurry up I'm going to see Maaaster…no, no not that way, the other way, nooohhh, ooohhh…" Try to picture the deep chanting from the movie Eyes Wide Shut. His less than exclusive girl friend completes the regimen at a proficient pace.

It was over very quickly, the closeted observer was chewing on his fist to stop from laughing at what happened next. The head droid finished sooner than expected and excess residue was deposited on the back of his trousers, which were dropped to the floor, but was not noticed until on his way out except not by him, it was seen by his friend and the observer. Wanting very much to be early, as always it seems, to see the hamster, the head droid simply belted up and strode off to the car, shouting more instructions over his shoulder, "Wait by the phone, I'll call if need anything later on…"

The femme fatal exclaimed something about fine point writing utensils as the big junk rumbled off as both she and the under-droid burst out laughing. They made fun of the head droid's trite way of speaking. "He's going to see Maaaster with cum on his butt!" They both laughed hysterically, no doubt releasing a large amount of cult induced stress in the process.

Some twenty years go by, during the intervening span all the Moo history happens and finally I reconnect with old buds, thanks to those who started the Yahoo board and kept the Anti-Moo growing. A friend of Joe relayed this story with full permission to tell it to anyone as often as possible, I can only laugh and laugh and laugh. Good times, good times.

MORE HANDLING, MORE EARNING WAYS

That winter was the coldest on record for nearly a century. Temperatures of minus twenty-five with wind chill approaching minus eighty. Still, school stayed open. The Mopar was frozen in the apartment building parking lot strategically located about one mile from school. School, eat, sleep, work, school; even a blizzard was a welcome respite.

Joe called down; whoops I mean "over" to school, we were admonished at length not to say down when describing our future even though the main droids had used "come on down to school" for years. Every once in awhile there were these behavioral corrections disseminated from Kim to instantly become the new mantra. Like stepping into school right foot first, the explanation takes about an hour; same as with calling over to school, or asking if anything is needed when you do. Once they get you to thank them for stepping in the room during a lesson, it's all downhill. You can't wait to find out how to be more correct.

On this miserably frigid Saturday morning Joe called into school and was told to get there as soon as possible. "Be alright to say," he began in the required Moo-speak.

"What, what's up, it's freezing in school and I haven't eaten yet, my concentration is on students, where's yours?" demanded the head instructor. Joe blurted out the car he drives was frozen and was concerned about fixing it today while the stores were open so he could get to work on Monday, to earn cash, to be able to handle towards school...

"Why not walk over anyway, and get some practice in, and then when others come in they can lend a hand," suggested Joe's mentor. Joe bundled up and staggered through the drifts to school. Hadn't done this since was a kid, he thought. And there's a 7-Eleven on the corner, got enough for coffee and a fruit flavored sodium roll.

Once at school, some power was out and only a few lights were on. No heat. Nobody came in for a long time, at least not to practice. After a couple hours one new instructoid course did show up and since he was lower rank than Joe, was allowed to assist. He took Joe to the parts store for new plugs, wires and distributor kit. They'd fix the blue beast tomorrow when it warmed up and the wind had lessoned. For tonight Joe crashed with his new helper and his roommate, also a new instructoid wanna-be. They ordered in pizzas and played dive and roll over their couch as the wind chill picked up again.

The next day the storm was over and Joe set out to revive the Mopar. A few other cult brethren arrived mid-stream and the instructor factor kicked in whereby results are driven by stupidity as determined by the quantity of droids present. During the operation one of the plug wires dropped near the open carburetor, the air cleaner assembly had been removed. I think we were trying to let the starting fluid dissipate. Well, the ignition was left on and Swoosh! The oil dipstick launches like a bottle rocket across the lot. Why the motor did not blow up, I don't know. Every gasket remained tight, compression obviously good.

"Do it again, do it again!" chanted all the young Moos like kids playing in a ghetto. Joe declined the opportunity to provide further entertainment and finished the job. The propulsion experiment must have warmed and loosened the beast better than a mobile starting unit as it cranked up on the very first turn after three days of icy gridlock in the windswept lot. That Mopar became a legend of its own during our era in the Moo.

BIRTHDAY TIME

Our schedules were kept consistent during the rest of that winter until spring reluctantly showed up. One day in late March we were notified, unusually in advance, we would be going over to the Vess street house for Master's birthday party the very next Saturday. This house was owned by Forrest but soon after taken over by the cult. When he was excommunicated, he lost this nice five bedroom home, his wife and son and nearly everything else, including his sanity just as many would who bowed long enough to Kim.

It doesn't happen all at once. It is a slow process, the boiled frog analogy. Put a frog in warm water he's happy. Increase the temperature slowly he'll stay in, trying to continually adapt. Turn up the heat too high, throw too much cult crap at him at once, he'll hop out and leave and maybe tell other frogs not to go near the cult pot. So the smart, effective cult leader, he slowly raises the temperature, waits until you adjust then after the new norm has been established, further refines the cognitive dissonance so it doesn't seem that bad. What was once uncomfortable is now tolerable. You reinforce your new beliefs.

We assembled early at our location and piled into transport for the journey to Naperville. Parking in the school lot and everywhere else along Ogden Avenue, the members from all districts, fourth section and up, were invited. We grabbed the groceries we had been instructed to purchase beforehand and waited for final transit over to the house.

Vess street house was at the end of a cul-de-sac behind the Midas Muffler on the south side of Ogden Avenue across from the school. There was a beaten path through the large wooden lot to the rear of the house but we would take turns shuttling over in preferred cars so as to not arouse local ire from two dozen or so vehicles parked along the street. With more than thirty of us all clustered under the tent draped over the back porch, we'd make enough noise anyway.

Once at the house we were ushered through the kitchen into the back yard. It was cloudy but not too cold, torpedo heaters had been set up and Master Kim was in the backyard supervising the arrivals. A line formed and on queue from regional instructors we shook hands and asked if be alright to wish happy birthday. Kim would grunt, "Hmmm," in his trademarked hue and give the impression he was looking you over to see if you were worthy of being there.

Higher belt instructors were scampering all over the place. Mostly just trying to make it look like they were busy handling. Each time stepping out of the house bowing towards Kim, who was seated in a high back leather chair, swiveling around to constantly acknowledge the comings and goings.

There were several large barbeque grills set up and a pit with a roasted pig turning on the spit. The instructors had been up most of the night setting things in place and preparing the feast. It was time to eat, so Kim stood up and announced he was giving all of us an opportunity to be around since Chicago had earned. Other locations across the country would be opening up soon, so now was the time to celebrate.

We formed a curving line trying to stay under the tent from the occasional mist and be nearer the heaters. Kim and Forrest stood near the meat dispensing area. With a noted deep chuckle Forrest would ask each one in the offing, "Do you want light meat or dark?" Light was freshly roasted pork and dark was a slice of honest to goodness Hippopotamus rump from the Weber. There were also exotic jerkys and piles of kimchee the spicy Korean cabbage and a good spread of potatoes, steamed vegetables, bread and the like. Next question was, how hungry are you?

Either way, whether you answered very hungry or not so hungry; Kim used his hands to deliver out mashed potatoes and other stuff, laughing each time. Whatever was on your plate you were expected to eat it, standing up. After the serving was completed, the only ones sitting in chairs were Kim and a few select highest belts. We gobbled as best we could, the hippo resilient to our cheap plastic forks. The pork was hot and good as were some of the hand baked deserts brought over by the minority of female students. After a few more banquets and holiday gatherings we would gravitate towards the display tables of certain students from certain schools as we knew the lineage of cooking ran strong in particular families.

After about half an hour the higher belts had finished eating and began to have some fun. Forrest asked Kim if it would be alright for one head instructor to eat the snout of the pig's head. Kim smiled and said yes, then said no, too many lower belts around. So Forrest asked if he could dispense more of the potatoes still wrapped in foil that had not been eaten.

This received a green light and aluminum spud missiles began zipping intermittently around the camp. It became increasingly difficult to continue eating because as soon as a nice mouthful was ready to be uplifted off the plate, there would be another incoming potato. Then the rank system engaged and lower belts became shields for those who had obviously been through this before. We scooped up what we could, swallowed and ran to the other side of the yard. Kim then discontinued the game since it would look funny to the neighbors; which undoubtedly it did, folks on both sides of the adjacent yards were looking on inquisitively, with spuds clanging off the fence.

We were ordered to begin clean up, put away the food and handle the garbage. Everyone started to move instinctively. You did not want to be caught without something to do. In short order we were told to step inside, it was now early evening. We were encouraged to play the board games that were scattered about on the floor. Kim sat on the couch and watched everyone play on the floor, like little kids. It was silly. And, you could not, NOT play. You had to participate or be slapped about playfully but effectively. The Monopoly had no money and half the pieces, the chess and checkers weren't much better, there was no point to this. Joe remembered reading stories of prisoners in concentration camps having their hairs pulled out in bunches, then being ordered to arrange them in groups of thirteen each. Joe wanted to leave but that wasn't an option.

At last Kim started to talk and that ended the game session. He went on and on in circular broken English sentences about how Chung Moo form transforms the body so it does not age as rapidly. He said he was near fifty yet he looked like what, twenty-five? And yet felt like eighteen, plus how many of you have seen me move? He asked the crowd, "It's not like fifty year-old, is it?"

All the higher belts, the ones who had presumably seen Kim perform numerous amazing demonstrations, nodded and together intoned, "Yes, Master." We had only seen little snippets of the master's ability thus far so we trusted to our seniors. The room was so crowded, everyone packed in the living room and in the adjoining kitchen, kneeling on the floor, Joe's legs were going numb and many others were visibly uncomfortable yet Kim kept talking. It was not understandable, his poor English, when in fact he speaks very fluently when he wants, this was discovered; the rambling on, the gestures, the use of "you understand" and of course we all murmured "yes, Master" at the proper times.

Kim stood up suddenly and motioned to the side. A box was handed over and inside were gold pins in the shape of the school crest, a tiger's head. Kim looked to regional head instructors who discreetly pointed who would get them and in what order. Joe was the last to receive one that day. Others who did not, about half the group were told more were ordered and would be given out soon; all had earned the right to wear the pins. We all thanked loud enough it could be heard down the block, let alone next door.

Finally it was time to leave and we quickly hunted down our coats and jackets and headed towards the door to find our shoes, all dumped in a big pile near the front entrance. As we stooped and bowed and thanked for opportunity to be around, Kim would grab each of our hands firmly and twist us out the front door, laughing. He was showing who was in control. Stumbling down the drive everyone was jamming their shoes on when a few higher belts came storming down the driveway to encourage us to dispatch faster. We emulated Dukes of Hazard getting into the car, any car, but we drove away slowly, as quietly as possible.

A few weeks went by, it was an ordinary mid-week practice night, several of us had just entered the school and were standing in the waiting room, waiting for permission to change or perhaps there was something to handle, we weren't sure but something was up. Suddenly the silver Mark IV pulls into the lot, and Joe says matter of factly, "I think the Lincoln is here." As the head instructors dart from the office, Forrest and Kim step from the car and immediately step in. Stand Up! yells the lead head instructor, his hip noticeably bothering him from over stressing the joints during years of Pal Gae.

Kim walks over to the office, bows at the entrance for a moment towards the flags there, then strangely heads towards the curtain to the main practice room. Joe and another assistant react instantly and scoop up the curtain and curl it up, holding it as high as they can, almost jamming it against the top of the entrance. Kim bows to the flags in the main room, his right hand covering his left first, glances at the students and says to those holding the curtain, "How you going to bow?" Interesting conundrum: standing on toes, uniform in one hand, curtain in other, master of the universe questioning you.

He goes back into the office with Regional Instructor Forrest. We are ordered to take the belts off our uniforms and hand them over. We do. There are murmured discussions in the office. Kim leaves after a few minutes with the customary fanfare as abruptly as he arrived. Upon stepping back into the school, the head instructor says, "Master is on his way to check schools in Canada; he just stopped by to sign belts."

Well, there are none and there never were any Moo schools in Canada, it just said so on the bottom of the flyers Joe and hundreds of other wanna-bees in Chicago put up all over the suburbs. But we didn't know that at the time, we never questioned. Kim's signature on our belts held about the same meaning; a good deal less in retrospect. But right then, we all thought we were special.

MORE MOO LIFE, FLOATING ON AIR

Throughout that spring and summer we Mooed on. Doing Moogwa on golf courses became the rage. When the last student departed after group each night we frantically cleaned school in anticipation of getting outside. Efficient little Moos, we had several choice spots picked out near the cash collection center for our nocturnal circle walking ritual. Some places were close to where one of the subgroups of assistant instructors lived, others were on the way home or had attractive qualities such as abundant parking where we could hide a couple of junk cars during weekend Mooing.

Moogwa at night posed obstacles but these were just more of a challenge to any self-respecting Moo. Trespassing issues were not worrisome, it was getting caught and revealing the exercise or being watched and somebody stealing from it we were most concerned about. What jokes, we really thought someone, anyone would care. Crouched down low, arms thrust out with wrists pulled back in a mock sparring position, walking in a circle and laboriously breathing. Rolling that belly out and in, out and in; then the dramatic timed switches. We would have five, sometimes seven or more cult members plodding along a fairway or on the eighth green for half an hour around midnight on any given day; the leader calling out "switch" at the agreed time for the pod to flail their appendages in synch, crouch back down and stumble along in the other direction. Trying to connect with nature, we were.

Practicing Tong Nong the supposed ocean form and other Moo prances on secluded golf courses or parks was also a favorite. It caught on quite well within the cult. One higher belt, a friendly assistant head instructor who would testify against the organization at the Tax Trial, mentioned he was observed by residents of his parent's subdivision. He liked to get in Tong Nong right before a thunderstorm, hoping to take advantage of the approaching energy. Silhouetted by the back drop of lightning flashes, the antics were fodder for neighborhood gossip.

"Those devil worshippers were in the park again last week," one housewife would say.

"Oh that's just little Tommy (Smith), you remember him, that nice boy from down the block, he's part of that martial art team, you know the ones who believe their leader can fly," another would chime.

See, that was the underlying theme of the Moo. To prepare you for the next step up in beliefs. When you first sign up you are told about Kim winning the fabled All Asia Championship in 1956, which in reality never happened and you are told about all his exploits as a child in Korea. How he lived in the wild for seven years, with tigers in caves and all the trials and tribulations he went through to become the eighth generation master of the art of Chung Moo Quan.

Then you hear the real story of the jump side kick. The big picture on the font of schools shows a man performing a jump side kick on a roof top of a five story building. The other buildings in the backdrop are from the Four Lakes Village apartment and condominium complex in Lisle, Illinois. The picture was taken in the mid-seventies during construction.

The jump kick looks cool with the setting Sun in the background and no doubt it was a feat jumping off the top of the air conditioner unit five stories up and landing back on the building roof.

However, once you have suitably advanced in the organization and are voted as clear enough mind to understand, it will be explained the picture is indisputable proof of a building to building jump at a distance of well over thirty feet. Then, once that sinks in, it is further explained he was actually jumping up to the top of the building as the photographer waited, the picture taken merely by chance for it would be impossible to see such an event and not be mentally affected. In fact, we are told, the person who took the picture went insane and committed suicide as he could not handle what he witnessed. Luckily for us the picture survives. But don't go explaining this to lower belts for they would not understand.

Over the years the cult would further embellish the story. Mr. Kim standing in front of the chosen ones selected to learn the 1500 year-old skills, telling them he jumped eleven stories in Asia before coming to the U.S. in 1972; that he again jumped this time eight stories at Four Lakes and was capable as he continued to develop of jumping over more, but he never shows, the mind can't handle. Not that it's a cult or anything.

The way this is explained is a term described as Kyong Gong Sul Bope or literally, rebounding off the air. In Moo theory, as one jumps into the air and kicks, with second and further subsequent alternating kicks if performed correctly, generates lift, thus the appearance of floating. This requires moving at very high speed thus the "mind can't handle part" and there is a limit to how far and how fast a physical being can move lest the respect line with nature be broken. This was explained as the sound barrier at a distance of several hundred feet. Yes, this is what we were told and believed, at least minimally.

This was way into the future for us, so don't think too much about, now you see what you may have a chance to learn, if you qualify. Look again at the photos and the descriptions on the walls it says right there, Kyong Gong Sul Bope (floating on air), Wae Gong Bope (ability to move like any animal) and Nae Gong Bope (nature or internal power).

Well, if it's written on the walls, it must be true. But Joe just wanted to practice and hang out with the buds. Thus he Mooed on. He practiced the Moo forms, practiced the bowing and thanking, worked overtime and extra jobs to handle course; Moogwa-ed at night and went to the movies on the weekends. These were cheap and acceptable to the cult handlers who would check us by asking, what are you doing this weekend? We were expected to be readily available in case something was needed.

Pizza delivery was another en-vogue activity. It kept us busy, brought in extra cash and provided free food for higher belts. If on pizza patrol you would be expected at least once a week to bring something over by school but not directly to, in case lower belts saw an assistant working as a delivery boy; that would not be good, their mind would drop. Thus, pasta coordination was another innate skill set developed as a Moo. They had another assistant, a new up and comer, meet you a few doors over. There'd be the bow and thanking at the exchange, the lower belt in awe of your abilities to handle, meaning you paid; while students changing clothes after a hard workout would also be amazed at the magical delivery with perfect timing. Must be okay to be an instructor, I guess, was the desired effect.

Another logistical challenge was moving apartments. It was a good thing as a Moo to find a new place every year; you didn't want to be too comfortable. This would prepare you for more responsibilities as a higher belt. Rent a truck? No way, no need. You have a fleet of MUVs you can us, which unfortunately for Joe, was the Mopar's fate.

Moving involved strapping everything onto the roof of cars and somehow making it to the new place. Furniture, mattresses, all of it tied down in ways the Beverly Hillbillies would have been proud. This was for two reasons. One was no unnecessary cash would be spent, and two it kept you humble. What are you, higher belt or something, you need a truck? Just use the cars, yet another reason to drive a junk.

Moving a school was more important. Any of these events were to take place on a nail day. The details were not explained until we became higher belts, past first degree. Consequently, we relied on head instructors to tell us when these days were. It's not like we couldn't have figured out the pattern, we were told not to worry about it, so that was that. The calendar as we know it, according to Moo, is really arranged in a different type of segment. The goal, if one is going to live by nature's ways, is to follow the real calendar, not the one that everyone else believes. Nail days work like this:

On days one and two bad things come from the east, on days three and four from the west, on days five and six the south; which leaves days seven and eight, bad things come from the north. The north is the worst so when you arrange your sleeping quarters make sure your bed headboard or if sleeping on the floor, make sure your head does not point north. East and west are best. East means remembering the past, which is why we bow to the east when practicing outside and the west means looking to the future which explains why we end practice facing west, when practicing outside or at home. There are three viewpoints, where you were, where you are, and where you will be.

Days nine and ten are neutral so these are the only times when it is permitted to nail or drive one object into another. No hammering or repairing or any sort of repairs could take place unless it was a nail day. One might think that's not so hard to figure out, but the trick is when to start the cycle and of course they were exceptions and this had to be officially proclaimed or else you would be nailing on the wrong day and the results would surely cause doom. For example, December was a complete month of nail days, but only on certain years. This of course was decided and directed by Master to make sure everyone got it right.

So when it came to a major operation such as starting or moving a school, nail days were an absolute requirement. Handling the pictures of Kim, the certificates, and cleaning around these areas was performed only by at minimum, a third degree and only on nail days. Every nail day cycle the regional or head instructors would drive from school to school and see that this was done. It was a mark of accomplishment when it was decided you were of clear enough mind to "handle this part."

Mouth to be clean and rinsed, hands to be washed, seven immaculate paper towels laid out on the clean glass desktop. Bow to certificates then proceed, spray Windex from a separate bottle kept in the desk for only this purpose onto the towels and never ever directly onto the certificates themselves. Use the towels sparingly with the final one for drying the displays.

There were two certificates of Kim, plus two of the next highest belt, as a rule a regional or head instructor. This was the "name on school" or owner, in case liability became an issue, and then those of the instructors who ran the place. These last sets were placed lowest on the walls to show position. Two certificates were used, one was engraved in Korean, superficially showing registration to Asian governments whatever that meant, and the other was in English for the morons who paid in U.S. cash dollars.

They were fancy looking, silver and gold inlays in well-to-do frames, probably cost a hundred bucks each to make. However they were worthless for authentication or accrediting purposes. They were there for show, to make it look like they meant something, to give false stature to the school. There is no registration system in the U.S. to Asian governments for martial arts, no Asian Chung Moo organization, no fifteen hundred year-old secret tradition handed down in an unbroken line; no schools in over one hundred countries.

Yet we bowed and we thanked, Moogwaed and brought in cash. We convinced others to do the same. Here's the proof it's real, it's written on the walls, see? The cult members say proudly to all naysayers: where is your school, your history? We were looking at the world through Moo glasses.

PART IV

I WANT TO BELIEVE

"Never underestimate the power of very stupid people in large groups"

—Phil Steffen

PART IV–I WANT TO BELIEVE

MOVING THE SCHOOL

So it came to pass that a larger facility was needed. The truth was the current landlord hated the school. Rent was chronically late, police reports of people being roughed up and the shenanigans of students standing out front in bare feet, holding bow position, the yelling and noise from classes; the neighbors had had enough too. With pure Moo breeding we were told we needed more space and a more visible location with better parking.

Down the road a half mile, north, as it turns out, was a newer shopping center set back from the street with a much larger lot. A furniture store had gone out of business, the ten thousand square feet being separated into smaller units. The second smallest at fewer than two thousand would be perfect. An expanded front room, bigger office and a spacious practice area, but without a back room this time, was the plan. Commercially the focus was on student facilitation and processing. The larger waiting and nomenclature display areas gave that away, plus the improved parking made it a choice location.

Haggling with the landlord and dealing with the low ceiling, despite village ordinances were minor issues that could be dealt with later on. After several weeks of arduous late night, sometimes all night handling, mostly waiting around until it was mentioned we could do something; the new place began to take shape.

Lessons and groups were still being run through the older smaller facility while construction and renovation were being performed at night, plus on weekends. This phenomenon would repeat itself many, many times over the years in Boston, Pittsburgh, Dallas and Houston, Orlando and Seattle. It was the same every time. Orders on when to move and what to do emanated from the top. Kim controlled everything. Any idea, suggestion or plan had to have his approval. He would purposefully wait until late at night or for weeks given the situation such as signing a lease or to give permission to proceed with a project. If things didn't work out that was someone else's fault or their problem.

One night, with midnight fast approaching, a team of underlings was dispensed to begin painting the background of what would be the main sign hanging atop the new school. The specially selected plywood was stacked in the open unit next door; we were told we had permission from the landlord to freely use the adjacent space. In reality we simply took it over a few weeks earlier and began storing all manner of supplies; paint, wood and carpeting in there.

The team began the set up, moving the saw horses into place and cutting the wood, next drop clothes were set up and the paint stirred. Boom! The front metal framed glass door slams open and the head droid screams out: What Are You Doing! You No-Minds! It's After Midnight! And so it was, our work was for naught, we would have to wait until the next nail day, and then wait for permission to begin the painting. What should have taken a week at most for average people to accomplish takes Moos two months; this is the legacy of eight generations of tradition.

Finally after weeks of delays and screw ups the new place is ready. We move, of course on a nail day, and it's in the middle of a late winter storm, snowing heavily. Vans and pickups are commandeered from lower belts, co-workers and passers by. We would have used draft animals if they were within reach. That's all we were to Kim and the higher belts, bipedal oxen as a means to accomplish further cash intake.

All the protocols were followed, all the rituals adhered to, the old place left as just a shell; with large holes in the walls from weapons panels or sections of partitions too enthusiastically fastened in place with over-abundant liquid adhesive or multiple sixteen penny nails when that location was the focus. But for now, it was the new place. We questioned leaving our former home of learning in such shambles. Our teacher replied it's the landlord's problem; he has spackle, doesn't he?

Kim showed up well after midnight, still within the newly revised and updated nail day schedule. See, the day does not end at midnight, it ends at four a.m. Why? Because that's just the way it is, when you become higher belt you'll understand. Besides, between midnight and four a.m. is when higher power is watching most closely, so be sure and be extra exact, understand. Um, but what about during daylight savings time? Does the day then end at five, or should it be three a.m.? Did this come straight from higher power too? Joe got a hard time for asking that in the coming months, for now though, the task was making it through this moving project.

There was a rite performed where we stood outside on the sidewalk, facing away from school. The sign that we had worked so hard on hung behind us, neatly against the roof line over the main entrance. It had a drawing of a jump side kick and proclaimed in large letters Champion of All Asia. In the window was a large photograph approximately three feet square showing the building to building jump. When the ceremony we were not allowed to see was completed, only Kim and the highest two regionals were inside; we were summoned back in.

The new school, although facing west, a good omen, required the flags in the main room and the certificates in the office to be placed on the north wall, no other way around it due to the dimensions of the unit. Everyone would be bowing multiple times per day and putting concentration towards the north; which was a bad thing. Kim explained in Moo-speak, he "had to use certain other higher concentration" during the move-in and establishment of the new school to alleviate this problem. As we filed back in and stood in line, Kim announced he had "taken mind out of old location and put mind in here." We all felt better, nothing to worry about now. We had accomplished moving the school.

Pizzas arrived almost on queue. Dozens of them, it took two pizza guys to bring them in, making multiple trips. About ten were thrown several feet across the room in a stack by Kim to an unsuspecting instructor. He caught pile the best he could and thanked. It was going to break up early several of us concluded, sharing thoughts mentally, not speaking. Food is being handed out, and that's a good sign. The pizzas and higher belts took off down the road to a nearby safe house where first degrees lived. A dozen or so of us, from several schools, were invited as well, told to meet there and eat our fill. This we knew we could handle without further direction. A caravan, lead by highest belts present of course, snaked its way through the unplowed streets of the developments to the modest rented sanctuary.

However when we got to the house, the food vehicle and the two responsible weren't there. Must have lost their way in the snow, they'll be along in a minute was the consensus. The Moos who lived there asked if we brought the pizzas, and then the phone rang.

"There's trouble! Everyone back in the cars!" yelled a first degree after answering the call. We jumped in the vehicles, Mopar in front this time, not knowing what to expect and raced down the block, sliding along to the convenience store parking lot. The two with the pizzas were sitting in their car looking dazed and rather confused. They had stopped to buy soda drinks for the clan with change that had been handed to them before we left and were accosted by a couple of locals at the store. Our brother Moos fought back and didn't lose any pizza to the attackers. However, they had not handled convincingly enough and were ordered to stand back before Kim and the others at school that night. All the killer royal style the defenders had practiced and professed in the past two years had let them down in the face of some common punks.

One of the two would lead a school for five or six years with mediocre success, in the end told to get an outside job and he still could be part of the organization. He provided state's evidence during the Tax Trial. The other would be as they say, "in and out," of school during the next year, eventually leaving and convincing two others to follow. He would make second degree in Moo but have a very long probation; years before he could test next rank. Ultimately after he left Moo he became mixed up with the wrong type of people, apparently.

Bob disappeared nearly ten years after he left the cult, his body found in a secluded wooded preserve, one arm wrenched from the socket. According to some, he had made inquiries of which the cult was not happy. The Moo was implicated in his death and investigated by county law enforcement, but no link was proven. Still it fueled the controversy.

REACHING NEW HIGHS (OR LOWS)

Spring time arrived and with the new location for Joe's alma mater came an increase in informations to the new school. But with no back room and the low ceiling, nine feet high at best, weapons practice was difficult. It was too hemmed in even with double the floor space accustomed to previously.

The decision was made to raise the ceiling. It was a huge undertaking, beyond our capabilities. It was explained to shut up and quit complaining and no, we certainly don't need any permits or authorization to push the suspended ceiling up to the top of the plenum, and don't worry about more supplies or instructions in how to work with the materials; you've got Moo.

Of course, it was a disaster. The plan was to erect platforms placed at strategic points in the nine hundred-odd square foot main room that would hold up the ceiling at the current level while all the supporting wires from above were clipped, except those most critical. These things were over built anyway; a little sagging for a few hours or even a few days is not that big a deal, right?

Well, we measured and clipped, and laddered around and adjusted and planned for over a week; working for hours each night after school lessons had completed. Our personal practice was secondary. Ran into a few problems, the ceiling could not be fully lifted to the new desired height due to plumbing, heating and ventilation connects and other concerns in the plenum. Two senior Moos developed the solution, a domed or barn-shaped design. It would slope along three sides but square up to the main wall with the flags. This would require new cult-approval of course. The already modified and destabilized ceiling sat atop us for a few days, gathering momentum for its counter attack.

We had begun on the last previous nail day and this coming Saturday was the last weekend nail day for awhile to come. We asked if we should wait until after school to complete the task but were admonished for suspicion of just wanting to sleep in. We began very early, had to help the guy at the 7-Eleven make the coffee that day. We stared up at the challenge in the dark waiting for the daylight to take hold; we had switched off all the electrical breakers to the room and removed the light panels the night before. Now we had to get the practice room resembling some kind of credibility before one o'clock when school opened for the day.

By ten a.m. we were about ready for the go. All the supports were in place with the longer bastions waiting nearby; we had plenty of manpower, about eight of us total. Kim would boast that with one phone call, he can make over one million start to move, you wanna talk about man power, he often claimed. So with our crew here we should be able to raise a few tiles if we were worth our salt.

Initially it worked, the final tie wires were snipped by those on ladders, and the rest of us held the supports on the now floating metal framed roof above our heads. My personal B-plan, per Joe's advice, was to stay under the two-foot square plywood support nailed on top of the lashed together two-by-four given to me. As we slowly pushed up in unison and the longer supports put in place, the Hindenburg principle kicked in. All that hard work crashed down in a few seconds. One of the ladders caught on the carpet, wasn't moved fast enough and the top step snagged the wavering contraption on its way up. The whole thirty by thirty-foot plus square launched to one wall and a few tiles buckled, then the frame, fatigued from the week of supporting that much weight without help from above, began to fold.

"Push it up, get it up!" yelled the highest belt leading the project, a construction worker. Turns out it was concrete construction but that's just as well. We stuck the platforms into the carpet, wedging the ceiling up at its new predetermined height. It floated there for a few seconds as tiles and frame pieces continued to descended like shrapnel. Nearly one in five of the ceiling tiles had fallen or was badly twisted.

The office door opens and the head droid, the one who before had decreed us no-minds for not starting on time, the one who had ridiculed us for wanting to wait until after school, was swiveling out on the chair to lend us a mental hand, to provide us no-minds with direction.

"Uh, keep handling, school opens in one hour," was all he said and shut the door.

The ceiling was up and not going anywhere. We concentrated on getting the thing tied to the roof supports to keep it there. The broken pieces were picked up and stacked outside the back door. We assessed the damage. There would be lots of holes until new tiles were acquired, we needed lights and to finish the clean up. Permission to vacuum was granted and with five minutes left before opening a few lights actually worked.

We were ordered to continue re-installing the lights. We got yelled at again for being out of uniform. Thus we changed and by the end of the afternoon, as students adjusted their practice sequences to accommodate ladders and no-minds working above, all the fluorescents were operational.

We had already raided the unit next door of tiles and frames when needed to fabricate the arched nature of our new design. We went for broke. That unit became the source for any replacement tiles still needed, their dumpster out back filled to overflowing capacity from the zeppelin crash the day before. When an explanation was demanded from the property manager, the head droid slyly indicated he thought he had seen some guys go in and out but he wasn't sure who they were. Yet another landlord set up for five more years of Moo-misery.

CON-TINUING ON IN THE TRADITION

For awhile things returned to a level of comfort. We practiced, received additional steps in the main forms of the Moo, including more weapons forms. The once hectic life became a plateau. We would go to work, hand in our paychecks with the list of our required needs and be handed back spending change. None of us, Joe included, kept good track of how much we paid, we just brought it in trusting higher belts to record it in the tally of satisfying our course obligation. We went out in groups and most of us by now, lived with other Moos who were also on the path to a better life. Sharing rent and expenses made sense, but having to every time go out with Moos and not having any outside friends was confusing. Keeping us as busy as possible was the cult's best defense. There was no time to discern whether or not the skills and techniques being shown us were really the best possible source as they claimed.

How would any of us know what is a royal style or not? As we progressed in rank we spent more and more time handling or working extra jobs or running errands than we did practicing. And self-defense or sparring was intentionally secondary to practicing form, unless there were newbies around then it was permissible to spar so long as not too many bumps and black eyes showed up, that would hurt school's reputation we were told. Protective equipment was not allowed at all, as Kim said the schools would turn into just another Tae Kwon Do shop; funny how the champion of all Asia would be concerned about that. It was the marketing appeal of Moo that brought the better minded fatter wallets in. Our role was to set the example.

The reason we were kept so busy is clear now. The reason we

could not spar or practice as much as some of us wanted to, openly a least, was so that we would not improvise; to test ourselves and find out what worked and what did not. And this is absolutely key to understanding Moo. The self-defense is mediocre at best. Memorizing the moves does not a warrior make.

It's in the understanding and ability to apply sound techniques developed by instruction from truly knowledgeable teachers that makes a good fighter. Learning from a guy with two or three or five stripes on his legs with just a few years in a school that teaches conformance over substance is not going to help you learn truly effective self-defense. You are going to have to learn elsewhere. And that is what the Moo does not want you to figure out. To solve this predicament, they planned your waking time for you.

The Warriors movie had been re-released and that was a favorite at late night showings along with Rambo, Terminator and Highlander. Going to bars or clubs to practice dialoguing light-minded females was allowed so long as you received permission. If you were a higher belt, you would not be able to relax with too many lower belts around, so it was correct to clear your plans in advance. This showed respect towards your instructors by deferring to their schedule. A group outing was a preferential response during the Friday evening brain probes.

Any personal plan like a date was scorned lest you become confused by a woman. This requirement eased over time as the higher ranks were given permission to marry; by order of rank and of course, after blessings from Kim. He picked out and approved the rings.

As lower belts, before the weekend or holidays each of us would be asked what our plans were, in front of everyone else naturally. Peer consensus along with facial expressions from the higher belts weighed the responses as to who was most correct.

A good answer was stating what you wanted to practice, and that you planned to hook up with other instructors to see what they were doing. You had to have plans or you'd be told to call Saturday morning. If you had to work you would be expected to call late Saturday and then again on Sunday if couldn't make contact, as when higher belts were not home. No doubt busy out handling something.

MIDNIGHT LESSON

As summer approached the instructors in training were summoned to be at school no later than eight-thirty that evening, we could skip group. No other explanation was given. About seven of us were taking turns from the waiting room to the office where the head instructor grilled us individually.

"You have to make sure each punch; each move is full on every time for the entire night, no holding back, you understand? And be sharp! No mistakes! You understand?"

"Yes, head instructor," we each answered flatly when it was our turn in the cooker.

As we regrouped in the waiting room, the main droid stuck his head out of the office beads. But we were too far away to run over and hold them up; since with the large windows it would look funny to pedestrians we were lectured one evening, so he stepped out.

"Alright then," he murmured, "head towards School Five, Villa Park, few cars as possible." We piled into one van, arriving about ten o'clock after a pit stop. None of us had eaten since perhaps noon, depending on your day job.

The gold color Lincoln was already there, parked nose first, but with space reserved closer to the door for another Lincoln. The lot for the adjacent restaurant was filled with what looked like similar instructor-class throw away vehicles. Must be a big lesson we thought.

Villa Park school had also recently moved, not that there was ever any competition amongst higher belts or head instructors and the like. In fact there was a lot. It abounded. If one school passed fifty flyers in a week, another had to match it. If three new courses were signed, five were signed somewhere else. If two new tiger idols were brought over for Kim to sign with his mark of upside down king, larger and better ornaments would be brought in from somewhere else.

Kim would often say the schools in (wherever, pick a state, or country) were forever doing so well, the way the instructors move is fantastic, all he has to do is make one phone call and fifty will be here tomorrow. And, the form they have is different than what has been taught here, for a reason. That way not until you reach very, very high belt will you have even ten percent of the knowledge and form that has been passed. The truth was Kim passed bits and pieces of strung together steps from wherever he got them and passed them along as royal form. Over time he forgot how much and to whom. As the cult grew in size, it was easier to make up new stories explaining any discrepancies in until-then accepted doctrines than to correct his own mistakes.

On this night about two dozen students, fifth section and up were gathered for what exactly we did not know. Everyone changed in the back room then began to loosen up for what would be a long night. Looking around, there were a lot of new faces from last year. Not everyone makes it to first degree we were often told. As hard as you think you have to try, higher belts try even harder, pulling you up.

A yell from the front room let us know Kim and Regional Head Instructor Forrest had arrived. The other regionals, Tom and David were in the office. The waiting room was filled with head instructors, all third degrees. We lined up in the practice room along the walls, extending towards the waiting room. Kim seemed almost giddy as he drove up in the silver Lincoln and stepped from the car, resplendent this time in a dark blue jump suit. It was very unusual to see him driving and not Forrest. It would be explained by Kim that Forrest had a night vision problem (he didn't) and that other higher belts had certain physical challenges; this was exaggerated or twisted to suit Kim's needs. For tonight though, we were only concerned about the agenda and why the rush to assemble here at this late hour.

After a quick line up and bow, lesson started. Pal Gae for an hour, then Ta Bouk Chung, the power or volcano form for an hour, then sliding side kicks. This attack, a first section movement; is to the side from down low horse position, upper legs level with the floor, raise the font knee and slide the rear foot up to past where the front foot was while thrusting the front leg out in a side kick, then retrieve the front leg and step back down. Three times across the room was all the space would allow.

After dozens of laps the office door burst open and Kim steps out. It is 01:30 in the morning. Some of the folks there have wives, families and they probably haven't called home yet, there was no advance warning about the schedule. Wonder if the other hundreds of thousands of Moos in the over one hundred countries would show up on demand, as advertised. This time we do not line up, we are told to remain standing in formation, rank and file; but stand bowing, hands clasped in front in approved conduct.

Kim begins to talk, in his rambling, purposefully broken English approach. About how in Asia students have to try for years to learn what we take for granted. How we think we have it rough skipping lunch or dinner once in a while but people in other countries are happy to have dog food. How he lived in the mountains and was subject to very harsh conditions so everyone here would have a chance to learn.

Right then a commotion is heard on the roof, like branches in the wind or some raccoons. It travels the length of the school and is loud enough for Kim to stop speaking. He smiles and gestures towards the highest belts standing fairly relaxed at the front of the room. They bow and nod seemingly to understand. It was said spirits and otherworldly entities would follow Kim around in hopes he would send them back to have another chance at a life. Certainly we were witnessing this first hand.

Joe confided afterward he thought the regional instructors did not look happy, more like worn out. Apparently they had a long day. We had been told it was not easy being around such a high belt as Master. It was explained Kim used the term eighth degree, then subsequently tenth degree, to describe his accomplishments. Yet his true rank was immeasurable. How could one put a belt rank on someone like him? So the eighth degree or whatever was used just to help us understand.

After the royal explanation of how we are not worthy, he checks our kicks. There were six or seven rows queued up. On command, "Step!" was shouted out by the lead head instructor. We slide and side kick, slide and side kick with Kim walking down the rows, watching each student saying, "No, more this way," and he'd point at the student and make a gesture, the student would nod like he understood, looking down, not worthy to be corrected by such a high belt.

Kim said the way we were kicking we would never generate power for our kicks to be effective. "Some of you," he said, "have felt before." Joe remembered holding onto his forearm as a lower belt and of seeing Forrest side kick the student across the room who had cushions from the couch as protection.

We were told to line up, front to back, touching slightly; the master of Moo would show us a little bit of what he had. A fifth section who would eventually earn the position of Kim's personal attorney and along with that his own personal bankruptcy held up a couple of kicking pads at the front of the line. Kim then used his power, thrusting his belly out and into the procession. The motion traveled along and we each felt a little push move through us. How much was due to the multiplying effect of the line dynamics was not debated that night. We were in awe of being talked to by Master who had the supreme patience to wait until we were warmed up enough at three a.m. to spend his valuable time with us low lifes. After the kick boards are put away, we stand according to rank. Kim talks on, using less broken English.

"You so concerned about three o'clock, three o'clock, so what, other part of the world it's afternoon or certain thing. You only concerned about your case, your certain part, what you have to do, what about everyone else here?" He intones towards Joe and a few students near the center of the line, working the rank thing skillfully.

"What about the others, their case concerning," he continues, "that's selfish your part," and grimaces a little, putting emphasis on the guilt trip he placed on those who have already paid in thousands and thousands of dollars for him to live in luxury while believing they were leaning from royalty.

Kim announced he decided to "show little bit higher power" and asked if we wanted to see. Everyone of course said, "Yeeess, Master." To which he immediately admonished the group, correcting them, "You mean if have opportunity..." using that effective scowl of displeasure to underscore his point. Kim harrumphs one final time then pulls his right hand up to his shoulder, fingers to thumb and cranks the forearm muscle. Joe sensed everyone focusing. This is It! Seconds pass and Kim says, "Will take a couple minutes," again using that condescending smirk Moos enjoy. After about two minutes the forearm was larger. As the group before him seemed to mentally capture what they were seeing, Kim laughed and quickly turned his wrist out and away and released the build up. No doubt the result of time well spent living alone in caves as a child. Five years hence he would repeat the display to better minded ones, a more general audience of potential new cash contributors; a Moo marketing gathering at 11:00 p.m., not a full lesson until the birds come out, also seeking Kim's power. But the arm would fail to grow as advertised, yet Kim would be telling the lower belts, there it is, see?

For us though on this night, we were about done. Lesson ends with the bowing to all in the prescribed order and the thanking.

"Stand Up!" shouts Forrest. "Bow to Flags!" We snap to, the numbness leaving us momentarily until he says, "Bow to Master." This takes awhile as Kim purposefully looks everyone in the eyes, checking, probing, or just making it last longer.

"Bow to higher belts," Kim says, almost quietly, in a low rumble, "…and to each other." Then it came out, a thunderous scream of Che-Yung Moo!; with the applause and thanking of Master Kim, and of regional instructors, and of head instructors. And of instructors and of assistants; we were thanking ourselves at the end, like it made some sense.

After changing, now in the front room, the clock ticking upward at the evil hour of four a.m. we each had a turn in the office in front of Kim. The regionals were on the couch and did not get up when the students passed through, either to the office or out of school. They remained seated and bowed from there, one of the privileges of rank and of their own personal fatigue.

In front of Kim spread out on the desk was a print out, like a business report. He spoke in clear, fluent English with near unnoticeable accent. He said to Joe and the others in turn, "Keep trying and the next rank was not that far away." That was it.

We were hustled out of school and trudged home. Most of us slept for an hour or two at best before work the next day, more mental ways getting in, again. Only a few of those that went to the special lesson made it into school the next day. Seems they called in and had to work late, if that would be alright. Joe and I Moogwaed alone that night, both having been given a key to the school.

SIXTH SECTION TEST

We were told the test fee was $750 and to start bringing it in as soon as possible. A few dared to ask if first degree was therefore one thousand. Astonishingly this was confirmed without any backlash. Test fees could be problematic since it took away from course payments. Then there were also contributions to Master's Christmas and to Master's birthday on April 1st. The collection plate for these events started well in advance of a month prior, although over the years the emphasis moved towards only the highest belts in the school. As time wore on those with better jobs were steered towards higher positions, thus the amount of additional contributions did not decline and the risk of alienating lower belts not yet fully indoctrinated was reduced.

So with test fee nearly complete and armed with a full nineteen Kata and Tong Nong, Yuk Tong and self-defense practiced regularly; when the word came to be at School Nine in Addison by seven o'clock, Joe said he felt more prepared than for any test yet in Moo. Pass or fail he did not care, the process was at least by now more fully understood.

Addison was run by a very capable third degree, also a head instructor. Quiet and soft spoken yet he could move very fluently and taught a lot of self-defense to his students, moves we did not have. He was known to have prior experience in martial arts before he Mooed. In the past few months there had been an assistant rotation program to give teacher's helpers experience in different situations. Joe had been at Addison before when the head instructor was granted a few hours leave to have a tooth pulled. Upon his return he treated Joe equitably, not condescendingly as was typical in Moo. Joe was familiar with the operations there, knew some of the students and was comfortable with the highest belt.

Addison was a default location. Originally planned for another suburb to the East, the organization ran into difficulties with zoning and city council, and squabbles with the property owners. Seemed the Moo reputation had caught up with them. Another school in that area a few years earlier had been burned down by Mafioso types, allegedly. The story put out by Moo was the instructor had a wrong way type mind, so something happened.

The entire Addison school which was nearly complete before the last minute bureaucratic objections surfaced was moved in one night, the story goes. That would have been a Herculean feat, given what we had experienced so far. Everyone respected the head instructor there, he had been around since the inception of Moo, having known Forrest from when he was only a first degree and the school name was Kong Su, the Korean hard-form presumably nowhere near as advanced as the modern era Chung Moo Quan.

Kim had said this head instructor or his direct family must have done something wrong in a past life that he would have to try so hard, moving school and all. But he made head instructor and was well known for his ability to fight and that's all that mattered.

Sixth section test was rigorous. Five of us tested for that rank along with five testing for fifth section. The school was one long room and situated in a small, older row of shops on a less traveled road. It was considered an oddball location but it supported itself, the head instructor was promoted to regional for awhile in Boston.

The test lasted over an hour and a half with heavy emphasis on self-defense and less so on form. In a couple of circumstances Joe had to rely on repeating moves previously used to escape or defend from a choke hold and other situations. The others did better, had more variety and could execute the moves more skillfully. Still Joe passed, scoring in the middle of our group. With sixth section accomplished and only one section of the belt white and all black trim on the uniform except for that first stripe, it opened a new view on things and new challenges.

In the very near future another new location would open, this one further north as the cult pushed out their frontier. Many of Joe's cadres within the herd were now handling group lessons frequently, freeing up the head instructors to concentrate on talking (selling) course. It was encouraging and at the same time mystifying to see lower belts as we once were, attempting to stymie the Moo assimilation process with the same arguments we had used.

I can't afford it, it's too much of a commitment, or I really like just what I'm learning now, they would say. The answers were of course, how can you put a price on your mind, your body; easy to make is easy to break; and you need to build yourself up. Still, the best was, it's up to you to decide, you can do what you want, but… The student then left to ponder his decision and left alone to practice while those who did pony up the cash were taught what seemed to be enhanced learning. Used car representatives would have been proud had they attended a seminar by senior Moo-account executives in action.

One night at the new location on the northern frontier, both regional instructors were in school prior to the main night time group lesson. "Step in," said the senior most regional to the sixth section assistant instructor. The third degree head instructor stood to the side, waiting.

"What is the most powerful thing in this room?" asked Forrest the senior regional.

Joe the assistant thought carefully, as much as a Moo apprentice can think anyway, and then replied, "Yourself would be the most power...." He didn't get to complete the sentence because he was spun around by the others in the room and grabbed, his arms held to his side while Forrest smothered his large hand over the sixth section's face, covering the nose and mouth. Joe nearly passed out then was released, suddenly.

"Air," stated the regional. "Air is the most powerful thing in this room." He continued, "You can not see it, touch it, yet without it you can not survive." Going on, the regional who had learned directly from the Kim said, "Master mentioned there are over ten thousand different powers on this Earth, I just explained one of them to you. Master has control over all ten thousand, you understand? Now go inside and start group."

The students got a good workout before the regionals and the head instructor stepped out to check form. After that personal lesson, talking course was easy. Joe could parrot with the best of them.

INVASION AT THE MEADOWS

The relatively new school in the north 'burbs was located in a lower middle class town. The homes were smaller, the cars not as fancy. But this means people there keep their money saved up don't they? The factory and machine shop workers, the small retail owners of an older community were perfect pickings for the Moo ploy.

This school built up fast, there was no competition close around. Serious martial art clubs, where the emphasis is on training to fight, use industrial warehouse space or second story lofts above older business districts as their venue. They don't care about 1500 years of made up history; they practice diligently, perfecting their craft. Whereas Moos perfect commercialization of the Moo product line in store windows alongside pet shops and fried chicken marts.

This store, I mean school, opened late in the year, a few weeks from Christmas. The beginning of winter was mild, new students were gained quickly. There was less focus on stories of Kim and more emphasis on passing form. Lots of new courses were signed.

Come spring teams of flyer passers from established schools were sent to the new territory. The bordering hamlets would be the next phases of expansion. There were a few notable schools of other styles in the outlying area, a confrontation was inevitable.

Arriving at our regularly assigned school one evening, not expecting anything unusual, four assistants gathered in the office to be told about that night's group. Except, we would be sent over to the new location to handle. Nothing else was mentioned. Something was up but no one would say. The assistant who was stationed there had been on the fence for some time, maybe he left and we are going over to reaffirm the 'you can be replaced by a thousand waiting for same opportunity' doctrine constantly drilled into our heads.

Joe drove us to the frontier; we stepped inside by rank order. The wavering assistant, a first degree, was inside working with students. The third degree was in the office, on the telephone and seemed angry. He cupped his hand over the mouthpiece, nodded to us to change.

When group started, there were three sixth section assistants; two first degree instructors and one third degree assistant regional Moo with about fifteen students in the room. This school was set up differently. The waiting room was overly large which reduced the practice room. There were too many chiefs with too few Indians it seemed. This must be a special lesson to homogenize teaching practices. We soon found out otherwise.

There was a commotion in the waiting room at the front door, someone had slammed it open and the bells rang wildly. Then what sounded like punches landing, but not before the three of us standing on the inside of the main room near the curtain to the waiting area sprang thru and found our third degree trading blows with the invader; who was now backed up against the far wall near the front entrance in what we nicknamed dingy corner.

The assailant, a Korean man in his late 40's had already taken a couple of hits, his face was bruised. Joe and another assistant joined in pummeling him when the front door was again flung open and held from the outside. A second intruder was attempting to jump front kick his way into the melee. He was caught and dumped back out on the side walk. Meanwhile the first invader had collapsed in a heap, his collar bone broken from a three-quarter side arm sudo attack (striking with the bone at the base of the hand) meted out by the third degree Moo. The junior Moos finished in subduing him, picked him up and threw him outside too, face first.

Three defenders stepped outside and began to pick off who ever else wanted a piece of Moo. One trespasser was partially stuffed in a trash receptacle by the assistant Moo who caught the jump front kicker. Two other Moos chased a couple dingys into the middle of the parking lot and jumped side kicked them after a brief stand off. After the skirmish they were beckoned to return by their third degree. An attacker was left on the ground still in fetal position.

Remarkably, the class inside continued without much interruption it seemed. Students were into their kicks, their shrill "kee-haas" drowning out any complaining by the visitors. The main Moo returned to the office as the phone was ringing off the hook. With the still unknown aggressor force regrouping outside, two more cars pulled up close by.

"They have re-enforcements!" Joe shouted from the waiting area. Kombs, the Ace Hardware machetes with red strips of yarn tied around the handle, began coming thru the beads, handle first, sliding across the floor.

"Pick-em up!" was the order of battle.

"Be alright," blurted Joe, relentlessly speaking in Moo, "it's Assistant Regional Head Instructor Clancy (not his real name, but trust me this guy has suffered enough from Moo).

"Protect the highest belt out there!" was the command from the office. We picked up the kombs and jumped outside, encircling the bewildered Tae Kwon Do students who on orders from their leader had accompanied him to put down the upstart cabal of Moo encroaching on his territory. Passing flyers on his block was some sort of insult, apparently.

The arriving Moo stepped from his car and quickly identified who he would hit, the guy with the bruised face. The Moo yelled at the guy to leave and when the invader, still reeling from his first encounter of the Moo kind didn't, Clancy punched the invader, a sixth degree black belt, square in the face then pushed him hard towards the street. None of the supporting cast of dingys, there were about six, perhaps seven, did anything to save their clansmen. Most of them scattered.

The lead invader screamed in pain and ran down the street, as best he could, with a few members of his group trying to keep up and several Moos in hot pursuit. Running in the dark along unfamiliar sidewalks, barefoot, clutching a big machete while in full Moo uniform as traffic rolls alongside gives one pause for reflection. Joe asked himself, what am I doing? Looking around, the fight was over and so was the chase. He lost sight of the dingys and the Moo posse and figured it was best to return should another wave of unexpected guests arrive.

Trotting back, the police were there, so the machete was ditched outside temporarily. Right then, the silver Lincoln roared into the lot, nose into the front door. Forrest stepped out along with the largest head instructor in the Moo inventory. At well over three hundred pounds, his main function was of butler and servant, a role he still fills to this day for Kim. This time he was there for window dressing and wind break, nothing more.

By now several other higher belts had made their way here and were attempting to appear nonchalant in their street clothes, milling around in front of the pet store or the ice cream shop, pointing at the window displays all the while keeping tabs on things via the reflections. They also discreetly asked pedestrians what their impression was of recent events, to which nothing of consequence was mentioned. Almost like the skirmish had gone unnoticed.

The police talked quietly in the office with Forrest and the main Moo, as group lesson ended, but with minimal fanfare and bowing. We handle the waiting room and students leave, a little curious but not worried. The supporting Moo returns from the chase and steps inside, his crew heads back to their school. But Clancy, still revved up, grabs a plain clothes detective by the throat. Stupid move, but he would be known for this. Wrong place, wrong time, and wrong action fully induced by Moo-think. Amazingly, the cops let it go. Forrest smoothes things over like he always does and we are interviewed briefly by higher belts.

Turns out, flyers were passed by another pod of Moos all around the Tae Kwon Do guy's place, which he had for over ten years undisturbed. He called into our school and threatened the main Moo.

Well, the flyers kept getting passed. The TKD students would tear them down and the Moos would put them back up. Say, that area in Arlington Heights is real good for getting flyers up, was the word amongst junior Moos.

After weeks of this the TKD guy calls and screams, "I going to kill you, I come over tonight!" Well, he stood by his word but the Moos out smarted him, laying in wait, except we didn't know that's what we were doing. Nobody told us; we were pawns, used by the cult because they knew we'd fight. Joe and crew hadn't passed flyers in that area.

One of the late arriving head instructors brought in a couple boxes of victory spoils, donuts from a nearby shop. After a brief respite sitting on the waiting room couch reviewing our actions that evening, consuming our jellied treasures, Joe and our clan wondered if we had acted properly, or taught them enough of a lesson.

The Tae Kwon Do guys did put up a fight, but retreated when confronted. Our ferocity took them by surprise, and their moves had no real effect, they made a lot of noise but their kicks literally bounced off us. In the end it was them on the ground, curled up, pleading not to be struck anymore. Joe had a very small black mark under one eye after elbowing a dingy who grabbed him from behind as Joe pounded the ground dweller. The elbowed recipient's feet flew up and swiped past Joe's face. He never felt it.

Forrest and the other senior Moos departed, they went to the hospital to check on the condition of the assailant. He would need several months in traction, his gang received mostly minimal injuries, but it was clear they were beaten.

Immediately after the pastries were devoured, a good sequence of Ho Bar Tu or tiger form was passed along, doubling the amount we had thus far. It was believed this form was the highest of all main hyung, or main forms, that any martial arts possessed. It was only taught to the most trusted and loyal students. It was said to change you mentally as well as physically. I'd go into the mythos, theory, stories and legends of Kim developing tiger form by living in caves with a tiger, one of the symbols used by Moo, but I gave up repeating lies long ago.

OUT FOR BLOOD

A few weeks go by and upon arrival at school, we are told to be at Naperville by ten o'clock for a special lesson. We are even let out a bit early to make sure we're on time. Auto pilot dialed into 7-Eleven, we bought Gatorade, orange juice and Hershey bars. We knew the beefy bean burritos would still be there on the return trip, if we survived.

As we entered school, Forrest nearly laughed, "You'd better be careful, Regional Head Instructor Sam is out for blood tonight." This lesson was sixth section and first degree only. There were about fifteen of us total. The purpose was to weed out those who would not give all, all the time, on command.

Tension was absurdly high for these special sessions. The lesson was over two hours non-stop, very intense hard-form workout conducted by all the third degrees. No deep breathing in between sets. Every Kata and then every main hyung form blasted through at full bore and at maximum down low joint destroying position. This night Joe did well. Those who were thought to be on the fence and had questioned school were singled out. They were screamed out more intensely than the rest of us. The entire lesson was physical to test the mental or perhaps the lack of it. We punished ourselves.

Concluding the lesson, we punched out with five hundred repetitions from bone bending low stances. The front windows reverberated. Before leaving, Forrest addressed us in the waiting room. We are reminded when Moo first started; it was practiced in a garage without heat for over a year. And how the early lessons were like this every night, before Master decided students were worthy enough to teach higher form. We are dismissed.

JULY FOURTH CAMPOUT

In the early years this was an assemblage of instructors brought together so no one would get too much of a taste for life outside of Moo during a few days of unstructured bliss and end up quitting. That was persistently a difficult thing for the cult to have to deal with. So keeping everyone together, even on holidays was better. Besides, don't you want to be around higher belts instead of all those no-minds, even your own family?

Having been on last year's escapade to Michigan where we traveled for hours and hours in a caravan, by rank of course until finally reaching the KOA campground quietly located next to the interstate, Joe was ready for the excursion this year. Except, he and a select Moo unit were going to be the advance team. The location was Wisconsin. No idea where in Wisconsin exactly, just expected to follow the car in front of him.

Joe had been discharged from his union job due to missing too many days, being late too often and the relentless phone calls generated as a byproduct of school. Misuse of a company vehicle for school purposes was the final straw. We had been allotted an aged green GMC pickup another student donated whenever it was needed. We loaded it with supplies and gear, a couple of sandwiches for the ride and headed north.

After carefully motoring for several hours we arrive. Nice place, secluded on the south shores of Fond du Lac. We set up camp and, a tent for higher belts and scout around. We eat what food we had left then make a startling discovery. We have almost zero money between any of us and no idea when relief will arrive. We bargain for firewood with the campground owners but are refused. Joe does acquire sodas and cheeseburgers for us from the on-site matrons.

Well after sunset the caravan shows up. There is a lot of confusion and tension. A couple notable higher belts, one a head Moo-droid, had quit recently and Kim wasn't sure the campout was still a good idea. He gave his permission to proceed only after the regional instructors explained all the students had brought in tents, food and were (disingenuously) looking forward to it; and then to cancel would be difficult to counter.

After an all night session setting up tents and making sure everything was in order, in other words just staying awake because no one gave permission to go to sleep; we prepared then ate breakfast. It took half the day. The regionals were busy being regionals and the other higher belts were each giving orders to every lower belt they could find. Some of the lowest belts became kitchen slaves and did nothing but cooked and cleaned for two days. Our crew was smart enough not to be seen and lucky enough to have such a high ranking bootlick for a head instructor he was busy following the regionals around asking if be alright. For what it did not matter, he was going to show his Moo-worth regardless.

Overall it was not that bad. After a specially appointed food-recovery team, we drew straws, had been compromised on return to our leaky tent which had half the required number of sleeping bags, from a late night mission to the food tent scrounging for goodies; the regionals passed an edict saying for everyone to cook their own, clean their own. That meant most of the higher belts had to fend for themselves too, but thanks to Joe's mercantile savvy, we now controlled all the cookies. Literally, we had a black market in Oreos that was amply lucrative in proceeds from lower belts to pay for the cover charge at a swinging little place in town we had scouted earlier. Saw a good band, had a clandestine beer and Joe snuck the big green pickup with five riding in the back, lights off for the approach to base before curfew. If anyone asked, we were out handling or getting in Moogwa.

The return trip back to civilization was uneventful until Joe was awakened by the fourth section driving the truck with the repeated loud questions of where do we turn? What exit do we take? Joe looked up from exhausted slumber and saw the I-94 road sign for Des Plaines flash past overhead. "That one," he said.

The fourth section hauls the wheel to the right attempting to still make the exit from the center lane and drives over the top of the front fender of a Volkswagen Beatle minding its own business until we smashed it in true Moo style. No one was hurt and insurance took care of the damage, but the fourth section was extremely distraught, knowing the severe tongue lashing he would receive from his assistant regional head instructor, a notorious hot head who would also end up serving five years time for carrying out his master's orders.

For now Joe's bud, the fourth section, saw his own career in jeopardy. Joe's friend would in time make first degree then leave, the cost-benefit analysis for his-self, his case concerning, having run its own course.

PART V

BLACK MOO BELT

"The only people who gain importance are those who crave it"
—Napoleon Bonaparte

PART V—BLACK MOO BELT

FIRST DEGREE TEST / NO TEST

Into late July that year it was proclaimed the schools would close on Saturday for the rest of the summer to give students and presumably instructors, more of a chance to be with families or to simply enjoy some free time. The real reason was the Farm was about to be started, but this was a closely held enigma shrouded in misdirection. More about the second cousin to Waco will be revealed in the sections ahead.

On the last Saturday before the semi-vacation days were to become effective we are kept busy all day, with minimal practice time. Handle this, go pick up that but be back in a few minutes. Higher belts' cars are washed and cleaned, something is up but as usual we find out as it happens. A caravan is arranged and we violate a significant number of traffic laws driving south. Of all cardinal sins to commit outside of school in the presence of higher belts, letting another vehicle cut the line between you and higher belt is top on the list. Obeying this is critical to your survival as a good cult member. On this day we once again force people to the side of the road while maintaining our path to a better life.

Naperville's parking lot is full; we park in the shopping mall down the street and hustle back on foot. The entire organization from fourth section on up is there, about fifty of us in all. It seems implausible now, how the masses never grew quite as large as advertised. In over one hundred countries, over one million students have, Kim would often repeat. The attrition rate was phenomenal. Several had dropped in the past year, more were forthcoming, the reason we were dispatched here was still unknown. Joe seemed unfazed, his norm.

"Shoes off, line up by rank, waiting…" the highest belt ordered from the office, poking his head out of the beads. He was handling the office, meaning tallying up the day's receipts from all the schools.

We stood waiting in the main practice room, still in street clothes, uniforms hanging on arms; the line started near the flags, and went completely around the room. Those of us with pins wore them. After a long wait, perhaps half an hour, the yellow Lincoln cruised up. Kim and Tom, the other head regional besides Forrest stepped from the car.

Several lower belt head instructors jumped out to open the Mark IV's doors and commanded Stand Up! as the entourage entered school.

Kim wasted little time. After checking the receipts, he stepped from the office into the main room and motioned the others in. We all bowed. For some strange reason things seemed relaxed. He spoke only briefly, Forrest was not there as he had "mistaked." Whatever the mistake was, it was not explained. Instead mis-spoken English, gestures and charismatic nodding and the approval seeking phrase "you understand?" was used ad nauseam. Towards the end of the fifteen minute circular diatribe, Kim made the familiar references to opportunity and more schools getting in, of opening the gates; all his hollow promises of ever more learning that was never realized.

We unanimously bowed and thanked. Lesson was over. We still waited in the practice room, being allowed into the front room in groups to put shoes back on and to step into the office for a review in front of Master. Another mind check, Joe hated these things.

He was one of the last to be sent in, more concerned about a ride home and dismayed by the treatment of Forrest in front of everyone. Spread out on the desk was green bar computer paper, some kind of report, but with minimal printing. Pluses and minuses it seemed were being added up right there. Tom, the lead regional present, after asking permission from Kim, pointed to a line appearing to represent a certain in-duh-vidual's score.

"Hmmm," Kim started, using that low voice to sound impressive, "The way I look, beginning from today, starting to put on first degree stripe, you understand?"

Looking away, Joe felt his eyes dropping uncontrollably towards the floor. Being promoted felt hollow, the goal of first degree obtained without passage by rite of fire, as if rank were bestowed without qualifying for it.

Kim interrupted his thoughts, "You earned, understand?" He uses the basso-tone voice effectively, the way a fat dog keeps inquisitors from getting too close to his food bowl. Menacing and controlling, it was his decision who to promote. How well we had done up till now, efforts at special lessons, mistakes, payment towards course; all pertinent data set before him for his judgment. At least that was the desired illusion.

"Yes, thank you, Master," Joe replied. He has since confessed this was a mistake and makes him ill, to re-live calling Kim master. Master of what, exactly?

Nearly everyone there that day was promoted in the office in front of Kim. Sixth section to first degree, first degree to second degree, second degrees told they would soon test for third, if they stayed true and continued to try hard. Kim was careful not to water down too much the effects rank held on small group networks. It was supposed to be just a little beyond reach, that next rank, that next symbol. You had to draw out a little further each time. Some existing third degrees became assistant head instructors that day, a new differentiation between full head instructor and the standard main instructor handling a school.

We went to eat in a quiet stampede, several groups of eight or ten all showed up at the same restaurant. The local sports team taking over a full extra room at the local Greek owned diner. Beefy bean burritos discarded in favor of steak. Head instructors doled out a few dollars for the meal. It was noted a well-liked former head instructor was not among us. His wife had won out it seemed. He had to make a choice, either continue with career in school or stand by his wife and family. Despite the promises of a better life, the two choices were diametrically opposed. Consensus was this was why Kim was trashing Forrest. We contemplated what was in store now that we were first dans.

MOOING ON

Into the following year the assistant rotation program fizzled out. It brought up too many unanswered questions, like why form is taught one way in one school, or why certain lesson coding sheets for recording cash intake are or are not used and how they are used. Having people travel around then ask about what they saw to their higher ups afforded more prime time television watching for the master. The intelligence gathering worked. He discovered which places were disciplined, which were relaxed and who needed a talking to, and best of all he expended very little energy.

A couple of new forms came out. Both of course were super hush-hush as they had been for centuries and it was up to our generation not to let anyone except those specially selected to witness the practice.

One was called Shim Yoke. It consisted of a stick about five feet in length with a piece of rope at each end and one in the middle, which was slightly longer. Sand bags were at the ends of each rope. The form was to hold the arms extended in front with the big dowel rod level with ground. Standing in a high horse position, careful not to put too much strain on the lower back, the ropes are curled up around the stick using a grasping and cranking motion with the hands and forearms. Keep the elbows straight, no-mind! Keep going until the outside bags touch the wood pole. The center one, for balance, should be still hanging below.

Now let the ropes unfurl in a controlling grip until the bags touch the floor. Repeat, but do not bend the elbows. It takes a good deal of focus to perform correctly and it does build strength. The first time most of us could do two, may three repetitions. Within six months we could do sets of ten. But since this makes the body like Godzilla, a lot of speed forms and fast non-stop ocean form was required in the same practice session lest the body lock up. This happened to a few of us. Bowel movement became an issue in severe cases.

But like all things Moo the importance also faded with time. The Shim Yoke was kept in the practice room for everyone to see. Most folks could look at it and figure up what it was for. Boxers, weight trainers and gymnasts have used similar for many years, but then the Moo marketing would kick in. That's a high-level form you will learn only as a higher belt, if you make it on certain course. That one, choose from the following, a) Develops amazing strength b) Requires more mental than physical practice c) Is a secret only Moo has or d) All of the above. The main thing this form did was to pump up the skinny twenty-something instructors with a little physique in lieu of more protein in the diet. It looked better standing in front of lower ranks with arms folded across the chest if you had just Shim-Yoked. But the additional strength does not last, it is external development, not the fabled supreme internal the Moo claimed it has.

The other intergalactic mystery was called Ba Gua Breathing or Nae Gong breathing form. Nae Gong was said to mean internal energy. Like raw charged plasma, it radiated straight from the solar system and could be controlled and transferred by only the most clear-minded and mentally advanced. Kim was said to be able to stand on a mountain, catch lightning and direct it. But this takes tremendous internal development, something Kim was born with so to help us out he is opening the gates and passing along so much higher forms that in Asia there is uproar.

As a matter of fact, one seventh degree in Hong Kong complained too loudly about Kim teaching directly to the Westerners, so he was stopped, just as Bruce Lee was. Nobody dared ask what that meant. We all knew what happened to Mr. Lee.

Nae Gong breathing went like this: stand in high horse position with one hand at eye level and the other full extended past the groin. The hands face each other, palms open. While breathing in, rolling that big Moo belly-in-development out over the belt line, the hands start to approach each other compressing the energy. As the hands cross past each other they turn over, exhaling and switching positions. Repeat and breathe, roll that soon to be gigantic belly out, then in; out, and then in. Keep the neck relaxed or you will pass out before you have opportunity to develop into a pudgy manatee.

After a few hundred repetitions you should start to feel something like nausea developing. This means you are doing it right. In the mountains of Asia higher belts for centuries have practiced this form all day long. So they don't eat much, they just keep Mooing. For us though, the main thing to remember is that ten minutes of this form equals thirty minutes of hard, down low Moogwa. When time is short from working all those extra jobs and handling, a good Moo can still be one with the collective in as little as ten minutes per day.

Please don't anyone try the above scenario as described, it is worthless as exercise and can be harmful to the body. It was copied, again incorrectly by Mr. Kim, from Tai Chi training.

THE PINTO

They were in the process of moving, but things were not yet set, in other words they had not been granted full permission from their higher handlers to sign a lease. Joe's small dresser full of all the clothes he had was stuffed length-wise across the back seat, the trunk filled with other crap. The misfit subcompact was so overloaded one night on the way home from practice he and another first degree at the time ran over some bad road at 01:00 and the muffler broke off, the main exhaust from the manifold now dragging along.

Fearing a brilliantly explosive end to their agonies, the duo pulled over and did what any good Moo does when he has a flat tire. You rotate the wheels and drive home. They reached under, grabbed the pipe, bent it outward like a dragster and tied it to the passenger door handle with a combo shoelaces and hanger contraption that should have been patented for its universal aesthetic appeal. The scramble for resources resulted in new discoveries as is often the case in Moo-ville, in their situation several dollars in loose change under the seats. In uniform, they pulled into the nearest 7-Eleven in nonchalant mode; no shoes, reeking of body stink and slimy exhaust.

Beefy bean burrito? Why not, how much worse could it get? Joe said to his compadre as first one then the other spilled out the driver's side onto the sidewalk. They cruised the final miles home at low rpm down the back suburban streets, bean-surprise and colas on the dash, with faded grins and stupid dreams.

During our coming up time, the transition between white belts to full instructor, it became more a quest to just make it to the next point, the next belt or through the next day. We never really thought about the full reality of handling a school. Our brains were on a pre-determined, pre-occupied schedule. At the right time, we would be given more things to think about.

ROYAL SWORD FORM

"Step in," said the recently named regional head instructor to the underling shortly after night time group finished. "Tonight, take all the rope off the komb handles and replace with this tape, instead, understand." This is a command in Moo, not a question to check understanding.

The reason was Kim, the eighth generation master of the royal line of Chung Moo, had noticed calluses on the hands of certain higher belts when he shook their hands and determined this was unacceptable. He asked what they had been practicing, and they indicated komb, the Moo sword form. Since Kim had recently made up and passed along a few dozen new steps within the past months, the regionals wanted to suck up as much as possible and be able to say they practiced more of the new form than any of their peers. Competition, which was not supposed to exist in Moo, and certainly not at the higher levels, was absolutely rampant. Kim fed off it.

All the weapons in the schools had to undergo an approval process by Kim before they could be used by anyone. Sometimes this took weeks or months, depending on how Kim wanted to leverage the importance. In a ritual performed in front of only the most trusted, loyal members to influence them with the unexplained mysticism; Kim would hold each weapon submitted and take out any bad thing or wrong mind by putting his own mind in. This was just another leveraging strategy, if you got to see this you must be well on your way to the inner sanctum. Every so often Kim would designate a certain sword or staff be set aside for effect. See, the approval process weeded out some bad there, whew! Lucky us.

All utensils making the grade would receive his mark of upside down king, which was actually the Chinese character for king, written inversely. The marking would be small, the uninitiated would rarely notice, but when they did, the branding strategy was a shrewd concept. Lower belts new to weapons training would be told it's a school mark, higher belts were told it was Master's mark to make them feel good about buying a seemingly quality product and instructors would get the full-flavored dogma of Moo. The reason this is complete tripe is because this tradition like so many others in Moo were recent inventions; differentiation of the product line, the new and improved bigger and better belief system that you are ready for now but weren't before.

Thus all weapons having been personally checked and approved by Master and certified as such by the proof mark were therefore another extension of Kim into the student's practice; an additional projection of Kim's image throughout the Moo realm. It was also a great selling point for course.

Just think of it. The Champion of All Asia (CoAA) personally handled this weapon and now because you handled your course, or at least brought down the beginning part of your multi-thousand dollar down payment; you are going to get into (some) number of steps today.

So here were these vetted, fully sanctioned machetes placed by his command in the schools, now judged inferior as the rope the CoAA himself specified to absorb sweat and keep the weapon controllable during extended periods of use wasn't after all, sufficiently Moo. No re-marking needed during the retro-fit, just handle correct ways, make sure wash face and rinse mouth, and be sure to bow to certificates before and after. If the gestalt isn't there, just go with it but once start, can't stop, have to be finished before leave school, understand?

Near dawn, all the rope is off and the tape is on all the handles. Another bright fresh day approaches. Just enough time to shower, shave and try to find something to eat before work, to earn more money for what exactly? Oh, yeah, Moo.

WHAT TO DO WHEN BREAK A MIRROR

My close friend Joe Smith offers his advice on handling broken mirrors. It's not just seven years bad luck; this is much more egregious if you're a Moo. If you break a mirror, you have to wipe dog manure on the broken edges, and then throw the treated pieces over your left shoulder into a moving body of water. We kid you not. This sacrament in Moo prevents the bad thing that was set to occur from actually happening. This was a validated, documented Moo belief to be taken seriously. Your future depended on it.

Joe explains: Broken mirrors, the way it was mentioned, is that mirrors are a gateway to different realms or dimensions, that it's possible for something powerful and not good to enter this world through a broken mirror; that animals such as dogs can see this and will howl or act strangely afraid if a broken mirror is close by.

Breaking a mirror in school was absolutely the worst as it had to be replaced that night. Many schools had spare mirrors just in case. A mirror broken in the home or car also had to be handled as soon as possible regardless of any schedule, Moo-speak for long days to keep you on the right path. It did not matter you were only going to get three hours of sleep at best, you had to find dog crap. It was ordinary conversation to ask amongst your peers about neighborhood canines and of course you knew where one good sized pooch liked to hang out as a backup.

There were instances late at night when groups of instructors on poo-patrol competed for droppings in certain areas that were over-checked, with no dog poop to be found. Nothing else could be done until the mirror was handled, no practice, nada. Often several parks or apartment complexes had to be searched in order to obtain adequate material to handle the task. Undoubtedly, some enterprising nuveau Moos substituted near dog-like product as in the dark and under time constraints, it probably wasn't inspected very closely.

A good measure of forethought had to be given to the logistics and process steps, you hold the mirror steady and I'll… no wait, I'll hold the mirror and you… lest the drive home get complicated. No wonder adherence to Mooisms put a strain on relationships, work commitments, daily life.

Advancements in the technique brought about kits in boxes in some car trunks that contained all necessary tools like the precious paper towels, rags and soap for cleaning up enough to get home. The critical concern was pre-establishing the location of a creek or stream, especially if you had just relocated. This was one of the advanced criteria to scouting a new place to live, along with making sure your higher belts had keys, but that's another story. The water had to be moving, not sure why but it had to be real important. If the water wasn't moving, it was trouble. We heard of at least one unfortunate soul, for lack of a better word, who had to retrieve his previous night's work and start over.

Thus, covering the broken pieces and it was stressed to make sure every part of the edge was covered properly with ample bongu, in other words shit; was paramount lest you were not handling correctly and what ever bad thing that was going to happen, happened due to your failure to properly wipe. It really sucked when at the end of several longer days, Moo-speak for trying hard; like late in the evening or before something you personally wanted to do, such as a date with a nice girl; you found out someone in your immediate circle had "something to handle." There were certain ones that were not allowed near any glass object after their second offense. You just didn't want to have to put up with it, but without question you bailed out your buds because we were all going through it together. In Moo terminology, eel don (to move as one mind), was our mantra. Kim was quite skillful at twisting Biblical passages to entrap people to worship him.

After a time, some of us developed an innate skill in the practice of handling broken mirrors and were sought after for their quick and correct handling, should the need ever arise. This could be one reason why everybody kept tabs on everybody else. I used to think it was because some of us had consistent better luck with women or our cars had more gas, but I guess not.

Later this week, the current Moo leaders will continue to espouse Moo-ness and lead the willing to even deeper understanding of how to handle. No doubt the form and actual martial training will be phenomenal as well. Think about that when you mention you've brought down your earnings for them to receive. If you are a sixth section or higher, you may want to ask about this, then see for yourself and you decide. We did already.

EVEN MORE NEW SCHOOLS

Another new outpost was put together in the far south suburbs. A common facet of cults is that progressing higher up in rank reveals new discoveries. Like standing at the ready in the correct pose; waiting for permission to hit a nail, or to paint or to sit down. Putting up a new school was difficult because things had to be handled with an exact approach. And there were of course, varying interpretations of how things should be done according to the highest belt there. Then another similar or perhaps even higher belt shows up. Everything stops, the bowing and the thanking for opportunity is chanted and when allowed, the work begins again. Quality and timeliness of Moo workers left much to be desired.

"Why are you doing that?" asks a higher belt, sipping coffee.

"Be alright to say?" replies the lower belt, not having slept since the day before.

"Yes," says the higher belt, impatiently. In holding a higher position, part of the requirement is to act like any lower belt is not qualified to tie your shoes.

"Head instructor blah-blah mentioned we should blah more like this."

"No, that's no good, stop doing that and do blah, instead, understand?"

"Yes, head instructor blah."

This would continue for days and days, according to the nailing cycle and to the whims of the highest belts there. After one all night session preceded by an all day no food spend whatever little money you have left towards higher blahs, we were late on scene. We had been granted permission to go back to the two bedroom apartment where five of us lived for a temporary reproach, but we had to be back on site early the next day, a Saturday, meaning regionals will be there all day too, understand?

An hour late and facing certain doom, our solution was to clock over 130 mph in a 260Z commandeered by who else, Joe, from lower belts the day before; making the thirty-mile plus trip door to door the entire length of the Tri-State in under twenty minutes. The radar detector was shut off it was making so much noise, we blew past cops sitting on top the bridges, they must have had less sleep than us.

Naw, it was because we were on a mission. Higher and better purpose; better mind, better body, see? Every time we got away with something we chalked it up as proof of being on the path to righteousness. We power drifted into the lot next door, arriving seconds ahead of the regionals' entrance that day, close enough to the door we got to yell Stah-Hand Up! We were so correct.

After a few weeks, as happened every time at a new location, the local martial arts community drops by to say hello and check out the way of Moo Doe. During one notable free introductory beating handed out to an inquisitor who tried to fight back, the Moos ganged up on him, three on one.

The information deployed a little-known until then strategy to escape. Not even the almighty Moos know everything. The visitor kicked his way out of the large front glass windows and walked away. The Moo of course denied this ever happened in the true legacy of the style, but were once again thrust into suspicions from a new landlord.

KIM THE RACIST

"God made the first man too light," Kim would start out, telling a small group of instructors at a private gathering. "So, white is no good. Next he made too dark, black not so good either, God said. The third time, turn out just right, God made Korean." This was Kim's best attempt at veiled racism using his charisma to offset his poor taste. Similar to his other claims of true, right, correct; best possible life and 1500 years of tradition, he was obviously phony here as well. He didn't think it was a joke; he wanted us to think he was joking.

Black people he referred to as well done ones. They were black for a reason according to Kim. "You want physical, go to Africa, there's many with better physical there, but no mind," he would often repeat. This is the reason he said there would be only one black higher belt in the USA. He has to give at least one a chance to make, Kim explained. Now that's compassion.

Jews were labeled hook noses, Gays he called Liberace types, and for women; almost impossible to make higher belt, it was considered against nature. Although to show he's fair, there was one seventh degree female in Asia, but this was a very rare case. Where exactly in Asia no body bothered to ask, it didn't matter, we were not going there anytime soon.

Funny thing though, with Kim being the CoAA and the highest belt in living memory and able to leap tall buildings and so famous in Asia he can not walk down the street, wouldn't you think there would be perhaps one or two or even twenty Chinese or Korean students in the schools keeping a low profile, keeping a lid on the treasure they found? Nope; very, very few Asians were ever students. Those that did come in were confused by the oriental-looking lettering on the front windows. Is it a martial arts school or a restaurant?

And that was another deceptive ploy by the Kimster. Make it look real to those who don't know any better, but not too real to those who do. The real players won't waste their time with a commercial store front dojo whereas the easy marks will gladly bring in their cash. To help shroud the riddle, make up a story for your followers about putting mind in and certain protection, watching over schools.

WOMEN OF THE CULT

As the single male Moo approaches first degree, the focus on controlling his personal life intensifies. He already has to call into school at least once a day. And call in on weekends. Any absence for school requires approval. Weekend plans, who he is going out with, whether or not he will have sex or get in, as the cult speak goes; is monitored and evaluated carefully lest the future main instructor, potentially running a school, lose his mind over a woman.

Woman were said to have a unique power making them one of

the few greater dangers to a Moo. Gambling was the other, since instructors need stronger minds and determination in order to make higher belt; the urge to win and beat the gambling house was a foretold pitfall of which to be wary. This is why once reaching a certain level, Master will take you to a gambling place and explain how to defeat it. This was obviously just another ruse. Kim liked to gamble and this is how he made it sound acceptable to you for him to spend all the money you and your friends brought in.

With women however, the threat is not so transparent. They possess an inherent ability to confuse man, essentially known as Ma-ow. Ever spend time talking to girl you have feeling for, but it seems like there is two of them? One is nice and the other is maybe not so nice, playing games? Well, that's Ma-ow. It's natural for women to do this so don't think badly of them, but if you want to make higher belt you have to learn how to handle it.

Joe describes here as only he can, how many often felt after being interrogated by higher handlers on personal matters, in front of their peers or other higher belts, even after reaching first degree instructor:

Did you go out last night?
For some time yes I did, regional instructor.

Did you see that one female?
As a matter of fact, I saw several in just a few hours.

Did you get in?
Yes, I screwed dozens of them in intricate positions as much as possible before reporting to you as I place that high a priority on your wisdom.

Did you wear a glove?
No, the girls I go out with are clean. However if she wanted that, why I'd oblige or want to find out more.

Be sure to always wear a glove, understand?
If I get that desperate to date someone you'd know, I'll wear two, made of nylon tire cord.

Which way your mind is towards that one? Don't lose your mind.
I have lots of friends, date some, and sleep with whom I choose. If you need assistance working through your issues, seek professional help.

You care for her or what?

Yes, someday we might marry and raise non-Moo offspring which I'll see most everyday. Unlike your false promises of more time to spend with family, I'll be with mine.

What do you know of her background, who she dates?

Her background is credible enough and I'm not as pathetically insecure as you, more importantly she chooses to be with me, if our schedules are mutually compatible.

Which way your future is? You want to date more prostitute type?

Well, I guess if I really want to reach higher belt buckle, am gonna need to know some. Got any phone numbers?

A former regional instructor, having spent considerable time around Master Kim reflected on the cult's norms in this way:

Even as far as handling women, this came down from Kim, "Women are like shirts, wear it for awhile see how it fits," or "There are only three types of women. Some women are like pretty watches," and on and on and on. I remember one day at the Farm (the future Waco-esque training camp) Kim was lecturing a bunch of us there, and he started to talk about women while his wife Jeanne happened to be there. It was Kim, his wife, and about sixteen instructors sitting on the deck of the Green House at the Farm.

Kim was sermonizing about the right type of woman, and he makes a reference to Jeanne and says even her, if she stops trying she will be gone. For one flash of a moment you could see the rage in her eyes, her head shot up, you could see she wanted to say something, and then she composed herself, lowered her head and continued on her wifely duties. This set the bar at a new level on how we as instructors could test our women in front of each other. We were cruel. It was insane, but it came from the top. The Moo organization is not a free thinking group. The closer you get to the top, the less free thinking they are.

The ex-regional offers another example: I was driving with a national instructor and his wife, we had parked and were walking past a second-hand store and the wife had noticed a lamp she thought would look good in their apartment. The national agreed. The lamp was forty dollars. It took them twenty minutes of talking back and forth to finally decide that they would not buy it because they would have to explain where and why and how they bought it, to other nationals and maybe even Kim, or worse yet Kim's wife and the other women. The hassle of buying it outweighed the need for the lamp. Everything we did at the higher level was controlled; who we slept with, when we slept with them, when we married, what day we got married. It is easy to say that I had control, but the truth is Kim controlled everything.

Another ex-instructor reflects: There was a head instructor who liked to do his own thing, sometimes he'd practice at night by himself. Since he was in terms of tenure, the third highest rank, he could get away with a little more than the average Moo. As time wore on and those that could make something happen, that is bring in cash, started to eclipse him in rank and stripes, he too sacrificed. As a head instructor back when regionals were still a novelty, he had the run of where he stayed and all the perks, having had been around for so long, all were reverent.

He met a woman. Somehow along the Moo continuum he met an exotic, smart, wonderful woman, with a professional career and it was outside of school. In those rare instances when there was not something to handle or pick up or simply wait; he met her. Seems intelligent good looking people tend to do well without Moo. Anyway one thing leads to another and he brings her to one of the sit-down Kim worshipping sessions they called a banquet. Stupid move, never disclose what you hold dear to the Moo for they will take it.

In this case, they told him if he wanted to make higher belt he would have to give her up because he liked her too much. What with the others passing him up, he told her good bye. Fast forward a couple years. Still not promoted, still being passed over, the dude meets another; not the same cupid's arrow but as a Moo, you play the hand you are dealt.

He was practicing more and more late at night, on golf courses, taking off on free time without other Moos. But because of his tenure he was let be. He was in truth spending time with his friend. The major Moo-moos had their own Moo to worry about, so they paid less and less attention.

Turns out they had a child and he was married to her, yet they did not live together. She accepted his Moo class of living, but then she became ill. He turned to the people and the man who had always promised if you ever need anything, and of course they dumped his ass. They made up the evermore tediously-becoming story of him losing his mind, not qualified to be a head instructor, that Kim gave him too much chance already. This guy gave his heart and soul to Moo and was ostracized because he got married without asking. It was saddening to learn he was not selected by the government to testify at the federal trial, still convinced John C. Kim was something worth protecting.

Another ex-instructor, one of several who revealed a similar story, explained how he was coached by his higher handlers on the truth that abortions are not a sin. If that life or spirit is supposed to get to Earth, it will find a way. This part comes straight from Master, so don't worry, nothing to think about. Just because she says she will do it, doesn't mean you won't have to drag her kicking and screaming into that place. If you don't want it to affect your career, you better make sure it gets handled, understand?

The bottom line was Kim didn't want anything to distract his followers from the cash generation or to draw cash from the organization. Kim would offer paradoxically, "When time is right and you find right one, everything taken care of."

Twenty years hence, not one of those closest to Kim is still married; with children, a home, a fenced yard and a dog. The utopia never materialized. Several of them had children; a few others were married now divorced. They do not live with their spouses and rarely see the kids. It's somebody else's responsibility to raise and pay for them, to handle that part.

HANDLING OF FINANCIALS

"L is for lesson payment, T is for test, DP is for down payment, understand?" said the now assistant regional head instructor to the first degree.

"Yes, would it be alright to ask?" Joe affirmed, curiously.

"What?" (A little sneer from teacher adds emphasis to how stupid is the lower rank).

"Not sure about why a serial number seven C-note should be placed on top on the down payment part?" Joe asked.

"No-mind, seven is for Chicago, besides how many stars are there in the big dipper, you already heard Master explain this, he has seven stars on his back just like the big dipper because he comes direct from higher place, understand?"

Well, it was like this, Joe and many others figured; sometimes you say you understand and hope you'll catch up on the details later, right? The payments were coded to evade scrutiny should too many questions be asked about how many students schools had, or how much money was coming in. It was in the tens of thousands every month. Not just in the dozen or so locations in Illinois but from those in Boston, Florida, Texas, Minnesota, Pittsburgh and Seattle.

During the Federal Tax Trial begun in 1995, the IRS purported that Kim and *The Kim Organization* as was officially published, caused over two million dollars in tax loses to the government. Unreported income was estimated at over six million dollars in just the five years leading up to the case. Because records were destroyed as a matter of procedure and training within the Moo; the conviction was for Conspiracy to Defraud the IRS.

When speaking on the phone, one thousand dollars was ten. Five hundred was five. Any less than one hundred was identified as cents. If a larger down payment was expected, say ten thousand or more from a better minded, more clearer ways student, meaning an eager up and comer; regionals would schedule a private first lesson, afterwards handing the cash to Kim personally as a medal of their worth.

All records were removed from school every night. Attendance was the only book left in the desk. No monetary recording was allowed. Instructors carried a briefcase with the papers, contracts and such. The envelopes with money were transported in the socks or down the arm if wearing a large enough coat. Once a week or every few days, depending on the level of business, certain records from the nightly transfer at the pre-selected collection points were burned. It was a cardinal sin not to completely burn any evidence.

Students were not given copies of their contracts, despite consumer protection laws. Over time the regionals or head instructors would amass piles of finely printed yellow and white bullshit papers and have lower belts sort them out. This was to appease the Kim should he ever ask to see the records, which on occasion he would, to keep an underperformer in line. He'd call up at midnight and demand all the courses for the last year be brought over, and then he'd ask meaningless questions until near daylight just as a drill to test perseverance as part of the Moo legacy. It says so on the walls, right next to volition. There, see? It says moron.

PAST LIVES = ROYALTY

Chung Moo Quan was translated we were told to mean true warrior; in addition to true, right, correct. Even as a low belt, the meaning of true, right, correct was emphasized. Kim would say, "You have girl over at house, and you want to be with her, but parents are in next room, how going to handle? True is you want her, but right is not to let parents know, that is correct way." In essence therefore, according to Moo doctrine it's acceptable to lie so long as you can make up a good enough explanation. I think most people in the above scenario would have deferred certain activity for a more appropriate time or setting. But in Moo, you don't have to do that. Why? Because you have a stronger mind.

The reasons the taxation system was wrong, Kim explained, was to look at all the waste of the money taken from the working class and compare to the well-known cheating by the rich, who of course, wrote the tax laws.

But Moo will change all that. As a member of this elite society, by having earned your position, all of you unquestionably come from some type of royal background. It's the only way you would have made it this far. Somewhere, somehow in a past life, any one making first degree must have done something right to earn the opportunity to learn Chung Moo. It is your destiny.

THE FARM BEGINS, AN EXODUS RESULTS

The Farm was ten acres along Book road in south Naperville. An existing house was renovated and another one, the Green House, built on the north side of the property. This building would have no windows along the north wall, to protect Kim from bad things. It would take six months to construct and another several months to finish it out to Kim's liking, with opulent carpets, cabinets and furnishings. Only the highest belts were allowed inside and never via the front door. That honor was reserved exclusively for Kim's mother.

The existing white clapboard house was renovated somewhat,

but this took much longer. It served as a commune for the regional instructors who lived there and for the assistant regionals who wanted to. The cabana, a converted tool shed was behind the white house and was used as Kim's command center when talking to lower belts or holding meetings, often belittling instructors for a small infraction he would go on a tirade about for hours. Or, when seeing the need to more firmly set the line, Kim would administer the death test; grabbing a Moo by the throat, collapsing the windpipe and choking him to the point of no return. "You have a choice, serve me or die, which way is your mind?" Kim would tell the candidate seeking a better life. Those wanting just to be let go were cast out, never to return.

The pond with island in the middle would take another year to build out completely. Initially, the dig was performed by an instructor promoted to head instructor because he had experience with heavy equipment and his parents were fairly wealthy. Hmmm, more opportunity if you can handle, as Kim would say. So he sat atop a Caterpillar for days nonstop, food was brought to him while he carved out another acre to about twenty feet deep with an island and provisions for a beach.

Apple trees and landscaping would eventually fill out the camouflage. This was to be a training ground and headquarters for all Moos in the northern states. Barracks would be provided in the renovated barn. Aside from the cultish aspects of comings and goings, the bowing and thanking protocols never relaxed. In fact, away from public view, with no lower belts around, they were more rigid.

That is until the surrounding neighborhood caught on to multiple cars entering or leaving at odd hours; plus all the construction, which drew curiosity. The dogs stationed at the Farm to keep the local high school steroid users at bay probably helped publicize the Moo as much as any factor. A large German Shepard named Major liked to jump the front fence and chase joggers down the lane. One morning he advanced into nibbling form and the attorney he bit sued his owners. Word spread in the Naperville area, there's a commune on Book road. Loud thanking and other cult rituals had to be minimized to avoid further embarrassment to those living there full time.

But this was years away. That first summer and into the fall, all available hands were employed for free at the Farm. This is your opportunity, this is your future. This is where Master will teach higher level training. That never happened. It was a place for Kim to live well and have lots of servants around to feed his ego.

After months of every night, plus non-stop weekend work at the Farm, three guys from Joe's pod decided to leave. These were difficult times, to see guys you've known for a couple years now, and been through some tough times with, decide to pack up and bolt. Although to this point Joe had not yet worked on the Farm; he was still drained emotionally, spiritually and financially by his Moo experience. But he made the decision to stay, having nowhere else to go.

His friends' departure did however prompt intervening changes within the cult. Instructors were treated with barely more dignity. But soon it returned to as it was. Below second degree you were nothing, not qualified for the rewards of Moo. This came directly from Kim, simultaneously preaching about the glory of being one of his chosen elite yet pushing you down and aside once you were drained of cash, or of use to him.

Living quarters were consolidated with the last remnants of the old school group. Of all those testing sixth section the year before within a few months of Joe, only a handful remained. The Chung Moo Quan system was real good at attracting new students, to get them to sign up. It had to be as the burn out rate was so incredibly high.

The rest of that year was fairly bleak, although the constant pressure lessoned around Christmas. Sufficient accomplishments had been made at the Farm to satisfy Kim's need to live in luxury. And he still had plenty of supporters to serve him.

For those that stayed in the organization, our practice was checked more regularly and the attempts to break us down mentally by long hours standing, listening to speeches and criticizing personal choices in front of peers regarding clothes, or food, or girls was reduced. Joe felt like turned a corner, for awhile.

CHE CHUNG

We used duct tape on everything; uniforms, school projects like kick boards, home appliances, even cars; with diminishing degrees of success. It was a right of passage as a lower belt, say around third section, to have a higher belt show you how to use duct tape to repair a crotch seam on your uniform or to fix up your wallet so you would not have to spend the change on buying a new one.

If Joe had taped over his briefs this night he would have been better off, he reflected. The form of Che Chung, or paper over wood, was supposed to be a precursor to Chull Sa Chung. Che Chung was supposed to be learned first, but here in the United States, Master wanted to faster build up students so, see how much opportunity you have?

The form was practiced using telephone books, covers removed, placed on top of the chung box in place of the bean bags. One did not have to drop as low and use the full body as much as in Chull Sa Chung and there was no herb mixture. You banged away, using high amounts of snap from the shoulders to the hands while turning the hands over in between. The focus was on the method of striking the paper and pulling back. If done properly a near liquid sound, like a pop, was heard and the top sheet of paper would instantly disintegrate. It was likened to pulling the skin off of someone's face. Phone books were good for this reason, dense and plentiful material; page after page blasted through, a mess to clean up but the hands toughened quickly. Needless to say, most of the public phone booths near a Moo location lacked the full compliment of reference materials. However, open hand attacks were more noticeably felt by informations or dingys should the need arise.

Joe and his re-formed pod learned Che Chung well after experiencing Chull Sa. But Che Chung could be practiced anytime, right in school as much as you wanted. After second degree access to the Chull Sa herbs was more readily available. Looking forward, Joe and the others decided to concentrate on the Che Chung form to better prepare them for the future.

On this night as the evenings grew warmer in the summer, Joe was nearing the illustrious one thousand hit mark on the second hand when it happened. The need to urinate was over powering. Nearly passing out on the way to the restroom, struggling to undo his uniform bottom in time, it flowed freely, uncontrollably; thick pulpy blood. It almost would not stop by itself. He had to concentrate best he could to bring the platelet fountain to a halt. He flushed and cleaned the toilet. Blood in school was not good, he wondered what ritual or conversation or whatever else would happen now. He had to pee again. Gonna be one of those nights he thought. There was a knock on the restroom door.

"Be alright to ask if yourself is alright?" one of the fellow Moos asked in the ever present Moo-speak.

"Yeah, I'm fine." Joe replied, rarely breaking custom. "I urinated blood and it won't stop. No big deal, I might sit down for awhile."

A long few minutes later Joe returned to the practice room to clean up the papers from the chung box and call it a day. Bladder on cautionary hold status, he walked slowly, insides felling like jelly when he noticed the practice room was already cleaned up, the box and books put away, the papers cleaned up.

"Be alright, assistant regional head instructor is on the phone for you," said the lower belt to Joe.

Reaching through the doorway from the practice room in the approved stance without having to bow to the flags in the main room, then again in the office and to the certificates; Joe spoke into the receiver with apprehension.

"Be alright to ask if anything needed?" he began in Moo-esque verbal submission to his handlers. At all times it was most correct to ask this when first speaking towards a higher belt, with few exceptions. Even under duress, it was important to use the polite conjugation of Moo.

"What did you do?" asked the voice on the other end, almost chidingly to Joe.

Joe explained and his coach, Moo mentor and cash drainer listened patiently for three full seconds before interjecting, "It is nothing to worry about, it will stop soon, it has happened to several instructors who were a little bit weak in that part. Go home and get some rest."

He hung up. Joe stood looking at the telephone base, pausing before putting the hand set down. He wondered what would happen if he ever really needed help. But for now, he had to make it look good in front of the lower belt who had placed the call.

"Yes, I understand, thank you assistant regional head instructor, good night," Joe said into the dead receiver.

They changed clothes and stopped to eat at the Moo equivalent of a Ritz Carlton banquet buffet, the $2.99 Slam Breakfast. Two eggs any kind, two pancakes, two pieces of toast, your choice moldy or not so moldy with two strips of simulated meat-like soy product shaped and formed to fit onto a plate that was hopefully exposed to hot water within the past day. During their feast, Joe had to use the washroom twice to alleviate the swelling. Less and less blood was seen, finally it ran clear. Another Tricky Day by The Who was on the car AM funk machine as they headed home.

OPPORTUNITY TO ASK QUESTIONS

Soon it came to pass, so let it be written, so let it be so; word went out among the Moo that Master would answer any questions about life, the universe, any thing any instructor was curious or wondering about; anything at all. Below a certain rank, second degree, Moos would have to write their questions down and their regional handlers would present and read the queries directly to Master. But above that rank, the droids could ask themselves, up close and personal, direct to the one who knows all.

After group lesson, Joe and other lower belt instructors gathered together in the waiting room to write out their questions. The deadline loomed, Joe would have to take the compiled list to regionals tonight. Things often went this way in Moo.

The reason Kim wanted to hear from the flock was not to help them better understand anything; it was simply a maneuver to see what they were thinking about and to ensure that whatever it was, it was no threat. He was constantly evaluating how much information was out there, who knew it, and who might cause him trouble. At lower ranks this would be more so in the form of re-telling too many of the old stories or of not understanding the current spin used to market Moo. The emphasis was to permanently keep the transforming mind pointed towards the school. The trickle down effect was to have the under-droids work on their questions together in a controlled setting with peer pressure working its magic.

"What if I don't have any questions?" Joe wondered, nearly aloud. Or more precisely, what if I don't want to ask any questions, I just want to practice? Lest his self-depreciating shrug be misinterpreted and reported to higher ups, Joe wrote simply: Dear Master, thank you for opportunity to ask questions. Be alright if did not have any at this time. He folded the paper in threes, careful not to bend the edges and placed it in his designated envelope, collected the others and made the call. The task was completed. He was ready to, in Moo-speak, step over towards higher belts, checking if be alright to ask if anything needed. Broken English sentences were preferred; it showed you were catching on to the expected behaviors.

Another reason to have the questions brought over was an additional level of mental inspection could be performed without the droid suspecting anything until it was too late. The slightest hesitation, or misstep in gestures or formulaic behavior could lead to a lengthy correction no matter what time it was. Before he turned the corner to the street of doom, Joe reviewed himself mentally. Remember to smile, he thought.

This evening proved uneventful, the higher Moos had been through the ringer themselves which was Kim's trade mark run-up to an event. Since the Kim was going to audience questions, well then, you better be prepared for whatever, understand? Joe presented the questions in their envelopes.

"How did this one seem?" a regional intoned seeking Joe's input on the appearance of one of his buds.

"Be alright to say, best I can see, all instructors are looking forward to this opportunity," Joe mentioned.

"Huh," was the regional's reply. "Okay then, see you tomorrow, take off and leave quietly so as not to disturb the neighbors," the higher belt finished.

Relieved there were no further issues for this night at least, Joe took the long way home and found Twinkies on sale at the Gas n' Go. He cranked the good speaker's volume.

A week goes by, and the lower belts ask Joe if he has heard anything about the questions they submitted. Now he's in trouble. If he goes and asks higher belts he'll be yelled at for asking too soon, for wanting and be called selfish. Yet if he doesn't ask and the higher belts find out lower belts did ask but Joe didn't then re-ask towards higher belts, Joe gets yelled at for holding lower belts down and blocking their path. And they'll probably throw selfish in their again too, Joe thought.

Continuing on in his reasoning he came to the conclusion there was only one correct answer at this time. He uttered what all good Moos utter when faced with a decision with no possible good outcome. "Waiting," he said to the lower belts. "I'll mention when time is right, or higher belts will. Now step inside and check students." Waiting has so many uses in Moo.

In this case it performed the primary function for which it was designed, holding up the position of the one who said it. The lower belts were satisfied they had been given some attention and now had something to do at the direction of a higher belt. And, they felt good about it because Joe was looking out for their best interests in keeping in close contact with regionals, all on their behalf. That Instructor Joe can sure handle, he must like us. Moreover, Joe saved his own ass because now there was little chance a lower belt would chomp at the bit and ask a question out of turn if they saw a higher belt first and even if so, they were told "waiting," that they'd be informed per the chain of command; so it would be their mistake if they did ask directly. Still, Joe would have to stand for hours and watch the lower belt get corrected, as often happened to him when he was that rank. Overall though, waiting was the best possible option.

When the results of all the questions were finally disseminated to the rank and file, the results were disappointing, a non-event, almost. The lower belts asked about other styles of martial arts and were given answers about how they stole it from Moo centuries ago. How other societies do have Ba Gua but not the real one; their way is watered down (the reverse is true). A couple instructors asked about stories they had heard a year or two before and were heavily corrected in special sessions in the weeks that followed. This is what Joe had feared, that somebody was going to bring up about the time Master traveled to the next life, when the seven sacred birds come and the Sun and Moon become one, and about life on other planets and whether or not aliens influenced humans here and what really happened to Bruce Lee.

Who ever brought any of this stuff up was in for a rough time, even though these and many other weird ramblings were common fare during the after-group adrenalin high speeches we often experienced as higher Moos practiced hearing themselves talk. It was just one more way to wear you down so you'd sign up for course or to puff up their self-importance. Joe and his close buds learned to put some distance from anyone venturing too far along the mystical curve.

The real purpose of this Q&A program was to weed out any that were confused or had questions, two key indicators of future doom. It was also to smooth over any problems so that as schools grew and more and more droids were in charge of cash collection without the benefit of the direct link to Kim as much as the early Moos had, the process could still be controlled. This was the true nature of holding the line.

In private, a few days after all the questions (or non-questions) had been satisfied and most of the first round of corrections meted out, Joe was pulled aside by his main handler who asked him why he didn't have any.

"I just did not want to take Master's time unnecessarily," Joe said. "Whatever I need to know will be explained, I'm sure."

His handler smiled, then said, "Well, just as an example of what is allowed once you reach higher belt, one head instructor did ask, 'Master, who built the pyramids?' And you know what? Master just smiled and pointed to his nose and said back, 'the answer is right here'. How about that?" the regional presented towards Joe.

Joe shrugged and looked down noticeably, "Guess I'm not at a point where I can begin to understand how deep that goes," he offered back.

His handler accepted this, still thinking he himself had witnessed some kind of miracle by being in the presence of supreme platitudes. As he escorted his regional to the car, Joe hoped he would not be too bogged down in this sort of complete waste of time if he did make it to higher belt. What was making higher belt anyway? He just wanted to practice.

PHOTO OPPORTUNITY

Summer was arriving quickly this year. No more freezing cold nights or early mornings trying to get junk cars started, soon we can practice outside again Joe contemplated. He would miss working outdoors in his union wage delivery job, now having taken an inside sales gig by necessity to Moo. He had a fairly decent place to live, steady income although Moo took nearly all of it; and membership among the elite royal blood descendants of true warriors. Joe was ever hopeful the next belt, the next rank would finally prove out to be all the things originally sought.

Calling in to school this warm afternoon, he was told by the regional cash handlers to be sure and be in promptly for seven o'clock group lesson. Obviously something was up, yet the group was nothing spectacular. It was immediately afterward Joe's spider sense kicked in. Students above sixth section were ordered to change and head for Villa Park. This was where the special late night lesson with Kim took place last year about the same time. As his carload approached the destination parking lot around ten o'clock that night, Joe was calculating the probability he and the others would make it to work on time tomorrow and whether or not they'd have something to eat prior. Going twelve hours without decent food was the norm for most Moos back in the day, going eighteen or twenty-four was becoming a strain.

Arriving students were hustled through to rear rooms to change. The higher belts from all schools were already there and tension was high, of course. It seemed as if some higher belts were acting that way on purpose to add importance to their presence. Egos fluctuated visibly as third degrees will stand tall until a fourth degree or higher rank third steps in to the room. This was uncomfortable to Joe and many other Moos. It should not have to be this way, he believed. Ah, must be my thinking is wrong; I'm the problem, Joe concluded. He finished changing into freshly washed uniform and moved in sync to the main room with the rest of the herd. It was clear now why having a clean uniform was stressed yesterday. They had been told to make sure of it, and stayed up late dutifully complying with the order. Tonight would be picture taking for school.

There were perhaps fifty students total, lined up along three walls of the main practice room. It was impressive, all the striped legs and black belts standing shoulder to shoulder. Regional Head Instructor Forrest checked in via telephone and it was said to begin, the other regionals informed us. We bowed in to the flags, then towards the office to the certificates, then to the highest belts and then to each other. It took a few minutes to accomplish the ceremony due to the size of the crowd. Everyone was intensely focused, but on what exactly we weren't sure.

It started off with two regionals displaying large weapons and one moving unannounced towards the other, who jumped up in the air seemingly in a spontaneous defensive reaction. Of course, as in all things Moo, this was staged and plotted beforehand. They were so far apart any contact was unlikely, and the photographer, a student, took the picture shots from where and when he was told. The Moos, as directed by Kim, knew how to make optimal use of camera angles and crowd shots obtaining the highest impact look with the most minimal of resources. The goal was to hit their mind, as Kim put it. Let's call it capturing the imagination.

The regionals went through various postures and made cool sounds with the blades of the garage manufactured weapons. A few more postures were committed to film and then it was the next sub-highest belts turn, and then the next in line highest ranks. The spectators were allowed to change positions every once and awhile, moving to the other side of the room and during these times Joe and the others snuck in some stretches and muscle relaxing moves, but very subtly so as no one would notice. There was no chance to warm up prior to the session, which now looked like it would go on for awhile. No food, no refreshment and no movement equaled stiffening muscles and joints. Carefully looking around the room, those in Joe's pod noticed others were pulling off the same charade. They smiled largely inside, near imperceptively towards their sneaky brethren.

The sub-regional and head instructors who had the most physical abilities were showcased in the jumping, diving and other feats. One noted head instructor jumped and dived over eight students using all landing area available. It was rumored that for fun he would sometimes do this over a Volkswagen. Another jump side kicked over five lower belts holding their arms out towards each other at shoulder height and still delivered a throat level attack to his counterpart at the receiving end. These were the guys Joe and his group wanted to emulate. Thing was, Moo didn't really propel the standouts in their development. These guys were natural talents; they were track stars and high school athletes prior to Mooing. Just as Kim used his innate abilities to masquerade, he lured others in now to do it for him, to capture the cash.

The sixth sections were put through basic warm-ups in front of the camera, like leg stretches, double jump front kicks and such. The idea being higher belts show higher forms. The strata where Joe and equivalent tenure found themselves in would perform last. This is because they had been around Moo long enough and been through a few late night lessons; their mind would not drop as much as some of the lower belts who had never before pulled an all night Moo.

When Joe's group opportunity finally did arrive, they were instructed to use a weapon they had seen but not trained in; the Jung Sul (sool) a medium length stick, approximately six feet long of hard wood about two inches in diameter with a small pointed spear tip. The shaft was wrapped with red cloth like a candy cane and more red cloth was tied in strips just below the base of the spear tip. The diagonal pattern of the shaft and the tassels near the business end were supposed to disguise and confuse the enemy, Joe surmised, if traditional Moo weapons philosophy held true.

The disconnect was an ingrained behavior in every Moo not to touch a weapon for which you had not been instructed. When told to pick up Jung Sul, half of the twelve or so first degrees hesitated. They looked again to the regional giving the order, and not until after receiving a confirming nod did they grab the weapon. Joe found himself in this class. The others must already have the form so he saw from them as to how to pick it up, carry it and stand ready.

First degrees were shown by a regional what stances to take, what postures to emulate, even though it was soon readily apparent to Joe none of them had any movement with the striped pointy stick. As a matter of fact it was found out not even the third degrees had more than a few movements of this form. Nevertheless several of the pictures from that segment of the photo opportunity lesson were used in the waiting rooms and displayed in schools for many years. Moos on parade we used to call it.

The lesson wore on until something like thirty rolls of film were used, higher belts at last satisfied they had enough from which to pick and choose over the coming days. The best of the best would be presented to Master for approval, but Kim the control freak would simply wait until the regionals had said their peace and then have all the pictures displayed before him so he could emphasize his role of supreme arbitrator in the Quan. It was his Quan and nobody was going to make marketing decisions except him.

Well past four o'clock the requisite ending bowing and thanking, and thanking and bowing was finally accomplished and students were sent out; being told to do whatever it is you do, as the early morning light of day shown its greetings on the junks racing home.

One sixth section came to near blows with those he was

transporting back to the rendezvous point where other junks had been left to avoid over crowding at Villa Park. Stubbornly refusing to answer why he was running stop signs and ignoring the advice of his fellow higher Moo, two first degrees in the car with him turned the ignition off and grabbed the wheel as the vehicle was moving, guiding it gently towards a nice large tree.

This was an assault on the sixth section's manhood, he was already stressed beyond what he could handle but having to answer to anyone right now was beyond his capabilities. Before he could do anything stupid, he was restrained by the three other first degrees in the back seat. After the talking-to received the next day, his first degree test was delayed by one year, putting him well behind others who had started with him.

Joe and another first dan lived with a second degree, who had been handling school full time for the past few months and was still back at the lesson. Nothing much further was going on, it was a status thing. Lower belts were consistently kept distanced from higher belts and this time the dividing line was main instructors and up.

Joe and Scott left the student driver sixth section to his own devices and jumped into their conveyance at the transfer point for the final leg home. After the Mopar had journeyed to the scrapper some months earlier, the newest rusty rocket had a 351 Windsor with a four barrel and a decent factory stereo. A complete oil change would never be performed on this vehicle during its remaining fifteen month service life in Moo. There was never time.

In efforts to make it home in time to shower, shave and still hit the 7-Eleven for breakfast on the way to work, the black sheep of the Starsky and Hutch genealogy proceeded with full afterburners on the last final sprint to the commune. Local law enforcement might have wanted the autographs of the pilots, but instead were left to find the 351-W cubes shut down in the middle of the overflowing apartment parking lot, the coupe left to fend for itself while the Moos scampered upstairs, safely inside. No flashing lights, no need to stop. But we do need to get to work. In an hour, after a shift change, the cops had other things to do. Joe and fellow Moo excused themselves to the officers while ordering a second cup of coffee at the nearby dashboard diner. Working two jobs, got bills to pay, the men in blue offered no quarrel.

ANOTHER CAMPOUT

For this campout in 1983, things started out as they had with past events. Long waiting and time spent re-checking in the parking lots of the schools, the caravans finally underway well after midnight when orders from Moo HQ gave permission to proceed. This was Kim's way of keeping control. In preference to traveling the world, teaching students and continuing his personal learning like was said, the real story was he hid out in the south suburbs, shopped and partied where he wouldn't be noticed and gave orders to his underlings until he felt they had stooped and groveled around enough, satisfying his whims.

Another all night drive finds us deep into Wisconsin, past the Dells. The advance team was led by another school this year and they had everything set up quite well. Roaring fire, food tent, coolers and sandwiches for the late arrivals were at the ready. All we had to do was unload and then…wait.

As an instructor you could not sleep until your handler decided he was going to sleep. Then you had to make sure if he needed anything or merely wanted you to get something. After you satisfied this errand, then maybe, you'd get to sleep. This came of course, from Kim. He routinely kept the higher belts up long into the night making them listen to his ramblings before he retired. Kim perpetually slept in but expected everybody else to be up early preparing breakfast, cleaning; busy handling.

One noted assistant regional head instructor was very keen on stooping and bowing and holding the respect line towards higher belts, therefore insisting any lower belts do the same before him. He'd cruise the camp ground, sandwich in hand then approach a table of lower belts and demand, where's the salt? Well, it's right here, in these little containers you hapless Moo. This is what Joe and the others thought, but dare not say lest they lose a stripe or receive a punch to the groin on the spot. It wasn't so much the physical hurt that was fearful; it was the stigma of being incorrect in the eyes of the cult.

For what it's worth, the disingenuous nature of this specific player was revealed when although in a different state as his higher handlers, he kept a small dirt bike off premises, stashed at a lower belt's garage so visiting nationals would not see it and be suspicious his mind was not full-on Moo. Besides, they didn't have a dirt bike or any hobbies, how was this underling going to get away with it?

The rest of this campout was uneventful, no movements or learning was passed; just more of the same old tired stories Joe and his group had heard many, many times before. Concentration was being put on the newbie instructor courses; who was sharp, who seemed like wanted to be around, who had cash and could do something (hand in money) towards the cult. The Farm would soon require full time attendance to make it the way Kim wanted it, so more cash had to be identified. The long term goal was to attract more professionals and those with better paying jobs into the cult. Factory workers and laborers were becoming passé. Their only future worth was if they could handle a school.

The journey back was faster every time than the ride there for the campouts. Joe and buds were cut loose early from the regrouping and stopped at a pay phone to call ahead and order pizzas. Junk cars, fast food, 7-Elevens, pay phones, and being kept busy handling does not a true warrior make, thought Joe as cheesy pies were wolfed down while sitting on the floor back at the sparsely furnished commune. He wondered how the guys he lived and trained with before they left the cult the prior year were doing.

Burp, "Pass the two-liter," Joe said to his cohort. They hadn't had this much fun since dodging the cops several weeks earlier. It was noted the Torino was parked again in the same spot as it was that night. They laughed and ate heartily, a small mental lapse from Moo reality.

Shortly thereafter Joe and three other black Moo belts scored moving into a large but older four bedroom bungalow centrally located between the schools and work. Seemed like an ideal place, large lot and rent was affordable especially when split four ways. A fifth was supposed to move in but never did, this blink in time of a house with fireplaces, two-car garage and multiple baths supplanted by the overwhelming need to Moo.

WEDDING SONG

Towards the end of summer, schools were closed again on Saturdays. Joe had asked permission, as mandated in Moo, a week in advance to attend a wedding of a high school friend. "The Moo did not want me to go," Joe confided, "I asked and re-asked without receiving any more than the 'ask again later' line we'd get when it was something they saw as a threat to our remaining loyal."

Finally, the day before the wedding, Joe's regional handler said it would alright but be sure and call in as soon as possible afterward, as there may be something to handle. The allusion was something important was up in the cult, which there wasn't; they just wanted to keep tight reins on their senior most subjects. Joe hadn't even RSVP'd as the personally tailored invite on the formal stationary asked. He considered what kind of friend he had been to the groom, a true comrade since junior year in high school. In the past, Jerry helped him out whenever he needed it, without question, Jerry had been there every time. Joe had not kept much in contact since his involvement in Moo deepened. It suddenly troubled him greatly he had no gift to bring, no nice clothes to show honor towards the celebration on his friend's special day. He was ashamed to step into the church, parking his rust rocket well down the street. Joe did not even own a sport coat to wear over his one shirt with all the buttons.

For a few short hours that beautiful day in his hometown, Joe stood across the street and watched the guests arrive, saw the tuxedos and long formal dresses, the families and well wishers who had gathered for Jerry's wedding enter the newly built church. He heard the traditional songs and the music play sweetly, experienced a rush of emotions from the crowd throwing rice as Jerry and bride emerged, graciously making their way to the limousine. They walked with dignity, like true higher class, Joe knew. As the limo moved away, he wished his friend the best from his heart hoping he wasn't seen as he shuffled back to the junk. He had not cried in years, not even when his father died. It felt good.

Joe sat in the parking lot of a convenience store a few miles away. He had not been back to this area in over five years. Slurping the last of the giant cup full of soda he bought with the change scooped from under the seat, he looked around at his past one more time, then made the call.

"Be alright to say," Joe started, "it's over."

"Over! What do you mean over? What do you mean calling up and saying it's over!" yelled Joe's handler into the phone.

"Be alright," Joe continued, keeping his voice steady and using proper Moo-speak, "the wedding is over, my friend is gone."

After a pause, realizing he had launched too soon on the subordinate, the regional Moo side-stepped with the unthinking, "Oh, okay then, come on over to school." The retrenching technique was evermore the same. Regain control of the malfunctioning unit by getting them back in the school environment, where they had power over you and where you had given them power every time you pledged it by bowing and setting your mind.

"Be alright, since school is closed today, I'd just like to get in some practice outside and then go on a date later on, if that's alright, unless there is something to handle," asked Joe. This was unacceptable, Joe was ordered to stop on by the regionals rented home, just to talk for a moment as it sounded like Joe had some questions. This was another ploy the cult used. But Joe wasn't falling for it, he was rung out. "Yes," he replied.

Joe spent the rest of the weekend the way he wanted. He had saved a few dollars on the side in case the car ever broke down and he was stranded, as happened before and none of the higher Moos he appealed to wanted to help get him. That night he hitched back home the twenty miles. He repaid the debt, but not for awhile. That seemed like long ago, for right now, he needed to take care of himself and reassess the current situation.

Joe never made it to the regional's to be checked that weekend. Instead he ate a decent meal at a roadhouse café and drove away to an old hangout to think and have a beer, something he had not done in over three years in Moo. Then he went on his date. He liked her but was keenly aware there could be no combined future for them so long as he was compelled to Moo. Considering the sum of the Moo cult's false promises and lies, why did he keep going?

He just wanted to practice, everything else had been stripped away he realized as he stepped back into school the following Monday like nothing had happened. He camped out a la mobile junk motel for the weekend. If the regional wanted to give him grief, he was going to have to do it within earshot of the entire school, and he would not risk that, Joe figured. If he tries to slap me around, I'll pull a knife off the wall and end both our problems.

He visualized how he would do it, the one real dagger on the wall, within easy reach. Joe had practiced hundreds of times grabbing it from the holder and moving with it when he was alone after the regional left the school at night. Now, Joe brought a shank tucked in his side waistband under his shirt as backup, and stepped in.

As the door chimes sounded and Joe stood there bowing towards the office, the regional was faced with one less question to answer to higher belts. Joe had not quit, he just needed some time off, which he took. The cult pushes people to their limit, backs off then pushes on. They say it's like forging steel. But it's really just to string you along for as long as they can. The lower belt, who had stood side by side the regional when he was attacked by the Tae Kwon Do guys, was cashing in a chip.

"Get loosened up," Joe was told, "time to start group."

PART VI

LIVING ON A PRAYER

"Minds are like parachutes, they only function when they are open"

—Thomas Dewar

PART VI—LIVING ON A PRAYER

I'LL TAKE SECOND DEGREE FOR $2500, PLUS OR MINUS

Another month goes by and Joe is told along with others of similar rank, they will test for second degree very soon. They are encouraged to practice as much as possible as the schools are still closed on Saturdays for another couple weeks and to bring in test fees, which will be mentioned to each one privately. It will depend on how far along you are on your course, you may have to keep bringing in for awhile, it's up to you they are told. Joe was alone in the practice room one night after group; the regional was on the phone comparing notes with another regional.

"I'm gonna make this one (referring to Joe) bring in twenty-five. Uh huh, uh huh, that sounds about right for that one," (referring to the student at the other regional's school). He hung up.

"Step up front," he yelled out to Joe.

Joe was informed what his test fee would be. He had no money, nothing to sell, nothing else he could give. He was completely tapped. "Be alright to work a second job for awhile, to earn and bring that in?" asked Joe.

This is not exactly what the higher handler wanted to hear. Why? Because then Joe, like any other overused bio-component, with a little extra cash after not having any for so long would probably make the mental leap that he didn't need the cult anymore. With money in their pockets most folks, even gullible ones like Joe, can quickly develop their own support mechanisms.

The regional, deciding how he was going to handle this dilemma said, "I'll ask Master which way, in the meantime, just practice and do what you can, understand?"

"Yes, thank you," replied Joe. At last, all he had to worry about was practicing. This was his sole focus for two weeks. Got in at least two hours every night and three hours on Saturdays, drilling hard; with at least an hour Moogwa on Sunday, and then just relax watching sports on the monochrome plasti-box. They ate as much beef and protein as could afford and beat on each other hard during sparring practice. Joe and crew wanted the second stripe badly.

The test occurred on the last Saturday before Labor Day. Six would test at once before all three regional instructors; two fifth degrees and one fourth degree, ostensibly the upper crust of all martial artists in the U.S. They would make recommendations to Master. Kim would set the line and establish the rank order amongst the new second stripers. Probation would range from none to three months. The regimen lasted just under two hours and was less strenuous than Joe imagined it would be. The pace of the testing seemed to indicate the senior ranks were checking more for exactness in forms or more importantly, in exactitude of scripted behavior.

Joe finished second in this class, this time he felt he earned. He had the expected bumps and bruises the next day with more than a few sore muscles. What they all felt was a strange nirvana, again going out to eat as a group, celebratory beef melt sandwiches for all, pass the iced tea. This group would stay cohesive for eons in Moo-time. Even though some would transfer to other states; the bonds formed this day would outlast the ensuring years of campouts, new school openings, banquets, special late night lessons, uniform screenings and even federal investigations.

Joe's distant grandmother passed away soon thereafter. She left him twenty-five hundred dollars as inheritance. Joe considered what he should do, trying to establish his basis point for the next few years. Maybe he thought, things will finally be getting better, at second degree we've passed all the mental nonsense used to weed out those not worthy of the higher level learning. We're all royal brethren now he convinced himself. He announced his trust fund to the cult. They were pleased and set up a transfer time as soon as the check from the lawyers had cleared. This was problematic as Joe like many Moos, had no checking account at twenty-eight years of age. Within a week the cash was in hand and he was to report to the parking lot of the Naperville school to meet a regional who had come out from the Farm.

"Don't bow outside school, how many times do I have to tell you," scolded the regional towards Joe, "it looks funny, now step inside."

The Jeep the regional was using had been transferred the year before from a student at Joe's school. The student got to keep the loan payment, the Quan got to keep the Jeep.

"Hand it over," said the regional. Joe glanced over his shoulder as he reached under his shirt where the envelope was tucked into his waist. $2,500 was the most cash he had ever held that was his, anyway. He had seen students handing over ten times more for a single payment. Now it was his turn to be stupid.

"Don't look around, don't count it, you make it look like it's a drug deal going down," the regional scolded again. "How much is here?" he demanded, staring at Joe intensely.

"Be alright, twenty-five hundred."

"Twenty-five?" asked the future felon once more.

"Yes," said Joe.

The regional returned to the Farm to bring the booty before the Kim. Joe returned to his semi-luxurious abode to make plans for another date. It was nice to have at least a simulated life of enjoyment. The phone did not ring the entire weekend which was odd, everyone at the house thought; until they discovered late on Sunday the plug had been pulled from the wall during a late night front room Moogwa. They slept fitfully, wondering who would be screamed at the most on Monday. After work, Joe entered the retail plaza dojo with apprehension.

"Step in here!" said Joe's regional to him as he entered the doorway. "How much did you say you brought in for your test? I should have counted it myself before letting you hand it in to higher belts, just in case there was a mistake," he said.

Joe re-asserted he was sure there were twenty-five one hundred-dollar bills, the top one beginning with a serial numeral seven. In fact he made sure to ask the teller saying he was a collector just like the Moos told him to, so the bank would give him as many requested numbered bills as possible.

"Well a hundred was missing, but Master let it slide; he knows your heart is in the right place, you've proven it many times." Joe was upset, he knew absolutely there were twenty-five C-notes in that envelope. The fault was not with Joe. It was with the regional in the Jeep; who would be caught at the same trick in subsequent years, but with much greater amounts of cash. He was paid back in full for his disloyalty upon moving his household in Texas to the new HQ in California. He had sumptuous high value furnishings received as wedding presents from his in-laws. Packed up and ready to go, Kim told him to go live with a group of fellow regionals, to share their house until the California house was set up. He never got use of his furniture again. Kim gave most of it to his kids or other instructors. "All comes from same place," Kim would say.

THE YELLOW PORSCHE

Joe and the others were charged from time to time with handling certain assets of the organization. One such item was a disassembled Porsche in the basement of the house he and a few other almost semi-pro hockey players rented. As a stunt to impress girls, they scattered around sticks, skates and old college jerseys for effect. When the phone would ring from the Moo in the next room they'd act like it was coach Esposito on the line and they were late for practice. Any lower belts in the vicinity were told their name was now Kenny Yaremchuck or Clark Kent-chuck and to play along. The car was as a matter of fact, a real racing Porsche and they were getting it ready for the next Olympics in Fresno, but the engine wasn't rebuilt yet. That was it there, in the garage. See, there are some of the parts, the rest are over here... This worked wonders in seduction we are told.

The real deal was the car was a down payment and one certain regional instructor who liked to have sex while being watched from the closet thought he'd tool around town for a few weeks with it and then tell Maaaster it was for course. Problem was, from the late night high speed use since other higher minds also driving the 911-T considered it was merely on loan, the negligibly cracked but repairable frame worsened so much the car turned to junk. Naturally the student was told we will only credit you $3,000 and not $8,000 as originally agreed, you had to have known the vehicle had a more serious defect.

Concurrently existing in a parallel wealth-draining universe, a team of Moo morons were hard at work taking the thing apart in a one-car garage underneath their neighbor's townhouse at 02:00 every night, after they had finished Moogwa and handling any broken mirrors that came up. The tool kit was a Phillips screw driver, a broken ball peen hammer and a discount store bargain bin all-purpose kitchen utensil. For jack stands fifth sections were used. They became tired after awhile but they were told to shut up or we'd connect the stray wires touching their zippers. We didn't think the battery was hooked up, but the car, if you could call it that when we got done with it, stayed put.

Then surprisingly we had to move, something about too much noise in violation of the lease. So if you're a Moo and you have to move what do you use? Rent a truck? No come on, always thinking of yourself and the extra $50 that could go towards school. You use your MUV.

What about furniture and mattresses? Hey you're a Moo, just strap it on the top. And drag that Porsche body with you. The stupid engine weighed six hundred pounds. One larger assistant who liked to fall asleep at off times was cajoled and tickled unmercifully into plopping it into the back of a borrowed Toyota truck. We explained if the engine wasn't moved that higher belts would ask him why he didn't pick it up like we told him to, and besides we'd make him eat spaghetti, which we knew he hated. It's fun being a big brother sometimes.

Twenty-four hours continuously non-stop since it was Friday and we had to work and then Moo again; we dragged the Porsche body on a dolly, through side streets the fifteen or so miles to the new abode. The new neighbors just like all the previous neighbors since the Earth began to Moo-cool were stunned by our arrival. The Porsche was further dissected, the interior placed in the nice warm basement for safekeeping and display to hot chicks who thought we could skate.

A week later the power went out in a massive storm which was a good thing, the phones went out as well, but of course the basement flooded and we had to deal with blow drying the interior parts before the lower minded outside-ways one came and bought his project car. He wanted everything except the engine and trany. He paid $2,000 for a pile of junk.

Then we got a call early the next Saturday morning, "Is that Porsche three point whatever motor in the paper still for sale?"

"Ah yes, why yes it is," Joe answered sleepily.

"You want thirteen hundred, will you take a thousand?"

"Show us the Benjamins; we'll help you load it up."

"We've got a hoist," replied the buyer.

"You won't need it; we've got just the guy to do it sleeping on the floor in the other room."

For awhile we thought he might have been scared off, but he showed in half an hour. We did the deal and life was ours again, until we had to answer to the fatter belt. You sold it for how much? What is wrong with your mind, you coulda got twelve hundred!

Yeah probably, but right then Joe and the others no longer cared, it had nothing to do with us and everything to do with Moo. Besides, in another few weeks, the Farm was gonna need trees. We just didn't know it yet.

ELVIS NEEDS BOATS AND THE FARM NEEDS TREES

Deferring to Mojo Nixon; although these events happened better than a half-decade prior to his explanation of why all those boats disappear in the Bermuda Triangle, it's because Elvis needs boats, Elvis needs boats... for us it was because the Farm needed trees. It was mentioned often about higher belts trying very hard again that summer so although we could not be around, there could be other ways to contribute.

The year before (1982) the major work began at the Farm; the moving of large trees, groundbreaking on what would become the Green House and basic upgrades to the existing barn which would convert into barracks or home for some. The apple trees were started this year to mask activities of the cult. A newly ordained regional instructor came up with this idea and so as not to be outdone in seeing the favor Kim bestowed upon him, other higher-ups stressed the need for more landscape. The word went out amongst the Moo. The Farm needs trees.

We mentioned the property we rented had a couple of flowering crabs and maybe the owner would be willing to part with them, they had overgrown their plots and were too close to the house. Sounds believable. We were thinking cash sale or barter, but instead we were told to start digging. These things were over ten feet high and their branches spread about fifteen feet in diameter. In the real world, you'd be talking hydraulic tree spade on the back of a tandem axle diesel; but no, instructors know how to handle. Besides, early on at the Farm higher belts moved much bigger trees and many of them we were told. We shouldn't be looking for the easy way every time. The more difficult the better, the more we'd earn.

There was no further thought on our parts although we should have realized this was theft by conversion. But since the landlord lived out of state, plus it was for a higher and greater good, we dug. And dug and dug and dug. We didn't have to handle by school as instructors since we had certain other part to handle, thus we dug. The ground was hard from lack of rain. On the second day a regional came by to check our progress. The tree would do well, but we needed to dig harder he encouraged. After watching us dig for about an hour he returned to the Farm to report it would be a few more days before this flowering beauty would arrive at Graceville. The trench went around in a circle not much larger than the giant shrub's canopy in a path two to three foot wide, until on the second night we hit clay. About three feet down and then things got tuff.

See, we'd work all day, report in, and then start digging. By this time, if you bent your back over, you would be level with the ground except you were in a trench and visitors or folks next door would no longer see you but they would see the mounds of dirt circling the plant. One guy inquired, we indicated it was something with the septic tank and he went away.

It was in the early fall, the weather stayed good and finally after five days of digging until the stars were out we reached the bottom of the root ball. We learned a lot about horticulture during this mission. If the main root is cut too close to the tree, it will die. The goal is to secure as much of the root ball as possible with the earth intact and then carry it to its new destination. How we would accomplish that next phase, transporting the multi-ton load, was not our concern nor was it our care, our job was to dig.

Getting under the root ball several feet down was tricky. The trench wasn't quite deep enough or wide enough to dig under it with long handled spades. We used hand tools, machetes and anything else to try to tunnel horizontal. Word from on high revealed knowledge kept in the closet for centuries that a rope with nails twisted into it will work as a saw and will only take a few hours; that's how they accomplished the miraculous movements of trees at the Farm.

We tried this but with little luck. The crab tree, probably as old as any of us, seemed to just laugh at our attempts to wrest him from his site. It would groan and nudge but never really move. It was a big tough sucker. So we improvised and enlisted our friendly 350 Caprice MUV.

It's late at night, in a suburban upscale setting and your neighborhood morons are driving a car around their house. They've got all their outside floodlights on and there's about five of them making lots of noise with tools at midnight. There's another car or two providing more sight and sound. Why? To tie a chain around the base of the root ball of the giant crab tree they simply must remove in order to maintain favor with those who believe the Second Coming will strike them down should they fail. As unbelievable as it was, no one complained. The neighbors must have bought the septic tank story.

The chain was strung from one side of the car's axle to the other and in between stuck under the undermost level of roots. The Chevy did not have enough traction to be effective and once again the big crab remained in place. Three of us jumped on the trunk for more weight but still no go. I remember the final play had us in the trench literally backs against the wall, pushing with everything we had, our legs, our guts until something was about to burst. With the tires spinning burning rubber and howling on the grass and dirt underneath, digging their own trench and still the damn thing would not budge after a dozen attempts. The air smelled like Sante Fe Speedway. We considered using an additional Chevy but instead in a flash of shear brilliance, concluded the shrub was not going to move, at least not by us.

The next day Joe used carefully chosen words and reported our assessment of the situation. He embellished that the roots were wrapped around something, perhaps the house main septic pipe and that it would be impossible therefore to move. Incredulously we were told to consider tearing out the pipe! He offered that in total, this was beyond our capabilities and so much energy had been expended on the project, we should try a different target. The woods near that house were full of candidates. We should have suggested we could raise some cash and go to a wholesale nursery, but felt that would have been pushing our luck. We were already exhausted and broke, we didn't need more grief.

Within the next week a posse was assembled and we went into the nearby woods at night to dig up a suitable replacement. There were five of us, we found a tree, dug it up and slid it back the few hundred yards in a few hours. Just in time to get some sleep and go to work, to get money to do what now? To make higher Moo belt. All the dirt fell off the root ball during the dragging process on the way back. What was left was just enough to satisfy our handlers but doom the plant. We watered it down any way and covered the roots in burlap.

The next day a regional came by in late afternoon to inspect our work. Mission one, the crab in the backyard, was authorized for abandonment and we then loaded the newly acquired specimen, a ten foot Pin Oak, diagonally into the back of the Jeep pickup. The tree had a nice canopy which hung over the cab while the roots were stuffed in the back. It deserved a ticket from the sheriff for being on the road but it was said it would be alright and he drove away, ridiculous as it was. He was not stopped during the twenty-odd miles to south Naperville and we held this as evidence that if handling certain thing and "your mind was in right place" that nothing bad could happen. We heard he was embarrassed to bring such a thing to the Farm; that Kim laughed at him and the tree was planted but it died in a short time, much to everyone's delight. This particular regional was not liked by most Moos.

The excavation was filled back up over the next few days leaving the back half of our utopian estate a mess. Four bedrooms, two fireplaces, two plus car garage with driveway for six more on an acre plot and a new cesspool in back. That winter's snowfall was substantial and covered up the earth moving, but the crab tree was done. It lost its leaves for the last time that year.

We broke the lease in Joe's name and moved out in late winter. Months go by and we learn one of our trusted buddies had neglected his obligation to handle Northern Illinois Gas to the tune of nine hundred dollars for six months service. We will never forget that you weasel, but mostly because you did not help us dig! You screwed off all the time. Yet, there was still more adventure ahead of us that year.

After a few weeks, we were selected to be members of an elite team on a multi-state mission to yep, secure more trees! Our worth as diggers was proven at least and Joe had experience driving a truck. Thus we were given another chance. We got to stay over at a regional's abode in preparation which was uncomfortable as it was unknown exactly what was in store for us. Sleep was fitful, food sparse.

We assembled at the Elk Grove school of Moo Doe cash collection facility, early the next morning before it opened on a Saturday in November and were briefed on details. We enjoyed a half donut each and relished in the cold on near-empty stomachs, fearing what awaited us.

A fourth section wanna-be had family property near Janesville Wisconsin with lots of trees of all different varieties so he claimed. A twenty foot U-Haul rental was on standby a few miles away, along with the two related regionals, their wives and two head instructors from the Farm. One of the latter would turn state's evidence; the other would gain a brain tumor by standing and delivering for Kim, defending yet another Farm in another state, the Ranch in Tomball, Texas.

Joe and a head instructor went and got the truck, the higher belt paid but Joe had to sign for the unit with his license. They returned shortly to join up with the rest. We loaded up some hand tools, some burlap sacks, the precious nails and rope to hold our quarry together, a few shovels and took off.

There were no other provisions. The head instructors rode in a separate car for the expedition, as did the regionals. Joe teamed up with the engine lifting assistant. The governed U-Haul junk made fifty miles per hour tops and took awhile getting there. Joe flashed the lights when the fat regional speed away but all he could do was try to keep up after the last toll. They had no money and the lead car was paying. Lost past Rockford about two hours out, not knowing where to go but hopeful someone in the entourage would spot them and lead them on. Other cars were said to be following for such an event.

About thirty minutes further the warning strips built into the pavement shoulder alerted them they had fallen asleep as the Interstate turns north approaching Beloit just before the Wisconsin state line. Joe said it was his fault and admitted it afterward. After realizing the trouble, hurtling off the road in a junk truck up an embankment, his first reaction after firmly grabbing the wheel was to back-knuckle his associate in the chest but hit his stomach instead. Joe apologized but was never forgiven. He did not mean to hurt his friend and I don't think I did, Joe said. "But it's not a very nice way to wake up. My intent was for us to be conscious during the next few seconds at least and this seemed a prudent method."

Joe related: Don yelled loudly but then ever more so as he looked forward. By then we were in the grass going up hill, slowing down to about twenty-five miles per hour or so when the surprisingly soft ground gave way under the left side and we flopped over with a notable crunching sound and slid for a bit. We didn't even make it half way up the hill, which was about the same height as the approaching overpass. We were in trouble for sure now, as tree recovery seemed in doubt, but we were still alive and so far, unhurt, except for my co-rider's indigestion.

My friend weighed a good two-fifty on a light day and was plopped on top of me professing his sorrow for this. He was panicky after I asked if it was possible for him to reach up and open the door on his side before the gas tank on my side blows up as it was leaking. His reply was that being sideways prevented his understanding of the functional operation of a door handle. Momentarily I wondered why I bothered to awaken him. I was able to reach up, grab the handle; both of us pushed open the door and we extricated ourselves. He was ticklish in a manly way so I made advantage of this. Then we scrambled up on top of the hill, whereby we gathered our thoughts and awaited our fate; looking down at the wreck while enjoying the view from the hill and the bright November weather.

Joe continued, "Even at this point my large friend wanted to argue. He wanted to tell the truth and admit we snoozed it. While I, being deceitfully practical, wanted to tell the cops when they came we got run off the road. No one was hurt, we didn't get a description, you know. It would go away. We would confess to higher belts our sins. "

After a few minutes state patrol sauntered by. The trooper's first comment, did you fall asleep, was rebuffed and they stuck to the story, both of them. The cop said often times people can ride it to the top, but in a truck it's difficult. Joe was cited for inattentive driving, but at the court date the officer didn't show so Joe got to take a road trip back near that area and some freedom for a day. It's a nice ride for normal people.

A tow truck was called to the scene and wanting to be reasonably useful, Joe grabbed a flare and with the trooper's blessing proceeded to take up position before the crest of the roadway's hill to warn approaching traffic. Like the second or third car coming along was the other regional and his wife. They had this really surprised look on their face as they passed by and saw the vehicle that would secure their future lying on its side, crumpled. Joe sensed their realization that their coup-du-foliage had been undone once again.

After the cop was finished and the totaled U-Haul was dragged off, they got a sandwich and a talking to. They went up the road and saw the first regional and his group pulled over at a wayside. His first reaction was where's the truck? Then he got pissed, really mad. But as Joe did not report to him he could not do anything lest he receive a correction from Forrest or worse from Kim, now scheduled to be in town. The shrubbery would have been a powerful offering.

Back on the road with tree search incorporated, the regionals made the call to the Farm and explained what happened. They spoke with Kim, who was not pleased. The mission was cancelled and we were about to head home. The hot tempered regional was convinced that a place he'd never been to had trees he'd never seen and now he would not get to fulfill his destiny. The student's parents who owned the land were never made aware of the plan. The regionals started to point to Joe, that he had failed everyone there.

He asked where were we supposed to sleep anyway, how would we dig up these trees as big as they were said to be and how would we then lift them into the truck? Couldn't we contribute cash and after a few weeks rent a real truck and approach a wholesale nursery for evergreens, or whatever we wanted?

Answers: You could have slept in the truck, that's why there's a shovel, and we can all lift. As far as a nursery, is that all you can think? What is wrong with your mind? This is the Farm, you understand? Go think about what you just said.

Within a few hours we returned to origin with the regionals still upset. Didn't evoke the good bye custom, no bowing just dropped us off by our cars and left. Joe was happy. Not gonna get a call tonight, nope. It's a Saturday and we don't have to report in. Went home and cooked what ever we had, lots of soup and cheese sandwiches. Man that was good! We had not eaten anything substantial in a day and went to sleep soon thereafter. No one else was home. Joe and I hoped they were all someplace getting a lecture. When the shit hit the fan, everyone else would disappear. They'd go stay somewhere else for a couple days until the regionals chilled out, the landlord went away or the electricity got turned back on. Anyway, stupid phone rings, it's after midnight and like idiots we answer. It's the regionals and there's one more thing to handle.

Have to write a letter, per the terms of the rental agreement, explaining the accident, and that we are reporting this so as not to incur additional rental fees or legal action. Higher belts didn't want to attract any attention to the goings-on at the Farm. Joe wrote the letter and as dawn was approaching left it in the mail slot at the truck rental. In about an hour he returned home and telephoned the handlers where we stayed the previous night. They wanted us to come over for coffee, to check our mind, but Joe said we had to go to work. Over the weeks ahead, he and the other worker belts mixed up in the fiasco would be heavily criticized for not being clear.

Joe seriously considered leaving the collective at this juncture but the handlers changed their attitude, briefly. It was just enough of a positive tweak to keep him in. Probably it was because Kim wasn't giving them as much shit as he habitually did; it was trickle down Moo-enomics. Looking back, Joe said he would have been much better off today in career, family; the total package. Instead over the next few years he earned listening to more crap from assholes and some half-baked secret form most any good Kung Fu school teaches correctly if one doesn't have their head up their asses like we did. Oh yeah, and what to do when break a mirror.

Turns out, this was an unauthorized adventure. The regionals had thought it up as something that would please Kim and had only lightly mentioned it to Forrest without fully disclosing the out-of-state details. After a few more days of being ignored in school, we were told, "After all that, all Master said was, 'where is your mind,' we did not get in trouble or anything, it was let go." This is good news we thought, that means no more lectures for awhile. Within days of this interstate escapade the desired shrubbery was paid for in nominal terms; those living at the Farm full time arranged for plants to be delivered.

Outcomes: The so-called higher belts, one for certain, really did not care what happened to any of us. Their over-riding goal was for them to look good in the eyes of Kim. If we could be part of that, well it was good for us too, see?

It took Joe years to realize we put trust in the wrong sort of people. At the time we did not see anything in its context we were so far gone, we were idiots, truly. It was a concentration camp situation where we kept trying to make it no matter what. Every once and awhile the guards would be nice to you and you'd think things will work out. Life will get better, this is just temporary, the ideal is possible if only we could figure it out, we just keep screwing up. Once make fourth degree we were told many times, you are handed a house. You'll have such a great life… Joe wondered if it would ever happen.

The remainder of the year was marked by another change in jobs for Joe and something really important to him and the others who had tested for second degree not that long ago. They received authentic thick black belts just like the regional head instructors wore around their growing waists.

These were brand new wondrous items, each with their names thickly stitched in fancy gold letters. There was a Korean label of origin on the belt and gold oriental symbols just like on the flag in the office. No doubt now there were schools in Asia, here was the proof! Additionally they received new uniforms with the full black instructor-level emblem on the back. They would have to sew on the black trim and stripes on their own. But they have ten days to get it done. Schools are closed for the holidays, merry Christmas. Just make sure to call in every couple days.

MOO LIGHT, MOO BRIGHT, BURNING IN THE NIGHT

One of Joe's roommates, Scott, with whom he had tested fourth section through second degree, would soon be on the outs. Before he left the cult for an extend tour of Atlantic City, Scott explained a mental lesson given by a regional shortly after the tree recovery failures.

During a huge electrical storm which knocked down trees and deluged the neighborhood, Joe and Scott sat in the dark on the large hurculon covered sofa a fellow Moo had contributed to the house. Staring out to the street and watching the lightning flash and blast around them, Scott related his special lesson. He had temporarily lost his school crest pin, the solid gold tiger with the symbols along the base personally handed out by the Kim.

"Think about Master's pin (everything was designated 'Master's' in Moo), focus your mind on it, it was said," Scott began. "Forget about where you left it, where you went or what you did; think about where it is now. Keep that focus on it, close your eyes if have to, but keep your concentration building on Master's pin. Picture it in your mind until it is burning white hot…" Scott relayed this is how the regional had guided him though the mental lesson, the same regional who had guided them both through ceiling tile replacement, landlord management and oversized dead tree transport.

"So, I did it. I mentioned I lost my pin, and he explained how to get it back. We were in the office and after five minutes I could not get it out of my mind. All the way home I thought about it, and all that night when I went to sleep, all I could think about was Master's gold pin." This from a guy who went through chicks like Joe did clean shirts. "It kept getting brighter and hotter until it was, literally, burning in my mind, Instructor Joe." Even at home or away from school, if you met on the street you referred to another Moo by their title, rank applied for household chores or meeting girls, too.

Scott paused for a moment as Joe considered what he just heard. Finally Joe offered, "Ya know, I believe regional head instructors did mention about certain mental parts were starting to be passed, I had no idea you got to try it, cool. So what happened?"

Ka-boom! Another giant bolt of lightning lands very close to the completely darkened house. "Well," Scott began, "I go to sleep with this image absolutely glowing in my mind and when I wake up. I know where it is. It's in the car. The very first thing I check behind the seat and as I pull back the front one, you know like putting something in the back, there it is, Master's pin is right there, just like I saw it, between the seats."

"Between the seats?" Joe asked rhetorically, "did you get in last night, in my car?"

They exploded with laughter, rocking the house competing with the echoing thunder. Just then the power comes back on, the ravaged Kmart stereo blaring out a Blue Oyster Cult song, something about someone's daughter in the middle of a dirt road. They decide to grab a pizza storm or no storm. They laughed all the way to the pizza place and back. One of the few times they could just be themselves and not straining to be correct.

SPRINGTIME IN MOO

As winter dragged on Joe and his housemates wore out their welcome with the absentee landlord. Rent was chronically late, the utility companies were complaining they had not seen payment in months, and the neighbors reported something wrong with one of the large flowering shrubs in the backyard. It was time to split.

They moved into another rented house, and two other black belts joined in. This lasted for about three months until Joe and two other second degrees obtained a more suitable abode, an apartment strategically located geographically between the schools in the area. Joe and the new pod were being groomed as the next generation of Moo-structors to handle schools full time. No more working a day job, they would mainline Moo.

The new complex was known as St. James and would soon become legacy in the archives of Moo history. By year end seven instructors would reside there in the three bedroom apartment, regularly sleeping in heaps on the radiantly heated floor rather than their own beds. They were evolving into den animals needing only a warm meal and anther Moo to be comfortable for the night.

There was a measure of comfort here for Joe and fellow Moos for a brief time. Higher belts had a lot going on with the Farm and the newly formed businesses to take the place of the schools as cash generators for the organization. Joe's new roommates had real furniture and a quality stereo and were treated a little differently since they had better outside positions, as the Moos would say. Compared to before, this rubbed off on Joe too. Now as second degrees they were allowed moderate freedoms, they did not have to report in as much, sometimes not at all on the weekends and things generally seemed livable, finally. It was if they had earned after all. Paradise lasted five weeks.

CAMPOUT DEVELOPMENT

Fourth of July in 1984 was a milestone in Moo cultural development. What used to be a cult tool to keep the flock faithful began to transform into a friend and family gathering where forms and teaching would be part of the planned activities. Previous attendance limits of fourth sections and up was expanded to more courses levels, not just instructor course and teenagers, if parents were along, could attend. If you had a girlfriend and she was correct enough, translated as approved by higher belts she would not somehow convince you to quit or want to spend too much time in the sack, well then she could come along too, but she better be prepared to cook and clean. This was the same with the growing late summer picnic and the future holiday banquets, one in the spring to coincide with Kim's birthday and the other near Christmas; both designed to supplant any consideration for outside activities or beliefs.

The campouts themselves would transform into what has more recently become tagged as the Weeklong Seminars. As a replacement for students contributing all their energies and money simply to camp out alongside their mentors, instruction fees would be charged and the focus would be on advanced learning in a retreat setting. If want to go can go, if not, no big deal, unlike having to go without much choice. In fact, back in the time of this episode, you had to have a really good excuse not to go.

The retreat aspect was still several years off and the creator of the less cult-like atmosphere much too low a belt and not yet in charge to where he could administer a better direction for his area of responsibility. He was a lot like Joe, taking up martial arts to strengthen himself and to learn self-defense; after this campout they became close friends besides being roommates, until David assumed new roles in the eastern region of the organization. Several close relationships would be formed between Joe and nuveau Moo-buds during the next solar cycle.

Joe and David had both been given immunity from caravan duties this year since the holiday fell mid-week and neither could get off from work, they claimed. So they were to drive up the following day. During the six hour drive through Michiana made in less than four by Joe and David in the 351 powered rust bucket, the Torino hit two huge potholes in a row while dodging rocks thrown out from truck tires on the Interstate. Luckily the heretofore uninspected spare tire was usable, the only problem being the trunk was so rusted; the jack and other artifacts had wiggled their way loose and were jettisoned at some point. The CB salvaged from the old Mopar came in use once again; a passing trucker provided a four-way lug wrench.

"Let's get new tires," said David.

"Don't have the cash," Joe replied.

"Don't worry about it," David reassured as they pulled into a Kmart, "I'll charge it."

Joe was amazed. They arrived just before dinner.

The main event during this campout was the night time beach picnic and Tong Nong lesson which took place on day three between the shores of Silver Lake and Lake Michigan just inside the boundaries of the state park there. The wily east coast regional, previously of the Addison school; had brought back a contingent of students and researched a really cool place for this happening.

The day before he had challenged all the students with relay races of intelligent design. The route was hopping up the sand dune on one leg, we were permitted to switch legs, then running back down before swimming out and around the regional standing on his toes about thirty feet from shore; then back to shore to hand off the stick to your team mates. Everyone really liked this one except the local regionals who hadn't thought of it.

And now the finale; how to sneak into a state park without breaking any laws. Simple, make friends with the rangers. The eastern regionals were observing these two attractive women in uniform at the nearby sandwich shop a short distance from the park entrance. A little dialogue and the plan was hatched. The Moo brigade would park at the shopping center down the block, then hike into the park just before closing and wait in the gully two sand dunes away from the beach and out of sight of anyone on the road.

When the rangers would come by, right before dark on their rounds at about nine p.m. like they told they regionals they would, so long as they don't see anything when they shine their searchlights and we clean up afterward; why our soccer team (a common term Moos used for subterfuge) can have their barbeque and make all the noise they want. But don't stay all night, that is prohibited.

Our clan followed these instructions perfectly. At approximately 19:30 hours the barbeques, blankets and gear were packed up, enough for a beach party of fifty. We had no idea where we were going or why, we were simply ordered to begin muster and so we did. The provisional caravan parks in the Walmart lot a half mile away, we load up and soldier into the park along a little used trail. Another half-hour goes by and we are in the gully, sitting like hungry pigeons on the ridge, watching the Sun fade and feeling our hunger grow. We know there's food but we can't get to it.

Several second degrees had gravitated towards David and Joe sitting on the ridge. This was noticed by the regionals to leverage the cult's potential. David would be sent east, Joe would remain in Chicago. Joe and buds shared candy bars they had stashed inconspicuously as soon as it was dark enough they would not be spotted.

"We are waiting," began the regional in charge, addressing the brigade, "for the rangers to pass by and shine their lights. When they do, nobody makes any noise, and nobody moves or else..." he laughed a little as he said that, taking the edge away. Everyone chuckled appropriately in response, then hushed.

The ranger truck crunched along the gravel road above and behind us, stopped a couple times and shined the lights. The last time it blinked once then remained out. The truck drove away, that was our signal, and the beach was ours.

The word went out amongst the Moos, "Get some wood." A dozen moved at once, and a huge pile was assembled in short order. Before long a pile as high as we could stack it, over our heads, was burning a ten foot square section into the sand. The regionals laughed and ordered us to bring it down some, "We need to cook on that," they said.

Instead a second smaller fire for cooking was organized as the idea of frantic Moos waving burning sticks in a lemming-like crowd was determined to be unwise. It was time for lesson. We lined up in five long rows facing east with the water to our backs and began Tong Nong. It was difficult to do in the sand. After each step, balance had to be regained as body weight shifted. Moving from one position to the next was much more strenuous as well since the sand absorbed your attempt to propel from it, unlike solid ground or the nicely carpeted practice rooms which serve as a spring board.

We each stumbled and fell at least once, plopping headlong into the grainy sand; got to our feet and hurried back to catch up with the cadence. Head instructors were in the lesson as well so one had to be careful where he leapt and landed. After an hour we were ordered to deep breathe. Big groups from multiple schools did allow the higher belts to see how much form was out there, how far certain ranks had in general and to assess whether or not it was being taught uniformly. Not that Kim ever cared about that, he merely convinced his lieutenants that he was by letting them run things on their own every once and awhile.

After a thunderous Chung Moo echoed from the sand dunes, we feasted on Rock Cornish chicken, potatoes and veggies wrapped in foil and cooked to perfection. The meat fell from the bones into our mouths. We lounged around on the sand and told jokes about each other's rusty cars, the ones we drive.

THE SUK CHUNG FIRST TIME EXPERIENCE

The first time Suk Chung was taught was at the Farm. We had heard about the movement, that it was the next step up. The progression was paper over wood, Che Chung, to hands of steel and wire, Chull Sa Chung; which used the legendary herbs to protect the hands and aid circulation while hitting the magic bean bags. The next level was Suk Chung, but it had not been anymore explained other than an occasional mention. Another higher form, Sa Chung, was said to be similar but in place of using a water surface, literally required pounding sand. Lower belt Kong Su methods were practiced with sand in buckets, toughening up the fists and knuckles.

Suk Chung was described early on as hitting the water in a precise manner similar in appearance to Chull Sa, yet technically very different to effect the next phase of development. To hype things up in Moo, it was emphasized that if one saw the movement and tried to copy it; severe, irreversible body damage would result. Perhaps not right away but over time it would and without the knowledge of Chung Moo Quan to guide us, all would be lost for the walking dead.

That summer day at the Farm with just a few hours notice, we arrived in small herds from isolated Naperville insertion points where vehicles could be left in town without attracting attention. We were shepherded towards the rear of the property to find Kim, Forrest, Tom and several other apparently higher belts leading a lesson, facing a group of instructors independently thrashing about in the pond. The group was facing east, with Kim supervising from the beach facing west.

We were immediately directed into the water, now realizing why cut-offs and shorts were the order of battle. Tom and other regionals paddled about and explained the form. Cup the hand, strike the water with an open palm and quickly pull back like Che Chung. The shoulder, arm and hand were all to be relaxed. When done correctly a high-pitched liquid "pop" sound results. The mouth was to be kept closed to prevent nervous system damage. The regionals moved around and we kept slapping the water. It was difficult in the crowded area to time the waves so a good strike and thus a good sound resulted. But we persisted and finally as a group, we were told we had the right idea.

After about forty-five minutes the lesson ended, the bowing and muted shouting occurred then Kim sent the regionals around to touch points and relieve any built up circulation restrictions that could impair our ability to (choose one) reason effectively, function normally, urinate freely in the pond, notice nervous system damage, any or all of the these. It was further explained that Suk Chung could be practiced for a few months time and then the pressure-relieving points could be adjusted, but it must be done properly and if any questions ask your higher Moo.

Points were touched on the top of the upper shoulders near the collar bone, midpoint on the main upper arm, and forearm meridian. Then points along the length of each arm were massaged in assembly line fashion by the regionals. Each point in that order was rubbed to stimulate circulation and the final top of shoulder implant with full-length arm rub ensured the nervous system and circulation were functioning properly. Hands quickly warmed up and tingled as circulation returned. Several other higher belt instructors from Minnesota, about twenty or perhaps twenty-five were also present. It seemed that getting in this form was a rarity, even for higher belts with pond timeshare access.

After a brief pause, the games began. The first was Kim in the canoe chasing everyone around the pond. Only Forrest seemed exempt. It was inferred these visitors were the lower half of all Minnesota belts temporarily joining our Chicago contingent. This was found out to be false. Often ranks and accomplishments of other states were inflated to instill a greater beyond mystique about the cult. However, it seems obvious that many higher belts knew the truths but maintained the fraud. The guests were in fact all the higher ranks from the Northland.

Meanwhile back at water world some tried hiding under the wood planked footbridge between the heart-shaped island (built so because Kim cared so much) and the shore. This seemed a good tactic, as the loaded down canoe could not fit under the bridge. When he approached we swam away and Kim would have to paddle around the island. We then swam back under the bridge. Finally Kim ordered several instructors to run across the bridge which could not handle the weight and with the fluctuations in the individually rope-tied floor planks, soon proved to be just a launching pad for instructors into the pond; much to the delight of Kim and Forrest standing nearby as the structural behavior of the rope bridge performed as expected. Dodging a branding by the canoe paddle by hiding under the bridge lost favor with the rest of the herd; the cost of our fellow Moos gaining grief at our expense was not worth it.

Joe was told that higher belts spent many, many, hours and days designing, building and maintaining that bridge. It was built from very heavy rope and one inch thick boards with cables supporting the cut down telephone pole pier supports used to anchor the starting points into the shore and island. It was nearly destroyed within a few minutes by the thousands of instructor-pounds wildly fleeing back and forth. Saw a couple good spills and one horrible sounding splat–splash as one instructor slipped, then face planted off the planks and plopped head first into the pond. Bit of a headache but otherwise alright. The joke was immediately made about 'rock-head' being an advantage, which seemed to get a smile out of Kim. Black belts can be real suck-ups at times. Rock-head was a favorite term used by higher belts to describe any misbehaving underling Moo.

Throughout this festival, we noticed several things: Kim used the paddle upside down when in the canoe. The vessel still moved at a good speed, noticeably faster than any fleeing swimmer. After a chase but upon being overtaken, one last resort was a quick, deep dive with a change of direction sub-surface twist and then make like a porpoise some distance away. However more than a few were paddled upon air intake and slowly floundered about, half sinking and groaning towards shore. Each whack was met with symbiotic groans from the on-lookers who feared the same. Collectively we all felt each hit each time. We bonded shamefully; the way ocean going mammals watch orcas eat their friends.

The use of a bb gun from the canoe was when the best hiders really showed their stuff and were able to stay underwater for very impressive lengths of time. No one was penetrated with shot, as it seemed Kim was a good distance away and not closely aiming, but a few glancing zings caused fear amongst the herd. When bb's whistled past, instinctive evasion tactics like diving had to be well-executed lest your noggin find hard wood awaiting upon surfacing.

Whaling up some air and holding onto the bottom sections of the aerator pipe was popular until Kim began prodding the depths with the paddle or boat gaff whenever nearby. Joe and I became much better swimmers that day after watching a few unfortunates being half dragged into the canoe for a symbolic light touch. Again the crowd reeled from every fleshy-sounding hit. Kim didn't beat on everyone; those known to be rougher received the most attention.

This chase game lasted over an hour and then we were ordered out of the pond and onto the backyard area that was supposed to be used for training but never was. Our shoulders were each individually coated down with vegetable oil by the dude himself to protect against sunburn while engaging in the next activity, chicken fights. Each participant was required to kneel before Kim to accept the oiling. Joe recalled a very eerie feeling right at that moment.

The system was bigger ones on top of not-so bigger ones, except for certain privileged higher belts. This gave higher ranks the advantage over the struggling lower belts. The feared combination was two notoriously large regionals.

We were paired off, mounted up and then saw the competition. Every regional was matched on top of a head instructor and looked hungry. At the starting chuckle from Forrest, a collective wolf-shriek evoked from the twenty-five odd fleeing combos as we all frantically tried to escape, all in the same direction like panicked cattle. Kim himself was on Forrest's shoulders at one time picking off stragglers from the frenzy.

Not being that large, but adjudged capable of handling his partner who was a good seventy-five pounds heavier, Joe's initial "oh crap" verbalization made them a primary target. Quickly assessing the situation and relying upon innate street survival skills, Joe scampered the hell outta there as fast as his scrawny little body could go. By the approaching Flintstone-esque plodding of big feet coupled with the scream of Joe's topside being blasted, they knew the jig was up. Their only option was the island safety zone if his upper armor could make it. They almost reached the bridge before being shoved off the shoreline, but the pond seemed like a haven, for now.

Other combos were not as lucky. There was complete carnage on land and they heard their cries for help but thought it best to sit it out in maritime shelter. Except by then Forrest was in the canoe and headed their way before they could climb out. Chased back onto the beach, new partners were awarded and the fracas continued for about another half-hour. Many different combinations were ordered and there was some good roommate bashing amongst the groups. Towards the end Joe was paired with a noted head instructor and they sought some brotherly payback on other teams, although this was frowned upon for the most part.

Soon after this everyone ate well, lots of roasted potatoes, grilled beef and veggies; we played sit by the fire and duck from the dog, plus practiced fleeing from the roman candles being shot at us, which was grossly entertaining for Kim.

Towards evening's end, during the fireworks chasing game where Kim shot roman candles or big, really big Nike Zeus-sized bottle rockets at scrambling instructors; from a side view one could see the rockets shoot towards the crowd then at the last second veer up to a higher altitude but on the same overall trajectory thus over flying the crowd, creating shock and awe. This happened consistently as if by design or from the result of some external guiding force, almost as if he willed the rockets to just skim over our heads. It was weird.

In addition to improved scuba, another positive takeaway was that at the end of it all, after the constant, non-stop moving all those hours it brought back memories of being about ten or eleven years old out past dark in the summertime playing in the streets or on the baseball diamond. When we didn't care about anything else but to just keep on running. We could go endlessly and not have to worry about being tired because it seemed like we'd never run out of gas. As children we were in control, but now it was the cult. Several of the groups were older, past forty and some had physical limitations, yet everyone played with abandonment.

I think most of us have experienced similar in a range of situations. Extended work projects, wilderness or skiing trips, moving a family or regretfully handling a disaster. Being around friends and sharing a common powerful experience, to a certain extent like a military exercise, built strong bonds between many of us. But it was the crap about Chung Moo Quan being the only way to do it because it was due solely to Kim, or is his name really Park, that makes it completely unpalatable.

SHADOW AND THE FARM DOGS

Sometimes around the fire pit, higher belts would gather instructors to sit and enjoy the fire, sometimes. Most of the time it was a sibling pressure session. Small firecrackers or the occasional bottle rocket shot from ten feet away. The trick was never to move. A flinch brought several more of the same. I once saw one higher belt take a rocket up the sleeve without expression. He was not shot at again. Some of us were frequent targets nonetheless.

The one dog, named Shadow, was different. Shadow was a highly spirited yellow Collie with really sharp, pointy teeth. Shadow could be vicious when properly motivated. This is how the dog survived with the much larger and fiercer German Shepard named Major and the other dog, a part Rotwieler-Lab-Moose mix on the Farm, both of which were very mean animals. Instructor Jeff, who lived in the Barn, would have to full blast punch them in the head to get them to stop fighting. These dogs would jump over the fence and chase joggers or bite instructors who came to the Farm infrequently. We quickly learned not to keep Liv-a-Snaps in our jackets anymore. Hitting a dog was not allowed; you just had to put up with it.

So, there are these shark dogs lurking in the darkness beyond the fire pit, and Shadow near Forrest. Whenever Shadow was called over there was a noticeable change in everyone's situational awareness. Forrest would grab a hold of the inbred, narrow muzzled canine, shake him, get him agitated then point and release this Collie rocket at any instructor in the circle. Shadow would leap out snarling and snapping away at anyone in his path.

If you didn't move the dog would relax and chill and go back to the firing pad. If you put a block up, like an instructor I knew did, the dog would sink his teeth in. I had never really seen a canine tooth pierce an ex-state class wrestler's forearm before, it was pretty different. My friend was largely unhurt; he just had this really shocked look for awhile. We teased him unmercifully about it for years.

Times like these, the barbeques, the camaraderie of the hard lessons, they were good times and am glad for the friends I knew. However, I realize we were deceived into believing in something that was if truth be told very sinister, we were being used. Once in awhile a couple of good times were supposed to cancel out the bullshit, I guess.

After Forrest was demoted, the dogs' behavior and personalities changed dramatically. They became very docile. Word was Kim used the whammy on them. It was weird.

EXPANSIONS AND TRANSFERS – THE REAL STORIES

Joe's new roommate, David, would leave all his belongings behind and head for the new Moo frontier at the East Coast a few weeks after Fourth of July. This was his opportunity, his chance. We were told by the newly promoted national instructors Forrest, Tom and Ken; that Boston was doing great, the potential for schools unlimited and the reason for the growth was those highly educated wanted to learn what Chung Moo had to offer. Kim himself said the people there easily recognize the value of Chung Moo. Instructors like David who had college were going to be the future, the rest of us had better watch out or we would be passed up.

The real story, not learned for another twenty years as the cult began to lose its senior members was that upon arrival, David was told he screwed up, this was his last chance and that he couldn't cut it in Chicago. He was forced to make a choice, what was he going to do? Be alright to handle, he asked. Two hours off the plane, no confirmed living quarters and two suitcases full of clothes, David steps into the practice room to run the group lessons at one of the schools in Boston.

Under his guidance during the span of years, the East Coast would become the powerhouse of Moo and provide most of the temporary growth in the organization. There would be less emphasis on cult activities and more focus on training.

Those sent to Pittsburgh, Texas and Florida would go through the same thing; being told this is your last chance, you have to earn now or never. Whereas the story told to the buds left behind is they are more qualified, this is why they have opportunity.

MEANWHILE, BACK IN THE MOO

Joe and the other second degree instructors were now handling schools full time. The regionals they stepped in for still had their names on schools, in other words were the owners and stopped by several times a week to ensure all was well, that students were still paying their courses and most importantly to retrieve the cash and deliver it to Kim.

The days were long for Joe and his fellow newbie main Moos. The regionals put additional pressure on them by making them run meaningless errands or arranging to meet before school then not show up, only to scream at the instructor for being late for school. They tried all sorts of antics. Switching cars was a favorite. The regional Moo would show up, characteristically in the middle of groups lesson if he could manage it so as to disrupt any reverence the students were building towards the new instructor and then insist coffee be picked up, and to have his vehicle checked. Better yet, let's switch vehicles; I'm on a schedule I won't be here that long. This was a ruse, the guy would camp out all night long since now he had something to do, he was "handling" and having fresh coffee and food brought to him. As a result, what ever spending cash may have been given to the lower belt instructor a few days earlier was now being used to support the higher belt. The cult giveth and then the cult taketh away. Just like your rank. You want to lose a stripe? You better handle.

The average instructor had very little spending cash, and was not given a paycheck. Cash was meted out as expenses arose. They were given the barter equivalent of approximately fifteen thousand per year in 1985 dollars considering rent, food and clothes. All this was "handed to" the instructors. What I mean is pants for example, if a higher belt no longer used some clothes, since he had gained so much weight, these would be handed to other instructors. Gifts from parents or relatives were often turned in to the Quan for disbursement amongst those that could use it. It's one thing to occasionally raid your roommate's wardrobe for a clean shirt or the like, but to rely on the whims of the controlling organization which mandates all your activities; well that screams cult, doesn't it?

There would be group outings were nationals would take ten instructors to a discount shopping center and pick out clothes for them. This came from Kim, who liked to control his minions and dress them up in attire of his choosing. Track suits for example, or every few years, take them to a suburban mall and buy them winter coats. Kim would wait outside with a few nationals close by to serve as body guards and the regionals would help the instructors pick out a coat. It was ridiculous, grown men asking if be alright to try one on. Then at the register having another grown man pay for your coat. Imagine you work at the store and see this, what would you think? The soccer team is back again?

However once a week, as a rule Thursday nights, was the instructor lesson. This was when the nationals, the holders of the direct line to Kim, would check instructors' form and teach new movements. The correct Moo term was to pass new movements since only Master can really teach. That's a whole other story. Kim never taught, he only alluded to teaching. He even said he only checked (reviewed) the highest level nationals once every year for twenty minutes because "there was nothing for him to check." In other words not even the nationals were at the level where they could absorb the teachings of one so high a belt as the Kim.

The instructor lessons were grueling late night affairs not starting until after 10:00 p.m. and not ending till well past midnight. School hours were 11:00 a.m. to 9:00 p.m. so the goal on Thursdays was to have something to eat prior to the instructor lesson. The wildcard was guessing when the regional would show up to throw you off balance and not let you eat, or drink, or use the bathroom. "Handle that part later, always thinking of yourself, you are so selfish." Joe must have heard that a hundred times he said, more like a thousand, probably.

One of the perks of being a main Moo was the Chull Sa Chung was to be available as much as you desired, you only had to ask. This the second degrees of the time did with glee, the nationals allowed them to use the herbs and the magical bean bags every time it was requested. It quickly became a weekend favorite for Joe and crew. It also meant the regionals could not disrupt them as it had national level protection. Over time as more second degrees began handling schools and the higher ranks stepped back to assist Kim with the Farm and the business that started up, the attendance at the Chull Sa parties grew substantially, everyone wanted in. There were so many instructors the period necessary went from two hours for a group of five, to four or more hours for larger groups and the time spent working on the bags decreased so much so that Joe and crew began searching for alternatives.

FULL ON MOO

When Joe first started handling a school full time, there were two immediate tasks to perform. One he was aware of since it was spelled out by the highest belt in the land: file for unemployment. You told me not to go there any more, to quit, Joe thought. Yes, be alright, is what he said. Something for nothing and your Moo isn't free. He failed to collect as the Reagan era policy of outspending the Soviets equated to no more handouts for deadbeats trying to work the social safety net, like Moos for example.

The position of instructor, sought for so long became not a milestone of accomplishment but was instead the beginning of intensified cult servitude. Worse, continued Moo membership and any chance for further rank required espousing ever greater amounts of cult dogma to lower belts. Even though each time the story, or history or supposed accomplishment of the Kim was parroted; the speaker was internally debating his or her own set of Moo convictions.

The other task not so readily apparent was he had to break up with his girlfriend whom he had met at his last job; they dated for seven months, a record for Joe. He often stayed over at her place and she did not have a phone, at least one Joe could find by looking in the refrigerator or under the bed. No phone, can't call into fatter belts. Besides, I'm exhausted, gonna eat then sack out. It was Joe's escape, his island of sanity he said in retrospect.

So the Moos, led by the not getting any himself ever getter fatter regional, put the time honored celibate-belt tradition into action. Keep them busy all day, all night, all the time and there's no time to think about the squeeze. See, training really starts once you start to handle a school. That's when you are really on instructor course. Not until then. This was really a surprise to the fifth sectoid, sixth sectoid and first stripers who had paid thousands of dollars for their opportunity to clean schools and run errands.

Joe's five-foot seven-inch tall blue eyed soul mate would not give up so easily. She retaliated by bringing food out to his car in the

Moo lot twice a day. "Be alright to say," an instructoid course would stammer, "looks like that one blonde hair female is back putting things in the Air Wolf." The Air Wolf was an early 70's black 350 Chevy Impala with modified air intake and equipped with state of the art JC Penny radials. At moderate speeds the coupe would scream around corners, the dull flat primer painted the entire length of the rocker panels reminded instructors of the aircraft in the then-current television program. Any resemblance to the pilot on the show was coincidental.

Joe had been told by fatter belts not to let students' mind drop if they see you with a pretty girl out on a date. "Don't let your girlfriend come into school. Their concentration should be on their practice and on their course," he was lectured by the fatter belt owning the school. After waiting a few minutes to ensure she had left, Joe would tell them to bring in the food. Instructor course lived for this; the picnics on wheels would include chicken, pasta, and home baked cookies. Soon they all wanted to meet Sherry too, mostly because they got to handle (consume) whatever was left over at night's end, although many times the tradition of aerial food dispensing was passed down in the true Moo approach, flung at high speed. The underlings also enjoyed fueling up the Air Wolf and readying it for the night time power runs to main instructor group or the rotation meetings where the cash was handed in.

When the Chevy fell victim to the instructor course maintenance program, his still devoted girlfriend's turbo Trans Am was a good substitute. Joe had to be careful in not letting higher belts see that car. He often argued with her about wanting the Chevy back in time after the occasional Sunday romance so as not to be caught. Explaining to fatter belts the Air Wolf had broken down was predictable and accepted. How he got around wasn't a real concern to them. Explaining to his girlfriend his so-called higher rank instructors took her car and won't return it for awhile, as was known to happen in Moo, would have been just another headache Joe did not want to deal with.

It wasn't the incompatible schedules as much as it was the shoddy treatment of girlfriends or spouses required by Moo that ended it. Falling asleep on the phone late at night at the end of another impossible week was forgivable. Not showing up for dinner at her parents because there was something more important going on by school or jilting on even inexpensive Christmas presents was not. "She didn't believe me when I told her something came up at school, or that I had no money at all. She told me it was if they controlled my life," Joe recalls.

One day the food stopped coming. Instructor course was saddened most, Joe was too busy Mooing. There was a card at Valentines Day Joe got to keep and not be ridiculed about in front of higher belts as he made it home before the others did, back at the commune and got to the mail first, a rarity. He still has the card. "Just to remind me of how stupid I was," Joe says.

There would be a couple more friends Joe would experience and have to make it through, as the Moos say, during the rest of his Moo career. One, a student, was determined to be seeking power and position after her interview with fatter belts. Joe was told point blank to end it after five months. It was bewildering and difficult for them both. Good thing they were not in a cult or anything.

Another would be the first person in school on a bright spring morning, surprising Joe. She was getting married she came to tell him, more than three years after they broke apart. It was the confirmation she needed, to ensure she was doing the right thing. Joe was spooked. A female stepping in first before any male students was taboo. Now he'd have to report in, lock down the school and probably need to use salt and pepper, sprinkled in the corners in all the rooms to ward off bad spirits. The same was required when moving into a new place to stay, as instructor's rented abodes were called. Joe wished his ex well, then ushered her out and set back to Mooing. There was a time when she was all he could think about, but Joe had made a choice; one he would repeat several times before finally learning Moo was not good.

Joe recounted he did not realize how deep the tentacles of control grow in the Moo microcosm until several years after leaving. He was driving along and came to a stoplight near a street side park. There was a black Trans Am sitting there with a blonde haired woman, about five-foot seven, watching a small girl play. The child looked to be about two or perhaps three years old, also with blonde hair, the Trans Am looked to be about seven years, well kept.

It was a few blocks from where Joe and Sherry used to work, back in the day she lived within a couple miles, down the same street. Could be a niece or neighbor's kid, Joe thought. The little girl seemed talkative and inquisitive about everything. He checked around, found out she had gotten married to a steady, nice guy within a year of being Mooed by Joe. Joe's contacts said she was secure and doing well. After careful reflection, so was Joe for the first time in many years. He was genuinely happy for his former friend; thought the best for her but never tried to re-enter her life. Joe realized he finally did know what true, right, correct, meant; and it did not go Moo.

SUK CHUNG THE URBAN LEGEND

The Suk Chung form had been passed during the previous August. It was now November, close to Thanksgiving; few of us had the chance to practice the form. We were still under the impression that higher belts routinely practiced it and that only during the lesson a few months ago had its existence been revealed to lower ranks. The truth be told is by ordinary Moo process, any higher form or movement is almost never practiced for long if at all by higher belts. It is merely just passed along by most of them before they forget it, without ever developing a real sense of understanding. It was and is left up to the individual Moo practitioner to make it their form. In the case of Suk Chung it had been given out that one summer afternoon to regionals just prior to everyone else arriving at the Farm for the lesson.

Thus in November, when a head instructor said he would probably be getting in Suk Chung over the weekend, that he had a place scoped out and we could come along if we wanted to, we jumped. This was very rare, an invite by a higher belt and to refuse for any reason might seem disrespectful and we'd miss out on the eliteness label, so there was no reason to question or consider asking any other higher belt about it, although only one of the three that would accompany were his charges.

Asking about the coolness at that time of year, it was said to bring along ski or snowmobile pants or heavy work clothes and you'd be fine. It wasn't fully considered what could happen. We were a little concerned as it was cold, but we did not think the process through, blinded by that time from critical reasoning due to our conditioning in holding the line.

With strong volition, three warrior-spirited instructors threw some extra snowmobile and work clothes into the car and headed off about eight o'clock that night to meet up with the higher belt. Once together, they drove to an office center parking lot near the expressway. Parking the car, the Higher one lead them across the expressway on foot, over the embankment and up the hill about fifty feet to the fence shielding the abandoned quarry that was to be the practice site.

The impression was this was routine, even though it should have been apparent this had not been done before, at least not at that site. Climbing over the barbwire fence, which did not seem familiar to the leader, should have been a clue. Back down the other side of the steep hill it quickly flattened out to a pebble-strewn mud and grass approach to the water. The pond size was a few acres; a small excavation apparently not used in some time, the immediate area was a mix of old fields and new land development. Off in the distance about a quarter-mile away to the north was an ancient farmhouse with a few lights on. It suddenly seemed a lot colder. The air was dense, pitch dark.

The higher belt tossed off his clothes and in old sweat-bottoms only, proceeded to wade out into the murkiness. The other three did likewise, but in full protective gear each picking some personal space between them. It was hoped the extra insulation would form a type of wetsuit with body warmth kicking in. End to end the band of four were strung out over about one hundred feet in distance and they were, in essence, stupid.

Wading out it was surprising how the water was extremely cold around the ankles, soaking through to the calves, the knees, then Bam! The shockingly frigid water pounded their chests as the first drop-off in the slimy quarry bottom was discovered and each of the three stumbled, recovered, backpedaled, and then shouted nearly in unison at the body blow the pond threw them. It was as if the deep was sucking them forward into ever-more cold.

Regaining some composure by taking a wide stance, they all simultaneously decided to begin slapping the water surface, trying to do the form as best they could, shouting and exclaiming at each hit, the added verbalizations used just to keep going against the horribly cold liquid mass pressing in on them. The higher belt seemed unaffected, but was far away. In the darkness his motion and sound could be detected only minimally.

The first member, farthest south in the pond, knew he could not last for more than a few hits, his feet were going numb. The water's coldness had knocked all the air out of him and it was much too difficult to fight the water and try the new form, which if done incorrectly, shocks the nervous system in a negative way. Brilliantly now waist deep, he questioned whether this was the right place to be. Quarries are notoriously dangerous with the slippery slopes, unknown water depth and no one nearby. Pictures of the headlines: four stupid idiots, drown half naked in quarry marked no trespassing, film at eleven and a real vision of death closing in convinced him retreat was necessary. This was a lot different than the nice warn pond with gentile slopping sand bottom at the summertime Farm. Without question they had followed.

He decided to get in eighteen hits, a favored cult integer, not that the worship affected the choice, and then to bail. He could not breathe. Completing the hits he found wading out was nearly impossible, the legs did not want to move and the footing seemed more treacherous than going in. The numbness in his feet was getting worse and he still could not breathe well. Pneumonia would have been welcome, as long as they would all escape safely. Fear of not getting out began to grow as the near-point of exhaustion had been reached too quickly. Gotta remember to eat better Joe was thinking, more steak.

Number Two was also now just coming out of the water and visually confirmed what they each must have been feeling. Except that number Three and the Higher one, they were still in the pond.

The First one said, "Not sure about yourself but this is no good, it's too cold."

The Second one agreed and said, "I had trouble getting out."

The First one nodded affirmative then added, "We've got to get the others out, we'll pull them out now if we have too, I don't know how they can take it."

"Me either," said the Second. Then, "Yes, we have to stop now or we won't make it."

Turning towards the pond they could see number Three was not doing well. He was wavering near motionless; his arms lose by his sides. One and Two waded out the ten yards or so off the beach to number Three's location, hoping not to repeat the indoctrination stumble and relive the shockwave of lead-like cold attacking the diaphragm again. The water was still excruciating but lacked the stun effect; their senses had dimmed.

"Come on," they said to Three, "let's go, we're outta here."

"I can't feel my legs very well," said Three as One and Two assisted him out.

Back on shore he sat down and tried to dry off while One and Two made an instant mutual non-spoken decision to approach the higher belt to ask permission and suggest they leave. Wading out again it seemed Higher belt was also not moving, possibly using a finishing technique the lower ones did not know. Hesitating a few seconds, upon reaching his location One and Two asked if Higher one was okay since he had ceased moving in the same manner as number Three exhibited moments earlier.

Unresponsive to verbal inquiry, One and Two could not make out Higher one's words, which were badly slurred. They lightly held his forearms and walked him out. Back on shore it got worse, he could not speak and nearly collapsed. Disoriented, he was incapacitated as group leader. One and Two took control, the line had been passed. They would get out of there and suffer any consequences at another time.

One and Two helped Three and Higher belt assemble back into the additional damp clothes and while holding them both up, began walking them up the hill towards the southeast fence corner entry point. Climbing back up was much more difficult, the wind had picked up, they were all soaking wet and half the group could not walk well. The pond retained a couple of shoes in vengeance. About halfway up, One and Two grabbed Three, got him up the side to the fence and told him to wait. They went back for Higher one who was sitting in the cold mud, fumbling with old shoes, trying to put them on the wrong feet and moved him up the hill by half-carrying him. Where there is a will there is a way.

Entering the place they had easily clamored over the fence, this would now be near impossible as they'd have to carry Three and Higher one over the barbwire topped eight-foot chain link. Initially they thought they could stuff the others back over. This was tried briefly but it was too unwieldy. Three was trying to climb but Higher was a babbling mess, unable to fully use his arms or hands. He still could not talk.

"What are we going to do?" yelled Two into the wind.

The reply was either fuck this or watch this, Two wasn't sure while One was already untying the bottom of the fence links near the post. Together they tore back enough of the fence to get them out. One and Two then lead the other half of the team down the embankment and towards the I-5 expressway; the one that runs right through the heart of Naperville.

Standing alongside the shoulder, gauging the traffic flow trying to re-acclimate to the speed at which everything seemed to be moving and still soaking wet in the November breeze; they waited for a slot to launch across the first three lanes to get to the median. Once there, they sensed they would make it back. The headlights were intense.

Two held onto Three, while One grabbed a hold of Higher one and shouted to the others: Go! Go Now! Move Damn It! The first two made it to the median with the following provision right behind with blaring horns monitoring their progress along the way. At the median Two helped Three over and had him wait. One handed Higher dude to Two, then One jumped over and picked up Higher dude back from Two across the barrier. Two then jumped over, grabbed Three and the curious quad of hapless idiots plodded as best they could, six feet on the ground and two air-steeping across the final three lanes to the grassy safety on the south side of I-5. They continued to stumble back to the car, over one more small fence and loaded everybody in. They were indomitable, soggy cold and miserable.

Three was still experiencing a loss of feelings in his lower legs but said it was getting a little better. No doubt the jog back helped. Higher one was still ranting although he could speak our names and kept saying, wow, wasn't it great! He seemed internally animated. Driving back the few miles to the initial staging point someone pointed out a bank sign that read thirty-nine degrees. Funny, now it seemed to make sense. Hey, ya think it's too cold out to do this? Nah. We could only guess the water temperature. What dopes.

Once arrived, the three instructors helped the Higher one into the house. By now he was slowly improving, could speak more clearly and move under his own power. "I'm gonna go take a shower," he spat out and left us in the kitchen of the small bungalow. After about twenty minutes he returned and again remarked, "Wasn't it great, wasn't it great?" The three asked with due reverence they were concerned about his condition to which he replied, "Was I out of it? Was I out of it? I must have been really out of it, huh?"

It was believed at the time that pushing oneself to the limit then beyond was the optimal achievement for a true warrior and no doubt he had been there many, many times; what with his reputation and length of service. So we questioned ourselves that perhaps we had mishandled. The Higher one then began to demonstrate Kong Su kata very slowly, pushing strongly into each position and moving his fists closer and closer to each of our vital points in succession. At no time did he ever ask how we were doing even though it was clearly apparent Three was still having after-effects and there was no understanding on Higher dude's part of our concerns during the time at the quarry. By then Three, like the other two, had enough. They left.

Back at the commune, each took their own long hot shower and tried to eat something. Number Three was still experiencing internal cramps in his midsection and legs. He had been in the water several minutes longer than the rest of the trio. We had another decision to make, should we try to see him bear it out, and not risk further trouble or go around a higher belt to seek help? Three was in need, Higher dude could not help. With measured trepidation the consensus was reached to call the Farm and ask to speak with Forrest.

After briefly explaining the evening's events and group current physical condition, One was instructed to drive with Three to the Naperville house so Forrest could check him, but to call when in proximity as per standard procedure. Doing so then upon arrival at the house, One and Three found Two had also been summoned as he answered the door, apparently breaking the established Naperville road speed record by a good margin. The Olds 350 was nearly pegged most of the way there.

It was immediately apparent there was a real battle going on inside. Two looked genuinely worried. Forrest commanded the trio to step over. Forrest was there along with two future parolees and they had Higher one cornered on the other side of the room. The big house was up for sale and devoid of furniture on the first floor. Higher one looked as if he had been wailed upon significantly. He was bare-chested, dressed only in another pair of sweat bottoms and displayed what appeared to be several larger handprints about his chest and sides. Both of the regionals looked very concerned, brows intensely furrowed, glaring from opposite sides towards Higher dude as he stood with his hands folded in front of his groin. Only Forrest spoke. Stepping in the three of us pondered our collective fate.

When number Two had first arrived, Higher dude was being slapped down the stairs by Forrest with the regionals following. Forrest bellowed from the second floor for Two to enter, then continued admonishing the miscreant.

Forrest berated him, "He," pointing to Two, "can handle you right now! You want to see?" Turning to Two he ordered, "Get in sparring position, Now!"

In an agonizing nanosecond pondering why he had to take position vs. his direct superior, Two steeled himself and was ready for the go should the order be given, just please don't make me do it, I don't want to do this, he thought.

Forrest growled to Higher dude, "You're done! You're through! This was your last mistake, you're out," and he pulled his right hand back on high, twisting it a certain way such that the two regionals and number Two began to turn away as if they knew what was coming next, a Nae Gong blast. Forrest was said to have been given this power by the Kim, of internal energy that could burn through you from across the room.

The doorbell rang. It was One and Three arriving. Two was ordered to answer and let us in. Stepping over we heard Forrest repeat that Higher dude was on his way out. We felt very bad and tried to explain, although meekly, we should have known better we just didn't think it through and could have asked some more questions. But none of us wanted to contest the proceedings going on. Forrest made mention of earlier times years ago when over some dispute Higher dude had acted as if he wanted to hit Forrest in anger, possibly for some mental correction meted out.

Forrest said, now calmly with a tinge of pointed disgust in his voice, "Do you remember that time, back at old School One, in the back room, you wanted to hit me, and all of us were there (meaning the regionals) and we all saw it, but I just said I hope you can be better. Well, this was your last chance."

The prevalent danger was that in an organization which absolutely did not permit any modest questioning of authority or discussion of means; disaster could easily result and did at numerous times in history. The many failed businesses, nor need mention lives destroyed from the Tax Case results, were of the same flawed genetic composition.

Forrest left Higher dude standing in the corner flanked by the lower belt regionals. He came over and checked number Three and the others thoroughly by the mental retinal scan looking into our souls if you will, checking pulse, rubbing points and talked to us for a few minutes. We had absolute confidence in Forrest, if he said we'd be okay then that was good enough. We were dismissed and stopped on the way back for something hot to drink but did not talk much.

Upon finally arriving back at the commune for good that Sunday night, the other member living there had just gotten home and asked, "Hey, what's up? You guys wanna go out?" It was already after midnight, some guys just know how to party.

The next day, Higher dude was back at his allocated school, still in charge. Indirectly it was mentioned during the ensuing week that Kim had said the only mistake made was taking us along to the pond. Higher dude languished in the organization for another year.

After a few days number Three slowly improved and was his old double down-chung with the homies self again. None of the three had much of a taste for Suk Chung after that. Others in the organization never fully understood why, although the legend persisted it was not discussed much. The focus was on the future, so bright...

LEGENDS OF CONTROLLING THE WEATHER AND BEN HURR

The story was told of how centuries ago, a general in what is today Vietnam could control the weather and turn night into day. Thus he ruled the land for many years. It was said that Kim could do the same. That he connected with nature as evidenced by his understanding of higher forms: Kyung Gong Sul Bope; body light as a feather or can fly depending on who tells it; Wae Gong Bope, the ability to understand and move like any animal; and Nae Gong Bope, the ability to externally project internal energy in the form of heat, light or wind. The waiting rooms of every Moo school, even today, show pictures of Kim supposedly demonstrating these abilities. These pictures were taken at the same time and in the same field as the one shown in the front of this book. One would think that with such talents he could stage a simple vault a little better.

Further along the cult continuum, the story of directing lighting was told. When the Farm started, sod was put in place and rain was needed so… he made it rain but it was a gradual buildup thing and the adjacent areas received some too so it would not look obvious. Yeah, that might be a give away there's a cult on Book Road controlled by a demon.

Another time one year in late December, Kim wanted instructors around so he made it snow, it snowed over a foot, much of it in Naperville with little elsewhere. Locally heavy snow storms are generally confined to a small area but it was still weird. This was one of the largest gatherings at the Farm calling all second degrees and up, subject to approval. The Jeep pickup was used as a chariot dragging several toboggans, sleds and sometimes unfortunate ones who fell off the Jeep or other platforms as the train careened around the pond at a good clip. It was fun but dangerous. A few, mostly girl friends and not instructors, had the wind knocked out of them and were shaken up but were otherwise alright after they fell off. Easily it could have been different. There was no real care or concern for personal safety.

There was also a snowmobile used to pull sleds, but it was nowhere as extreme as the Jeep, which with Kim at the helm, would take sharp turns resulting in colorful disembarking, those standing by the wayside from earlier passes would then jump on the available slots. This went on for a couple hours. The objective was not to get caught standing around lest a regional convince you to jump onto Ben Hurr, as the procession was known. Terrorists, any higher belt than you, or yourself if a lower belt happened by, would sometimes jump on one of the sleds as they rocketed past. The result was a freewheeling tumbling exercise for both passenger and terrorist. My personal record was something like eight rolls non-stop due to momentum, laughing so hard I almost choked. Ben Hurr was dangerous, but we felt we were being looked after and physically in good shape, though several of us nearly lost balance in the Jeep bed, that would have been painful. So we stuck to the sleds when possible.

Joe said many higher belts seemed genuinely concerned when the sleds were first hooked up. Forrest just laughed and chided them to climb aboard. Luckily, no one was seriously injured. It was indicated that Ben Hurr was also used during the summer, on the gravel and dirt, which would not have been as much fun.

No form was passed; we were there for the chance to be around. Sporadically, Kim might speak to an individual, mostly to find out or check on personal issues, which now seems likely to have been for ulterior motives.

Did he care about everyone, or were we just there for his amusement? Tend towards the latter given his handling after a head instructor's wife fell off a sled. From a distance I looked right at him, it was like he read my thoughts, should be more careful.

TRAINING IN THE POOL

About once each year during the summer, Kim would have all second degrees and up or sometimes for emphasis, all main instructors and up, only those handling school fulltime would be invited over to the Farm. There was a large above ground pool about five feet deep maximum with an extended deck between the houses and the pond. This was a perfect venue to further condition the herd.

Games would be played; sometimes those from other states would be called in for a weekend. Red Rover was a favorite, with higher belts stationed in the deep end of the pool so that when lower belts were called over they would be assured a near drowning. Terrorist football was another. This also had no rules, but if the ball came towards you in the pool you best pass it before being submarined and held under. Joe and the other lower belts preferred the pond to the pool as there was more room to evade capture and torture.

If captured the prevalent torment was the foot twist or foot elevation technique where as your foot is brought up by the higher belt testing your metal, your head invariably goes back and down under the water eventually. Kim was supreme arbitrator and had use of a garden hose he would turn on full blast into your oppressor's face when he thought you had enough. This brought out the symbiotic pleas and guffaws from the rest of the Moo-manatees thrashing about the plasticized grotto, somehow hoping they'd find an as yet unknown passage out. Cut up fruit on plastic plates prepared by the women would float by on pool toys after an hour or so and if you could, you'd inhale a piece and submerge, eating like a shark underwater until discovered again and put back on torture display for the amusement of the higher belts.

Then the whirlpool game would start. Kim would order everyone in the pool, all ranks to start to run in a circle. After it got going Kim would then walk in the other direction and pull everyone in the pool down in the cross current. Joe and the others were awed by this, it was near impossible to stand up in the flow, however after hours of such exertion just climbing out of the pool was challenging.

Now it would be time for "game with stick." From regionals on down we would be paired off and tied together at the ankles like in sack races. Kim would then use a torch or flaming branch to chase instructors around, moving the burning spears like swords over everyone's heads as they scampered for cover.

One enterprising pair, Joe and a head instructor who got along well, often sought each other out during these episodes. They knew the Farm well enough to where they could legally hide yet still make it back quick enough when called so as to make it look like they were consistently around. They had a system. Even pace never mind the flames; count one, two; ouch that's hot, and one, two... ordinarily they'd make good time and be outta range but this night their cadence was too loud and they got caught.

They were lifted overhead and thrown back in the pool still tied together by an enthusiastic pod of fat regionals. Everyone was singing, what we don't know, but it was melodic. This was another Moo group dynamic. If somebody else was in trouble, or being tortured or being promoted or being tossed back in the pool, all was good because it took the focus off of anything you might have done. This means all your buds are eager to help without fail; helping to throw you in the pool or tattling on you next weekend, having spotted you with a beer without other instructors around.

After a quick toweling off, dinner would be served, again cooked up by the full fledged cult women, called friends; with everyone except Kim sitting on the ground. Using a log was allowed so long as it did not make one sit higher than any other upper rank belt and certainly not higher than where Kim sat. Food would be brought to him and he would sit like a king, surveying his minions. The pretense of position was a constant invisible force.

As it grew late, with a quick fanfare, the leaving ceremony of thanking, and shaking hands and escorting everyone to their cars would take place and we'd return home and pass out. Of all the promises of the Farm being a place to get into training and to develop deeper ways, it turned out to be just another control mechanism employed by the Kim. Very few actual lessons ever took place there. Kim never really taught.

He would show a quick series of movements to only the highest belt at the time. Very little explanation or correction, the main thing was to remember the steps. The rest would be "caught up later, you can only do ten percent correct now anyway," he'd say. The next highest belts would then get in their lesson and so on. Many times instructors would be shown Kim's newly invented forms by regionals before the head instructors had it. Just as students would be taught forms in groups by the nationals or the regionals if they had the new form, before instructors were trained and yet Joe and fellow main Moos were expected to check and then ask questions.

An ex-regional confided to Joe long after both had left the cult that Kim obtained much of his ideas for new forms and how to pass it along from movies, television or magazines. Of course, the experts shown there weren't doing it right, here's how it should look. Presto, new form, new name; now all we need is a history and legacy so we can sell it.

COLD FUSION COOKING IN THE MOO

Late one horribly cold winter night at the St. James commune, all the little Moo-moos were snug on their rugs except for one. Joe was informed by Moo code to "wait for change part handing later on…" It was a Friday and the eagle often flew in Moo well into the night. It was extraordinary to have cash dropped off, but it deflected additional cars and cult activity from being observed in the strip mall dojos by the rest of the population, the no-minds who would say nay about our precious Moo.

The other reason for the impromptu dropping by was for inspection from an in-direct handler, so a different perspective of lower ranking cult member goings on could be reported in more of an independent viewpoint to Moo central control. Throwing on the last of the precious semi meat-like steaks we had squirreled away, the objective was to be fed and dishes washed before the upcoming exchange. We'd be plump, scrubbed and happy, and there'd be no food to offer as we needed the cash to buy more, and the fatter belt dropping by would want to blast back to his own little Anti-Moo refuge.

The primary utensil of any Moo worth his weight in feeding other Moos was the broiler. Set on high-plasma-nuke, the meat-like things would be done soon. Crap, it's been a long week. Tired, bone tired. It was so freaking cold out. The wind against the patio door let us know it also wanted to get at our steaks.

No, I'm fine. You sleep for a bit, I'll wait for the fatter belt, just in case he shows early. Joe and homies discussed the plan. I'll get the steaks ready... I'll just sit here on the... couch. Zzzzz... watching for the fatter belt... listening to... the sizzle of our steaks and the warm glow of the fireplace... fire wafting out of the kitchen!

It had been well over an hour we estimated. Wake Up! Wake Up! This is Serious! The roomie plodded into the gritty kitchen expecting food and was dismayed by what Joe had created. With flames lapping against the wall from behind the stove, they were a few seconds away from either a nasty grease fire or a gas explosion.

"Is it done?" anther roommate asked, sleepily. Having already survived close Moo-encounters of the pond kind a few months before, they knew they could survive this event as well. They grabbed towels and with precision teamwork opened the flaming breach, took hold of the pan, stabilized it, and while the other threw open the front door, Joe set the pan down on the concrete walkway in the fierce cold and wind. He left a bottom layer of epidermal foot on the concrete, the cold tearing away flesh. The fire threat inside was over; we now just had to extinguish the flaming pan on the front walkway.

Imagine you're walking along and see this set outside. Incredible, next was even more amazing. We slammed the door to keep out the cold and retrenched with a very large kettle of water. We knew this thing would prove useful someday, just not practical for normal cooking, but then this was Moo. They exchanged commands. Hurry up, it's still burning! Crap does it stink! Alright, open the door! The air was crackling dry and the large pitch of water fell on its trajectory towards the fiasco. Shut the door! Booom!

We heard diminishing sizzle then opened it back up and gaped. Sssss... Ash fell from the roof line. The air was so cold, the remaining bits of our cherished semi-steak were so hot and condensed in grease, the water vaporized our meal and caused the pan to etch a distinctive outline on the sidewalk. The phone rings. It's the fatter belt. The pan is tossed aside and we hustle over to the nearby convenience store parking lot, stealthily bow and thank, and thank and bow and take the envelopes with the five twenties inside each.

We head back to the confines but veer off towards our favorite late night last ditch restaurant where no higher belt would be, at least not at that time. "What can I get you?" asked the pretty young waitress. Why, steak and eggs of course. Joe watched the kitchen the whole time. He was never allowed to use the broiler again.

UNIFORM HANDLING

Main instructors would take turns on this after the regionals in charge were too busy with the Farm. The smell of the silk screen chemicals and of the ink was very unpleasant yet had to be endured for hours until the required minimum quantity of units was handled. Sometimes a garage adjoining a house or sometimes the living room of the house itself was used. The drying area would be the rest of the house. The vapors would leech into everything. The speeding colors on the drive home remained vivid for days.

In emblematic Moo mode it was done on a shoestring budget, a couple of cheap ironing boards, free labor and don't screw up no matter how late is. The chemicals and ink handled by somebody else. For a cost of around twenty dollars the finished product would sell for forty five; times one thousand a year equals that much more tax-free to Kim.

MOO BUSINESSES START UP

Several were begun only to be abandoned. Headquarters and the research and Moo-development site was of course, the Farm. First there was Renaissance. An herbal business touted as being the next Herbal Life. Then came Orience, another herbal supplement enterprise which also failed miserably. Then two printing companies and a couple of lesser known entities not worth mentioning. Even today they are still trying to fulfill Kim's dream as entrepreneur.

The Moo business plan was continually the same. Use the quarry's capital for start up and let Kim tell everyone what to do and set direction, that is to say otherwise control and approve every step or any action before it is taken. As suck-up higher belts anxious to gain approval in the eye of their master; they lie, cheat and steal their way into the hearts and minds of suppliers, customers and ever more potential targets from the schools. But strangely, the products fail in the market place. So what? Start over, get new chumps, new cash; same idea but in a new neighborhood. It can't miss, this is your opportunity.

Joe and the other main instructors were often the guinea pigs along with the extended families of select higher Moos for the vitamin supplements, magic elixirs and personal herbal products. None of it worked as claimed, just snake oil with a different hook. After Joe left the cult there would be many reincarnations of the same tired scheme with several new generations of suckers and their cash taking the risk to try and keep the Kim living in luxury. The cult keeps trying new names for their herbal scams on the West Coast without success, the market there is too sophisticated for royal hucksters. Although they came very close to convincing a bona fide doctor in the Seattle area to contribute $200K for the opportunity to open an herbal spa. Instead, the cult turned to selling overpriced martial art related wares on their website, such as the authentic Moo meditation pillow for a mere sixty dollars.

BUGOLGI AND MANIPULATION

During the last Christmastime at the Farm cookouts Joe attended, he was put in charge of several Webers full of Bugolgi, the marinated beef, next to the Barn along with others when his close friend David, whom he had not seen nor heard from in more than a year, walked over. They exchanged hellos, good to see yous, and continued cooking and yakking. Good times. Next thing they know, Kim walks up with the definitive, "Boy, what doing?"

Joe said, carefully using Moo-speak, "Be alright, handling cooking part, Master."

Kim says, "Uh," glared at the duo and grabbed a bunch of finished product off the grill, shoved it into his future felon face and smirked, "they don't know the difference."

Everyone was upstairs in the Barn waiting for food. Joe and David had immediately ceased activities when Kim approached, they stopped talking. They weren't sure what he meant by saying, "they don't know the difference." Was it a cue they could eat and cook or what?

Kim turned and headed back to the Barn so they picked up where they left off, catching up on things, telling jokes and sharing stories when he quickly turns around and again approaches; this time more rapidly, almost menacingly. Kim repeats the edict and grabs more chow. It was if he did not want them conversing.

After eighteen-plus years, Joe confirmed that was the intent. How many Moo conventions did he break? Rules he set out, saying this was the royal way, about open communication, trust and deeper friendships.

I wasn't liked Joe says, because now I realize Kim knew I could see him differently. My friend wasn't liked as he was one of the few educated ones amongst us. We of near rank that lived or hung out together were told David had been sent to support upstart operations in another state as this would be to his strengths. We were told straight he matched with that area more so than the others already there. Essentially, he was sent there to hopefully fail, as he was different due to his college degree. In typical Moo cult fashion, can't have followers thinking now, can we. If he failed, well then, those left behind would not be affected. It would be explained as he wasn't ready, doesn't have what it takes, but the rest of us assuredly do, your chance will come soon.

MIDNIGHT AT THE MOO-ASIS

Ah yes, the much maligned but required midnight inspections. For the longest time we thought it was more of a hazing or just to keep us on edge. As it happened it was to see if we had a date or God forbid a beer in the house. It was because the senior ranks routinely got shit upon by Kim and they felt it was their absolute duty to dump upon us in like manner. We could never relax. Or so we made them think.

Never thought they were checking to see if extra cash or new stereos were around, anything they could confiscate and donate to Kim, but that would have happened assuredly. Perhaps we seemed a tad too happy with our lives. We practiced, we ate, and now and then squeezed attractive women. All was well in our fiefdom and we had a comfortable sub-cult, a cozy mental den for the pack animals we were.

Joe and I never pulled a midnight inspection on anyone unless it was mission critical. We were told the newer generations couldn't hack the pressure because they didn't get to see the grandhamster. But I say it's because they had more sense. They would not have put up with it. After awhile, as am sure other groups adjusted as well, we could figure out quite accurately when the next surprise visit was likely to happen. Most of the time.

Under alert status, we'd drop hints about practicing outside then change locations via our own internal code regarding meeting at restaurants or nightclubs. Our particular subgroup was harder to track down than our predecessors and thus caused just a wee bit more o' frustration for the fatter belts, which we enjoyed.

With a still classified early warning network in place, we could literally hear them coming and bail long before they arrived. When faced with overwhelming weight, the best defense is not to be there, whenever possible. If you knew a couple girls that could cook well enough and worked afternoons so they didn't mind late hours, you were set. You'd crash at their places on a rotating basis and still be in time for dessert. But sometimes we had to pony up.

One notorious visitor in particular would stomp over whenever he was low on cash and couldn't afford gas. He liked the fact we had to listen to him. After months of this every other weekend crap, he started getting gasoline from sub-prime locations that ultimately, we like to think, helped his junk run not so well in the winter. We figured there's a low chance we would be the nominees to have to go pick him up. We wagered correctly.

Another stupid regimen was the vehicle exchange program. It could be at the cash contribution station (a school) or at the house or some other pre-determined Moo-asis like a Denny's restaurant. You'd swap your briefcase, clothes and unload all the crap the so-called higher mind trudged along with him and put them in the car you drive, which of course was full of fuel as required. His would be coasting on fumes with a near flat.

You'd get your junk back in a day or so, bone dry of gas, but with plenty of food residues, wrappers, garbage and the occasional partial birth in the back seat. All this extra stuff that wasn't in the contract we signed on to what now? Oh yeah, Moo. Not that it's a cult or anything.

We pressed on despite years of this crap. We practiced harder; the higher ups practiced less as they tried to control us or otherwise wasted their time in front of Kim. We were more efficient. We took whatever they dished out. Eventually we reasoned, we'd surpass them or they'd drop. And we promised to never give out any of the shit we took. Hope stayed true to that at least.

The bitch was whenever fatter belts got it good from upon high, like when grandhamster was upset about the trend towards decreasing cash, you knew the shit pile was going to roll your way soon. So we adjusted. We kept the occasional beer on the balcony or ledge, evidence of female visitors out of the way and never any phone numbers, references to outside interests like motorcycle magazines, hunting, or any other thing that was not Moo in plain sight.

You'd strategically place the school literature or a flyer so it couldn't be missed. This was a keen double-edged sword since they'd have to do it where they lived too, which made it all the more difficult for them mentally. It hurts to learn they could not turn big brother off. It would be there staring at them, even when they slept, even when they were trying to give us shit for no reason, because they were fat and we weren't.

Then there where the pitch-o'dark phone calls on trivial, meaningless issues. Why yes, regional butt-hole, I'm not sure where assistant head instructoid Joe is at, he should be right back, anything to handle? It's like 03:00 and Joe just happened to step out for an ice cream. We considered making a tape we could play into the phone. During one such call well after midnight on some stupid issue I've long forgotten about, one of the group mimicked self indulgence and we laughed out loud to the great dismay of the chap handling the inbound call. Man, did he get an earful. In the end, it all worked out. We learned a great deal about real communication and how to identify early stages of sociopathic traits. But more importantly we finally saw through the illusions.

PART VII

REVELATIONS

"To be persuasive, we must be believable; to be believable we must be credible, to be credible we must be truthful"

—Edward R. Murrow

PART VII—REVELATIONS

MY STARS FOREVER

National Head Instructor Forrest, the number one fifth degree in Moo, was demoted in front of the gathering in the Barn during the Christmas break of 1985. He held too much power amongst the rank and file, too much loyalty and favor, and was starting to see through the Kim. He was stripped of rank and position after the rites of food dispensing, group eating and follow on reception line where Kim would shake hands with each instructor; checking their mind, looking for any subtle hint of defection or of holding something back.

Instructors ate hungrily, wondering when the chasing games or other silly event would take place with no warning. Or dodging a hurled potato, although this was becoming rare with the increasing numbers of small children around as some permitted unions within the cult were generating offspring. As long as Kim was in his command chair seated in front of everyone, watching the group eat and chat minimally, eating his own food as it was brought before him; it was not likely he'd push another instructor into another who would fall into another and so on until there was a pile in the closet, the domino theory of fat, multiplying the effect.

Other games played for Kim's amusement at gatherings were singing and skits or ridiculous attempts at telling jokes, everything was designed to please Kim. This was a twist on an Asian custom in tribal communities where small social groups bond in isolated areas. Kim used the tradition to serve him. Sometimes this would last hours until everyone had thoroughly embarrassed themselves dancing the polka or performing rap songs in front of the merciless group. If Kim laughed you were granted reprieve, your task accomplished. If not, you had to come up with something else. As fewer and fewer were left to perform, the last poor sods were often relegated to just standing there, letting the group howl at them, all in good fun, right. One noted performance had Joe and several cohorts rendering The Twelve Days of Christmas into a choir of disaster. None of them could carry a note, let alone harmony or rhythm. They were pummeled with vegetables and laughed off stage. The mess on the floor did not matter since they were the lower belts and would be charged with cleaning it up.

The games come to a sad end. Kim abruptly orders everything put away and he begins to talk. This was expected, a good hour was the norm. After the meal and the chance to use the washroom, Joe and most of the crew could stand all night. They were accustomed to the long drawn out circular logic of the ramblings of the Kim. At least this time they were inside, but no one was sure where the topic was leading.

Most of the group, it seemed, was half listening, even Forrest was adopting a more relaxed stance, which he was allowed due to his rank. It was the accustomed to sermon about opportunity, and how Moo is now in over 130 countries (a thirty percent increase over last year) and then, Bam! Kim points towards Forrest and says he mishandled the herb business called Renaissance, that it lost over two million dollars since start up and how he has mistreated some instructors. Forrest is ordered out of the room. The other nationals and regionals are shocked. They look afraid. Joe wasn't sure what was up at that point. There is confusion in the herd.

Seizing on this, Kim pulls the crowd together and announces that he has determined that everyone left in the room has an opportunity to travel with him, to make it to the next life. "It is better to leave Earth," he says in that low, deep utterance reserved for times of emphasis. But first, we have to earn.

"There will be," he continues, "eighteen to the right, eighteen to the left, my thirty six stars forever." He taps both his forearms as he is speaking, making it seem real. Kim then explains that nationals Tom and Ken have already earned. Kim turns and offers his hand; they in turn dutifully comply, but seem unsure of what they are agreeing to. Both would end up in jail, Tom for only a year on misdemeanor charges. Kim had him and one other plead to lesser offenses without the knowledge of anyone else so they would be out sooner and be able to run things for Kim while he was still in prison, sentenced to five years. Ken swallowed the whole story and also served the full five as a price for stardom.

Kim then sets the line by having instructors pass before him in rank, shaking each hand to test their strength and checking their look for loyalty. Joe said he never felt the brain probe as some others did he told me. Some were shaken up, Joe said. "Me, yeah I was a little perturbed and Forrest's demotion was hard to take, but I also had to really take a dump, so nature won out."

As the clean up was nearly over, Joe was granted leave to go downstairs from the Barn's loft where the festivities were held; across the courtyard to the basement of the old white house to use the toilet. The bountiful sesame seasonings worked their magic. Joe was careful to wipe up afterward as he had been instructed before leaving the group. As he was exiting the basement, who should be wanting to use the same facility but the grandhamster himself, dressed opulently in goat fur coat and expensive boots; walking slowly, carefully down the stairs, using that low rumble of "Hmmm," just to let you know he's there.

It wasn't known at the time, but Kim's back bothers him a lot. All that Nae Gong and Wae Gong doesn't help much when you're a phony. Kim's higher born trophy wife was waiting for him outside. They walked together slowly to the newly built Green House, both giggling. The master was ready to get in one time, hope he used a glove.

On the way home and for weeks after, no one spoke about Forrest. Some instructors perhaps did not feel as close to him as others, certainly there were those who coveted his position and favor and did not like having to report to him as they felt they knew better. They went to prison too. It was starting to sink in for Joe and the rest of the lower Moos there would be new leadership and expectations in the cult.

Forrest was officially demoted to sixth section. The higher you go, the further you have to fall we were repeatedly told. He spent another six months or so working around the Farm. One day he was simply not there any more. He left his second wife, the one appointed to him by Kim and his additional child there. During the IRS investigations and lead up to the Tax Trial, it was said Forrest was found in a mental health facility in another state, unable to provide any useful assistance to investigators.

During the lecture in the Barn, as Kim was explaining Forrest's mistakes, several of the children were howling and screaming loudly. They would not stop. Everyone tried to ignore them, giving the full required attention to Kim, expecting the kids to quiet down if they were let be long enough. But they didn't, the noise was unsettling, it grew worse. As Kim kept talking, making his points about Forrest, gesturing to the crowd for effect, seeking the approval he craves; the kids were going berserk.

Finally Kim pointed to one and said, "Cassandra, Chum Sa (Kim) have needle, you want needle?" Kim often boasted about his knowledge in the use of needles on pressure points to cure all sorts of ills, even stressed out toddlers. The little girl shrieked in ungodly terror, wailing uncontrollably and clung to her father, a regional instructor. The future felon and hip replacement target scolded the less than two year-old who collapsed in misery at his feet, sobbing. He would be divorced without visitation rights before he finished prison. Joe knew this was all wrong but was not in a position to resolve any of it.

The whole scene was extremely uncomfortable for everyone there, especially for Joe's pod for whom Forrest had held special meaning. They decided not to talk about it back at the commune. Instead, just focus on practice and on handling school. It would be sheer doom to be asked, and they knew it was coming, do you have any questions? The best possible answer was, be alright to say, believe myself and other instructors are clear, be alright to ask if anything needed?

With Forrest gone, the regionals gained new powers which led up to the CBS news fiasco, the Illinois Attorney General Lawsuit against the schools and the forced sale of the Farm. Thankfully for Joe, he had moo-oved on by then.

We remember being told to tell students, if it came up, that for sixth degree there was one mental test Forrest did not pass. He failed in underestimating the extent of Kim's deception.

FORMS PROMISED AND NEVER DELIVERED

Kong Gong Quan

Highest of the high mountain form, Korea is sometimes referred to as the mountain kingdom, this form was said to also be eight, twelve, fourteen hours long depending on what version. Only six "foundation movements" were ever shown, fifteen years go by and they're advertised again. Now, there's got to be more than six movements or it's a really boring form.

Ba Gua (Moogwa) Switches

Let's stick with the Moo-referenced spelling since it's more stupidly appropriate. There was said to be three hundred and sixty different provinces in "old time" China or Asia, which is interchangeable to Moos; and each province had its own switch, or method of changing, but only Moo has them all. Why? So the provinces don't gang up on Moo.

Why three hundred and sixty? How many degrees or sections are there in a circle? You walk a circle when you practice Moogwa don't you? See how much you don't understand. Ever wonder why current Moos only have the seven or maybe eight methods of changing, depending on how you count, that were passed out twenty years ago? Apparently no one has earned any more. Or, maybe it's because the extent of Moo knowledge isn't what they claim.

Tong Nong

Was supposed to be at least eight hours long with no movement repeating itself. Well, about one hundred and thirty-odd steps were given out. Depending on the speed it's about thirty minutes at a slow pace. Notwithstanding the Moos never explained alignment, weighting, torque, let alone breathing; these are just steps and mostly useless in a martial application. The Moo reply was it takes five to seven years of daily practice to be able to directly deploy Tong Nong effectively.

What it will do in the meantime they continue, is develop your beginning form in more effective ways. This is partly true. Try an hour of Tong Nong then practice your favorite blocks and attacks. You'll feel like you can really move and it will look cool. But, in order to be effective there has to be sparing practice and not the Moo choreographed patterns. So one hundred thirty steps has got you what? You'd be better off lifting weights, hitting the bag then free sparring.

Higher Internal Moo Forms

Many students make about sixth section, then let their practice drop but come back after a few weeks and have trouble keeping up with group lesson. If Tong Nong or any other Moo prance was a true internal form the development should stay with you longer. Moo practice is largely external; you loose the pump from the aerobic benefit of Mooing. Of course, the Moo will explain this as their students only practice ten percent correct at best, so it's their fault, not that the teachers ever had it suitably well enough to pass on.

Going to Asia to Learn Alongside Other Higher Belts

Tom White the national Moodroid went to Korea, once; to the Kim or is it Park, family reunion. Upon return he alluded there were so many fifth degrees he did not know where to stand. This was Kim's family so Kim made adjustments in the seating arrangements. Bet most Moos forgot about this hook, it was one that made the Moo so special, make a certain rank and get to go overseas to train. No one has ever done this; there are no international schools of Moo.

18 Weapons

Stop laughing. Look at three section staff or the Pi Yung Su (Si) for a second. The few beginning movements passed out in the last few Weeklong sessions were also the same shown twenty years ago. However, the sustaining hype has been re-worked. In another few short decades if you earn, you might see five or six new moves. Wait, Kim will grab a magazine not found here this week and alter something from it, for your benefit, if you bring extra down. Or just make it up after a little consultation with above power. It's not the movements so much as who is teaching you right? Keep trying hard and keep bringing down. You're not done yet, still not ready to stop believing.

Zen Archery

This ancient art was said to have been mastered by Kim's direct line ancestor, the Khan family. Yes, Kim claimed lineage to Genghis & Kublai. This was one of the reasons to have the Farm, the Ranch and just before the Tax Case the properties under review in New Mexico and Arizona. The latter of these were to have training grounds for special horses and we'd learn to ride bareback, make our own bows and arrows in the true Moo tradition and learn from the greatest of the great unknown master archers, the Kim; or is his name really Jack Park. The only limit on our future was Kim's telekinetic imagination and our willingness to believe.

WEAPONS START TO MOVE – OR NOT

Joe received a call at the house early on a Saturday morning. The front window had been broken and the school vandalized, a panicked sixth section reported. He was on the way to work and saw the shattered glass. Joe sent the alert up the chain of command and was ordered to secure the school with backup from the commune.

The fatter belts arrived soon after Joe and since it was a few hours before school started, and no students were around, they began their screaming. Joe stepped back through the shattered window frame and headed for the car. He had been handed change the night before and knew he could find a real job in short order. The regionals were in disbelief. They didn't want to have to clean up the mess and report a main instructor had walked, so they tried a different approach, they played nice. Joe realized they were acquiescing as much as their position would allow so he said what any self respecting Moo does to cover his ass, he said he'd ask national instructors "which way" (Moo-speak for pretending to ask for guidance) since they called just as he was leaving from home. They hadn't, Joe was bluffing, but he also knew one of the nationals would support him if only to tweak the regionals.

Suddenly everyone was calm. Joe began collecting the bigger pieces of glass and in short order began inventorying what was taken. He was dumb like that. So long as no one was screaming at him he'd do what needed to be done. The regionals sat on their thumbs and decided they had something to handle and left. Before school opened, the window was boarded-up, the office, waiting area and practice room cleaned. The graphiti scribbled in magic marker by the offenders was scrubbed and painted over that day. It was as if they didn't want to cause excessive damage, or they were in a hurry.

Within two days new glass was installed, and the missing weapons replenished from other schools. About a half dozen swords and long spears were taken, nothing of high value surprisingly. The replica Samurai swords with plastic handles although sharp and long bladed would have made too obvious a trophy in the neighborhood and were let be.

The main front window had been knocked in with the butt of an assault rifle, it was discovered. A teenage student with behavioral problems had a knife taken away from him and he wanted it back. The punk got a few of his alternative educational facility mates to borrow one of their father's guns and took their revenge on the school.

Joe figured out who it was, the student had quit some months ago and was heard bragging around his high school he had authentic weapons for sale. Joe asked fatter belts if the police should be made aware, as this was the big reason they screamed at him so profusely that morning, he had begun to clean up when the scene should have been preserved for evidence they said.

"No, don't do anything," word came back, "it will be handled differently." At the end of weekly instructor's meeting, every main instructor was holding back their rage at whoever would have committed such a heinous act against the Quan. We were in their towns helping them after all, teaching their children and giving them all a chance to be better. What type of no-mind would dare do this?

It didn't matter. Nothing to worry about, the newly appointed lead national explained. It was a select group that night, main instructors and up, only those that had been around for long enough to be trusted with vital information were in the room.

"Master mentioned," began the national, "that very soon, those weapons are going to start to move around. Don't think too much about, but once whoever took them sees the kombs and staffs moving towards him, pretty sure he's gonna bring them back."

After a time in most groups people are receptive enough they know the others to an extent whereby they can perceive considerably the reactions and thoughts their colleagues are likely to generate. Joe was not the only one in the room who was in disbelief after hearing the national instructor's words. Few of the many no-minds there that night continued to have faith with the same conviction held the day before.

A week goes by, and then a month and nothing is mentioned about the stolen weapons or the break-in. It could have been easily taken care of, restitution made and the school property recovered. But no, the master is going to use supreme mental powers and terrorize the thieves into submission. Joe receives a call at school from the lead national. After the requisite checking if anything to handle and how is everything in school parroting, the national explains Master made a decision not to use supreme higher mental form as it would cause too much confusion and bring wrong type attention towards school. Whatever wrong thing they did, it will come back to them; the national finished relaying Kim's message. "Do you have any other questions, Joe?"

"Be alright, not. Yes, thank you national instructor." Joe wished again he had a tape recorder to play that line back rather than having to use it repeatedly. It was beginning to make less and less sense each day.

SHOES – THE REMIX

There was a certain large assistant who was having a hard time Mooing. He'd try then get yelled at by his regional instructor idol and not understand why. He would quit his good paying but boring tooling job, the one he had trained years for; languishing alone in the apartment shared with other cult members while they toiled in their day jobs, convinced his troubles were not his doing. He was right of course, but his anger misdirected. He blamed his friends even when they offered genuine help. Few it seemed, would listen to him.

He, like most of us did not realize he was simply going through the Moo break down process, being worked on to ready the human raw material we were for whatever purpose Kim would ultimately devise. We all went through it, yet didn't recognize when it was being applied. Kim is adept, nigh a master at keeping the Moo brain-in-training occupied for a reason. Life was bleak. Performance, achievements in many areas suffered for those subject to the Moo-vironment. During this troubled time, the assistant stepped into school one day.

"You are late, what happened?" asked Joe of his subordinate.

"I stopped to buy shoes," he said and motioned towards his feet.

What followed was catastrophic. It's fifteen minutes before group, naturally; informations are wondering around the waiting room, the special private course students are running the fifth section amok, both phones are ringing, fatter belts are on the way and now there is a shoe purchase mistake.

The large assistant visibly slumped, in stark realization since it was the first thing he bought that day, they had to be returned. Absolutely had to immediately or something bad would happen per the understanding of Moo doctrine passed to him by his idol, a future felon who did not do well on camera. Even buying a stick of gum before he bought the shoes would have defeated the Moo-voodoo. But he had forgotten what he believed.

During these few excruciating moments Joe stood gaping in wonderment, taken completely aback to an extent nearly as great as watching the highest belt ever administer punishment to a near frozen ex-head instructoid. The ramifications of this screw-up were deep. Breaking a Moo code, above all a nebulous one, was infinitely worse than just about anything else imaginable.

Often times the assistant and Joe would discuss how to handle, how things and which things should be passed and at what level to students. Joe had come from another place and things were different here, although you'd never want to say that out loud.

See, it was the large assistant who had told me this very same Moo belief as told to him sometime earlier by his idol who was now enroute for the group interruption standing lecture debacle. Group would get started, thirty minutes into it the arrival would occur and the rest of lesson would be a dissertation of Moo virtues. Attendance suffered per plan. Only the chosen payees will make it through, they have to earn.

Joe and the assistant both knew money could not be handed for shoes, because if you gave someone shoes, according to Moo theory, it meant you wanted them to leave. His large friend's additional take as passed from his idol was if you bought shoes you had to buy something else first, prior to buying the shoes, and before stepping into school. If you didn't buy something else first before buying new shoes it was very bad, if you were a Moo. If you then stepped into school it was a huge mental mistake, punishable by untold horrible condemnation that would last and last and was difficult if not impossible to undo. The entire fate of your Moo career was in jeopardy from this tiny error. And, you would be yelled at.

Joe understood it was a good idea not to make a big deal about it, if you need shoes, you need shoes. If you feel uncomfortable about wearing new shoes into school, then don't do it. Early on they had agreed to each pursue their own understanding until it was clarified, then share. For the time being they would not pass this on to students; they'd probably get talked to from a fatter belt soon enough and they would deal with it then.

Joe never passed this conversation on to any lower belt although we at the commune did discuss it from time to time. It seemed like one of the many not fully explained items purged to us en mass. We were meaning to ask about it but never wanted to venture the exposure for fear of suspicion. See how much you don't understand? Can't trust, must be confused.

Joe and the large assistant had reviewed this exact issue on shoe purchase protocol within the past week and then still, after explaining his understanding, it was agreed, you have to follow as you see best. After all that he does what he does. It was if he wanted it to happen.

Well it did. Something weird was due to occur during these twice-weekly events, the pending fatter belt arriving at the middle of group, his trademark; and this was gonna be it. No, not the missing assistant through group lesson out refunding shoes, which was explainable, something similar happened often enough. The fact Joe did not check close enough beforehand was going to be the issue. And was it ever.

Post group, after several hours of continuous screaming with it ending by the fatter belt storming out of school without the envelope and informing instructor course and most of the contiguous geography about Joe's general incompetence, it wasn't shoe-specific, just a general rant; the large assistant confided, "I don't think I ever heard him yell at anybody like that before and I know I've never been yelled at by anyone else like that in my entire life, but you just stood there, without blinking."

Joe glanced over at his cohort as if he were a giant tuna melt sandwich standing on end. His measured reply was, "Did you take the shoes back for a refund?"

"Yes," was the large one's answer.

"Well, we're back at square one for today, let's pack it up and see if we can do better tomorrow," was all Joe could say. He went in the backroom and began Moogwa, selfishly attempting to escape reality. He had shut the door, the assistant knocked and asked if he could handle the office. "Go ahead," Joe Moogwaed back. You don't want to break form so you try to utter some kind of reply while still breathing laboriously.

After finishing and upon changing, Joe found the assistant already gone; however the office was correctly cleaned and set, Moo-speak for ready for the next day. The fatter belt was notorious for leaving a mess, this night it was spectacular. He also left an envelope full of cash from the day's intake, a huge error in the game of Moo.

Cleaning the office was the large assistant's favorite part of the day, his specialty. He'd take longer than others would, to do similar chores. But he had as Moos say, come up there, from white belt to first degree, so Joe left him alone. If given a choice between starting practice and handling the office, he'd jump at the latter; it was his connection to the attention of the fatter belt I guess.

Why he didn't mention the envelope was puzzling. For sure he'd seen it. Joe considered the situation then called the nightly rotation reporting camp and said he forgot to mention the envelope, which of course was crap but it would save him from more screaming at least for awhile. Other, more reasonable fatter belts were there and would likely just want the missing cash brought over so they could "figure up which way" (finish the counting) and go home.

Confirming the amount via the high order cloak-and-dagger verbalizations used for centuries, Joe booked a flight plan for the south 'burbs and hustled over. It was just one more night of inefficient Moo. He didn't know it then, but enough cash to feed and house the entire organization for a week would be wasted at a casino by Kim in the days ahead from the packet in Joe's right sock.

The next day, surprisingly on time to move around some and review the plan for the group lesson; the large assistant shows up wearing the refunded, repurchased, new shoes. Assuming the procedure was followed properly this time at least to the buyer's satisfaction, and wanting to move forward, Joe merely intoned, "Go change."

The group went well. No interruptions, good enthusiasm, the assistant performed some sales course demos, we had a new course signing and he even used the washroom when he said he wanted to. This alleviated the further need to also check on that part, lest he hold it too long and then fall asleep on the toilet after class. We'd then have the requisite explanation to fatter belt when he called for the results of tonight's episode of Where's the Assistant? Dynamic screaming, the type where the phone cuts out, could be expected during this part of the game show.

Late into that night came the anticipated follow-up telephonic probe to ensure the large one had unquestioningly complied with Moo shoe regulations. Joe flatly indicated he had, the other end of the phone hung up. Very late the night after that and into early morning, a screaming was again received, via the U-shaped plastic voice tube hanging on the wall at the commune, for lying to a fatter belt about whether or not the assistant had been checked on day two to verify the shoe purchase procedure.

Additional concern on this issue was defrayed by explaining Joe knew there was no way he'd make the same mistake twice; from his non-verbal communication upon stepping into school the second day, it was clearly indicated all was in order, instructor's honor. Thus, "Yes I had checked towards him and was satisfied to the best I was aware, more correct ways had been handled," Joe explained in Moo verbal etiquette. Again the phone disconnects.

To his utter amazement, Joe was promoted shortly thereafter, to third degree with record setting low probation; his proven abilities to handle noted as a strength by the even fatter, fatter belt. Rank, despite anything else, was because of attention to the cash. There would be no test, only promotion, in a group setting at the end of weekly instructor lessons.

If he didn't know any better and obviously he didn't since he continued to Moo, Joe conveyed; it was if an even fatter belt, the fattest one, the Kim, was listening in the whole time. It was all according to plan.

BETTER MIND, BETTER BODY

At the school to where Joe was newly stationed, he noticed the kombs had the old rope-covered handles. He asked, at the appropriate time, about replacing them as had been ordered at his previous station. "This is not the other school, understand!!?" Another Moo-mandated screaming session followed.

Not long thereafter, instructor course was getting in a lesson under the supervision of a very capable assistant. One who woke up quickly in a few short months as his opportunity to quit his high paying job, dump his girlfriend and leave his possessions behind to handle Moo in another state would be de-selected in favor of a real life. This assistant was qualified in all aspects of school and well liked by students. It was Kim's systems that let everyone down.

The komb form the wanna-be instructors were parroting this night has a stupid move built into it where from a horse stance, feet shoulder width part, legs bent at the knees, thighs approach right angle; the machete is pulled from high over head with both hands and thrust downward between the knees and up as it passes behind, as if to spear an attacker from underneath.

The problem was as a sixth section thrust the sword down between his legs the overly long blade stuck in the carpet and his hand slipped over the inferior guard, slicing three of his fingers about half-way through. Turns out the kombs were not supposed to be used, in fact the regional in charge had been ordered to take them out of school, but neglected to pass this tidbit along to Joe or anyone else.

"Be alright to say," began the assistant after knocking first, "there is a problem." The sixth section was sheepishly put forth, but he could not hide his pain.

"Let me see how bad," Joe began. The student, Jack, tried to oblige but opening his hand a fraction revealed a deep cut, possibly to the tendons.

"Okay, keep it closed," Joe continued, "did you feel bone?" The black Moo belt wanna-be nodded no. Two instructor course students were dispatched to first help Jack change then take him to the hospital. Joe and the assistant wrapped Jack's hand in paper towels and antiseptic duct tape. The student fearful he mistaked, Joe and the assistant fearful for Jack's injury and whether or not it could be healed.

The doctor who saved Jack's fingers and hand by performing micro surgery had been a student for one month at that school the year before. He left after the first conversation about special private course. Jack, under the careful guidance of national instructors, would file a Workman's Compensation claim as he was self-employed and could easily say he injured himself at a late hours job site. Handling the deductible and uncovered costs for follow-up would take several months and cost nearly as much as the down payment he put towards instructor course. It would be some time before he could again use a hammer or a komb.

Luckily for Joe when he reported the incident, a national instructor, one who would also serve five years for Kim, took the call. Thus minimal screaming would be endured from the regional fat boy. Joe was just about to head to the hospital, after nearly three hours of waiting for follow-up calls and being told to standby for further orders; when Jack returned to school with the other students. Joe calls back to the national, who by now was near Kim, and they both spoke to Jack. This buoyed his spirits immensely. Relax, you've got master charge, was an old adage repeated at odd times in the Moo. Kim was going to mention he said, what certain forms Jack would be given to rebuild his fingers better then new it was promised.

The trade off, Joe said with hindsight, offered by the all powerful wizard of Moo was not apparent until several years after he left the cult. No claim versus the school? Insurance claim you take care? Means more right mind you have, special form you will get in. In reality the hidden message was that form you were practicing hundreds of times has no martial applications, and besides that's not what we're about. We are about Moo. However, as you have right mind and have proven yourself worthy, you will receive guidance to fix what never should have been broken.

A couple of weeks pass and Jack's stitches come out. He got in the special form, passed in the true spirit of Moo Doc. The national called Joe and talked him though it over the phone for five minutes until satisfied all the slight nuances and technical details not disclosed for centuries were fully ingrained in Joe's memory.

The mystery form: Palm up, arm out on front, on table or desk or thigh, relaxed. Start with fingers fully extended then slowly bring in as a fist over a twenty count. Then hold in a fist for twenty count; then begin opening the first (and here's the most important part) concentrate on every filament and ligament, put concentration on every tiny feeling as you go, but don't over stress the injury. Only apply mental pressure as much as you think you can take when opening the hand. Once the hand is fully open count twenty. Then begin again, do this for ten times, three times a day. Joe would watch Jack do it every day in the office then ask him to make sure he was doing it on his own. The key was not to over-exert the damaged fingers. Eventually the wound did heal and Jack did regain full movement in his hand, thanks to the surgery and not to the magic beans fist closing. It helped put the student's mind towards healing perhaps, and one could argue pros and cons of rehabilitation methods. But to say the Moo or Kim has any kind of superior knowledge is a farce.

You need to understand there are so many accounts of students injuring themselves it is impossible to include in this volume. Another book could be easily written. Multiply by the stories told by the hundreds of Instructor Joes over the past thirty years and you will quickly realize that Moo is truly "wrong way exercise," the term they use to label anything non-Moo.

Joe blew his knee out while practicing on his own between lessons in school one day. The form he was doing so it was said, develops coordination and timing for kicking and was taught at middle belt up to instructor levels. It was a couple of movements put together to look like something if you worked it the length of the room, repeating each side ending with a locked leg kick, trying to touch knee to forehead after every three or five steps. He had this form for years and was reviewing it for that night's student group lesson, when suddenly there was a surprise pull from behind his left knee. He kept going but soon it was apparent something was wrong. It swelled so much that by night time group he could not walk to the front of class without anyone noticing.

There was an instructor lesson scheduled that night, Joe hoped a little rest would do the trick, plus a double cheeseburger and the magic acetaminophen he kept stashed in the car. A good day in Moo was no dingys causing problems, no regionals screaming and a decent meal before going to instructor group. Do a couple Tylenols with a Diet Coke on the way over, Mooing past midnight was no problem.

Temporarily it seemed to help, he did a couple more on the way but Joe was going to have to ask about this one he knew. During group, both nationals are there and they review Tong Nong, all of it. Joe can't keep up, lifting his elephant-sized leg above the waist is nonsense, but rather than say something he takes the screaming in front of everyone and is told to step out front.

In the office the lead national asks what is wrong, "You are moving like you have lead in your legs, why?"

Joe asks in Moo-speak, "If be alright, if can point to one part." The nationals impatiently grant permission. Joe rolls up his pant leg while the nationals looked on, confused, and he points to the back of his knee which is now so swollen his thigh, knee and calf are all the same size. Plus there's a cool looking blue streak from the vein that isn't cooperating.

The nationals smirk and chastise Joe for being stupid, it's his fault, why he didn't say something. Like they would have listened, or cared. He is ordered to stay home from school for the next day, another instructor fills in. The pain intensifies; his whole leg goes numb at one point. Applying a towel and hot water with Epsom salts helps immensely. The phone starts up; it's his favorite fat regional calling who immediately begins screaming for not answering the phone by the first ring. Joe is told to rest and not worry about school, but don't go to sleep, that's not correct as everyone else is trying hard. Master is aware of his plight, Joe is told, so don't worry, it will be mentioned what to do later on. For right now, keep resting, don't watch TV and keep reviewing mentally which students can get on course, keep mind in school, understand?

Joe goes back to the couch for some more hot Epsom salts and then takes a nap, laying out on the radiantly heated floor. This was the best thing he could have done. The slow heat along with the magnesium from the salts worked to loosen the muscles enough for circulation to return. At one point his toes were so fat they all touched and he could not wiggle them, the fluid build up was so intense. When other instructors made it home from school that night, the entertainment for the evening was laughing at Joe's foot and trying to tickle it when he wasn't looking. At least his knee felt better and he could bend it a little, although painfully.

Two more days go by before anything is explained, received as gospel in Moo, about Joe's leg. He opened school on Saturday but was told he did not have to change into uniform, additional assistants were sent over and they performed well. On Sunday night he gets a call from the regional with the word from on high. It was explained that it was like you opened your knee joint up, hit everything with a hammer, then put it back together; Master had told the regional. "The best thing for it is rest, and if you have them, Epsom salts; do you know what they are? They have magnesium, and mag… will…" Joe held the phone away from his ear so he didn't have to listen; waiting until he could say yes, thank you, regional instructor and could hang up.

The volume and frequency of students whose bodies became "stuck" after practicing Moo is legendary. Stuck could range from severe muscle cramps to internal organ failure. Kim did not know what to do, only to label the student as committing the error, it's his fault, he got stuck. Kim would delay taking any action until he had time to assess the threat to his cash flows and to concoct a story. When a student got stuck from over-exertion for long periods and lack of water, taking a hot bath and eating hot soup was the answer from on high. But don't face north and keep clear mind or something bad will happen.

In one case Joe was told by Kim via his favorite national, to deny culpability, on how to insert sterilized needles into the finger tips to make circulation flow to alleviate a student's dilemma of extreme stuck. For two days in a row this was repeated. Then, in a rare show of personal concern for cash flows, Kim spoke on the phone directly to the first degree student. The condition persisted for a week. The student, at the begging of his wife went to a hospital emergency room and was given fluids intravenously to prevent his organs from shutting down. Three months later weighing all the mumbo jumbo about a better life, the mysticism and the limited real self-defense and martial skills learned vs. reality, this first degree also declined his opportunity to move out of state and dump everything behind. He was better off, he chose wisely.

The cult would go to great lengths to ensure all remaining followers preserved their concentration towards the organization. This is the main reason people leaving the organization were not discussed and if brought up by another student, the defector was trashed. He lost his mind, went crazy; or could not handle, was not qualified, was selfish. Kim gives out descriptors to make it more convincing to the remaining saps to keep their eliteness alive. The Pa Doe or wrong path, is the label given to those who Moo and then leave. The truth is it's the devil lying, saying he is the holder of the light. It's authentic form like Louhan being twisted into Par Gae, it is Pa Kua being twisted into Moogwa, it is a jump kick on a roof being sold as floating on air. It's a back alley fight being sold as champion of all Asia.

Once on instructor course in Moo, by all accounts this guaranteed a direct connect to all the knowledge anyone would ever need for a better life for themselves and families. The truth is the opposite. It is the worst thing for anyone or their families.

The Moo cult, ever seeking new ways to suck cash from the working class, has been selling their new scam Master Key of Wisdom. Literature to help those find their way after the martial arts bit, the various herb sales bits, and the other scam companies failed. The Moo even spent other people's money to have symbols and slogans Trademarked in hopes of gaining more credibility for their lies. In recent years Kim has tried to hide ownership of the current round of business exploits and properties through the use of the Kim Family Trust held in his wife's name. Her name is often misspelled in legal recordings in hopes of deflecting scrutiny, another old Moo ploy. If he can get you to hold the assets in your name, that's fine too.

This fools no one, nor did the prophecy that red-tipped lettuce reduces high blood pressure. A forty-something year-old instructor course had to wait months for Kim to look that up. Or, the cure for another instructor's diabetes was certainly available in the Moo archives, but first he'd have to earn. Past fourth degree with over ten years in, he figured he had earned enough and took his head instructorship and three schools elsewhere.

GRIND HIS BONES INTO PASTE

During one of the daily telephone calls into his higher handlers, Joe mentioned that a certain black belt course student has quit in response to the rough, demeaning conversation the same regional now on the phone used towards the student the day earlier.

"He called in to say he was not coming in anymore, said he had paid for what he felt he was taught and doesn't want anything further to do with us," Joe informed his regional. The student was well educated and worked for a major corporation downtown. He was business savvy and told Joe the instructor, who was not educated and had no formal business training, that the contracts the school uses are invalid. In fact, the student continued, to try to coerce people into signing them is fraud or perhaps even theft by swindle, his lawyer would look into it if the school wanted to make an issue of paying off the course as demanded by the regional.

After relaying this information to his handler, the response was not exactly what Joe thought was coming. Instead it came from deep out of left field.

"You call him back at work, right now, and you yell at him real good, you understand? You tell him you will grind his bones into paste if he doesn't pay. You do that, and then call me back," the regional barked into the receiver at Joe. The line disconnected, the regional hung up.

Joe thought about this for half an hour or so and let an assistant handle the afternoon group. Then he ordered a couple of sandwiches, and walked next door to pick them up, something he infrequently did himself. Clearing his head, he figured out what to do.

"Be alright to say," Joe began cautiously into the phone, "be alright I did call that one student and say to him what you told me to say, I think he was scared real good," Joe said to the stupid regional.

"Yeah," said the regional back, "well good, it's about time you figured out we don't let people walk away from contracts so they can tell all their friends about it. It puts a bad word out on the street that people don't have to pay, understand?"

Joe was beginning to. It's why he never called the student at work. He really enjoyed the rest of his sandwich.

CERTIFICATES

About one month after third degree promotions were announced, Joe was home early on a Friday night, a rare event. He was not scheduled for rotation at another school to report in cash, new courses and to be checked himself. An assistant regional who would play a pivotal role during the future IRS raids was running the show that night for the northern sector of Moo world. Instructor course had been let out early under the updated let them enjoy their youth program now in effect. By ten o'clock p.m. on this nice late summer evening, Joe was camped with a highly radiated frozen pizza and two liter soda companion in front of the twelve-inch black and white.

As he starts on his third slice, the U-shaped tube of doom begins to chatter. The ringer had been modified by bending the metal tabs between the bells to lesson the noise late at night. It's the friendly neighborhood national; the level headed one who has been running the main instructor group lessons and pretty much the majority of the organization since Forrest was removed. Ken wants Joe at the

Lombard school ASAP, nothing to handle just get here and bring your uniform.

Lombard was nicknamed the fortress or simply the Fort by Joe and colleagues. It sits in the middle of an older plaza and with the thick pillars and stone façade out front, it holds a distinctive appeal. Joe and the other instructors who live nearby were handed extra keys by the national so they could practice at will, within reason. This location was ideal for many due to its central location and most of the main instructor groups were held there. The practice room was large, about 2500 square feet with a high ceiling and nice big Judo mat, a real one.

Upon arrival in just a few minutes, Joe finds the national alone. Another main instructor who tested first degree, second degree and was promoted with Joe the same night to third degree arrives as Joe is changing into uniform. They are good friends, have worked on new locations, banquet preparations and campout logistics many times before. In the instructor groups they often practice together. Both have extra keys to the Fort.

"What's up?" Joe asks Larry in confidence in the back of the practice room. "Why are we at the Fort on a Friday?"

His friend beams back at Joe and says simply, "Certificates."

"Okay, step out," says Ken the national. Both Larry and Joe were each photographed holding double swords across their bare chests, the tips covering up the points near the front tops of each shoulder.

"Some instructors are uneven," the national remarked, adjusting one komb several times to cross over Joe's right shoulder. Joe did his best to keep the sword in the proper position for the picture. He felt the need to explain how he had dislocated the shoulder practicing as a fourth section attempting to dive and roll over six students, when five was iffy and there was scant room to land or to get a good running start. He sacrificed his body when he landed poorly and misjudged his landing but still avoided crashing into the wall. He thought at the time he was pushed past his capabilities. It didn't matter much now aside from the misalignment of the welded joint he had for a shoulder.

Pictures were over soon and they were dismissed. They thanked and bowed and asked if anything was needed, but Ken had to report back himself. He handed enough spare change for them to have dinner, there was an all-you-can-eat steak and shrimp special at the Sizzler in Oakbrook. This was a perennial favorite as they had not been kicked out of there as they had in Lombard and Naperville locations for competition seafood smuggling out of the restaurant. Hey guys, you have to eat it here, you can't take it home.

The national explained the photographs will be presented to Master, and if accepted, will be sent on for approval for certificate. This might take awhile, because Master has to submit to Asian governments. But, Ken revealed, "If Master says certain ones should get in certificates, then pretty much it will happen." Larry and Joe were sent on their way to set a new record at the Sizzler.

After a few weeks in the middle of the afternoon, the national drives up to the school Joe was handling and brings in a box containing two large frames wrapped carefully. It is a nail day. Joe was relieved to see it was the national by himself without the screaming regional along for the ride. Would have just been extra weight. Those two did not get along, the national most likely ordered the screamer to stay behind and find something to handle. Just as well because the existing certificates on the wall would have to be re-aligned, the screamer's ego would also need an adjustment. His certificates would have to be re-positioned to make room.

The issuance and approval of certificates was supposed to be a key milestone in a Moodroid's career. It meant you were set. Physically, mentally certified to teach and handle and also financially. After a minimum of three years handling school full-time with certificate reached, the instructor's future family would be taken care of indefinitely. Only things to do are handle, practice and eat. Nothing to think about at this point except keep school strong, everything else is taken care of by the organization the way it has been in Asia for centuries.

In reality this was nothing more than a pyramid scheme. Moo financial success depends on a steady flow of new contributors putting ever more money into the system. The organization in stasis consumes more cash than it generates. Sometimes, if it was found out a student was particularly wealthy, their course prices and test fees for black belt and higher were grossly inflated. As it became apparent most of the existing instructor course in the pipeline were completely tapped out, a new type of certificate would be offered.

It was for those who still wanted to reach that level of achievement but would probably not end up handling a school full time. It was sold as there are many people who have law degrees and perhaps they passed the bar exam too, but they did not go into business as a lawyer. See? Moo is just like that, we're credible too.

In these cases the certificate filing fee was announced as starting at ten thousand dollars. Fees of twenty-five thousand were rumored and one needy soul with better mind and better education; was said to be willing as ridiculous as it sounds now, to bring in one hundred thousand dollars. Ultimately he didn't, instead he provided evidence to investigators during the Tax Case.

These huge fees stunned Joe. He worked his hands to the bone, and forked over every dime he had; enduring broken shoulders, ribs, near drowning, and stood on the line everyday trying to succeed in an environment completely hostile to true mind and body. He finished off his eighteen thousand dollar instructor course just before being assigned to a school full time after four and a half years in Moo. Now, three years in, he was completely broke. But, he had certificates.

With all sincerity I can say Joe was quite humble about his certificate going up; he only mentioned it to me after many years when we began to compile our exploits here. Most students did not notice the new certificates of their instructor; the regional who had the lease in his name did not tell students what it meant, the significance, the legacy. This is because he knew the certificates were made in the Barn by the nationals and Kim at the Farm after being sent out for a little engraving in pseudo Chinese-looking symbols. The English translation version means what ever you want it to mean.

Most students never got close enough to read it. One day a regional Joe had not seen in many months was sent in to handle cleaning the certificates on a nail day. Joe would also be given this duty as he was determined to have reached certain point of clear enough mind. The visiting regional had not been informed Joe had achieved the milestone, but he offered congratulations nonetheless upon seeing the newly placed certificates. Mostly it was good tenure for that regional too, since he had signed Joe up as white belt long ago and once broke his ribs demonstrating how side kick should get in when Joe was temporarily not clear as the Farm swung into full Moo mode.

It was strangely funny Joe thought, that by the time he achieved his certificate he was beginning to question a lot more things and realized he was going to have to come to terms with them if he was to Moo on.

I'LL TAKE PAR GAE FOR FIFTEEN THOUSAND, PLEASE

Category: Cash, for fifteen thousand. Answer is: Thank you for getting me on course, regional head Moo-structor. Moo-testant: What is, what point do you want to reach?

That's Correct! Suppose you were in a car accident or a party to a legal dispute some years back and received a settlement of let's say, seventy-five thousand. What are you going to do with all of it? Well, it depends. If you Moo, you are going to spend most, if not all on yourself to help you improve. And the Moo is there for you before someone steals the money and gives you nothing in return. You will earn rank in a little bit different way. This was the ruse to explain why some students moved so rapidly through belt rank even though form could not be remembered and strength of movements was poor. Moo was their Sheppard, they shall not want.

It could have been a trust fund, an inheritance, money the lower belt had skimped and saved for in their factory job or the fact the student made so much money hustling others they could not see he or she was being hustled by Moo. Maybe they were lonely and would part with their cash in exchange for membership where they could be accepted.

In one case, for ten thousand cash a newly approved instructor course received lessons in special eye movements to help him improve his vision so he would not need glasses any more. It had nothing to do with an accident; this was his long time personal goal and the Moo was going to help him achieve it, just like they were helping the other members of his family achieve their own personal cash contribution objectives.

A national instructor would call to make sure the cash, and the student, were in school at the time pre-arranged. The big Moo would show up, make sure the cash was there and just to play with the main instructor make a comment like, "Seems like some of it is missing, how much is here?" after flipping through the stack of C-notes. Then the coffee and donut offering rite would take place. Finally after two hours, maybe more, and the student looking for reason to leave, the super special restricted to only those most worthy lesson would begin.

In the back room, lights off, stand relaxed. Hold your thumb up to the farthest corner of clear sight without moving your head. Concentrate on the point at the top of your thumb. Hold the target at different heights and positions to make the eye muscles elongate and strengthen. Down low at five o'clock, then at three, then at one o'clock. Try for thirty seconds each point to start but as your eyes strengthen you can do more. By the time you can do two minutes without moving your head or eyes at any point; then your vision will improve. You probably feel right now, right? Using abbreviated English mixed with Korean slang parlance or if you're good, a Korean accent, adds credibility when working this hustle.

Now try the other side. Do this form three times per day and ask instructors if you have any questions. How's your family? When are they coming in again? I have to stay on schedule, was a little bit behind today arriving here as had other students to check and the same with right now, need to keep checking schools and students. No time even for myself. As higher belt it's all about giving back. Oh, and don't explain this form to anyone else, you understand. They did not earn.

Twenty minutes after the lesson actually started, the ten thousand and the national were pulling away from the ATM referred to as a school. Now and again that student might be looked at during the next few months. The main reason naturally, was to get the rest of his cash.

Another student, Miss lonely heart, desperately sought long term friendship and liked the physical workouts. Yoga at the YMCA would have been a healthier option but instead she chooses Moo.

Ignored until finally succumbing to signing black belt course six months after being in school, her holding off only led to more disappointment. Turns out she had stocked away a pile of dough from her really high paying job, had flexible hours and a good heart. More important for her future was an open mind and wallet. She believed Moo would help fulfill her dreams just as it has for hundreds of thousand of others just like her in over one hundred countries. See? You're not alone. For fifteen thousand, she would learn to be a black belt.

"There are women higher belts in Moo, not many as it is more difficult to make, but we think you've got what it takes," the pudgy regional explained. She called back and said she had some questions. The regional launched into the schpeel about reneging on a commitment, until he paused for a gulp of air. "Oh, what's that, you want to pay all at once, in cash? Well, yes, that will be alright. When can you make it in?"

When the student obediently brought in the money, in one hundred-dollar bills tucked neatly inside a plain white business envelope, her personalized Moo-fomercial lasted half an hour. Of course she was told to warm up first and that took another hour before the regional cash collector decided she was ready, the Benjamins secured in the office desk drawer. By the time the lesson took place, suggestive enhancements filled the void between high hopes and lowered expectations.

"See! See how it feels, I'll bet you feel it right now, don't you?" the not ready for prime time regional huckster chirped, emphasizing the fine points of the joint stretching bastardization sold as royal form.

"What you are learning," he continued, smiling as the student groaned into the low crouching stoop, arching her back and feeling the form get into her hips, "what you are learning is so much more advanced, like I told you before, you do this for even just a few weeks and your body will dramatically change. This is authentic, proven methods, not watered down. All that wrong way exercise stuff you see in health clubs and on television can trace some part of it to what you are learning here, right now."

Ever wonder how those guys on cable infomercials learned their trade? Well, no doubt it came from Moo. The only difference is you can't return Moo the way you can ship back freight collect unwanted giant ironing boards with handles. But Moo will tuck neatly under your subconscious until you're ready to pay more.

Kim arrived before a small group of instructors who were tasked to weekend rotation. It was a surprise visit; he was picking up the cash himself and not waiting for it to be delivered. He sat on the edge of the waiting room couch, leaning forward, keeping the weight off his lower back. Pressured to give out a tidbit to keep the master thing going, he offered this, out of the blue, "Certain instructors you see wearing glasses, once certain form get in, this will go away. Hmmm, pretty soon I start to explain which way towards nationals and they will pass towards those who need most first, then to all instructors, but first you have to earn. I give quick example…"

Kim rubbed his hands together and told the droids standing there to do same, then he held his open palms up to his face, covering the eyes to block out the light. He instructed the black belted audience, "Keep eyes open and look up, down, all around. But, don't show towards optometrist. They just take advantage. Charge too much."

Hmmm, optometrist you say. Pretty good for a guy who doesn't understand Engrish and needed interpreters in front of a judge. The follow-up to the special hands over face super-duper eye form was immersion in cold clear water to remove errant mucus and of course the staring at your thumb holding out to the side form. These were never practiced in a class for instructors. Instead they were merely talked about, alluded to yet still considered viable teachings by Moos, something to drum up sales.

Remember that Joe was told to check the eye movements of that one student? When asked questions, he said what all good Moos do when confronted with something they can't answer, "I'll ask higher belts that question." Eventually, via telephone, his regional furthered the question to the national who first got the student in the wallet draining form. In tandem via the chain of Moo command they would coach Joe or any other instructor in similar circumstances on how to check any special case student. What the student receives in Moo is simulated near-real instruction (see e-Moo Direct in the following sections). It is as good as you can imagine.

Towards the end of his time in Moo, Joe remembers walking in to the kitchen of his higher belt's rented house one Saturday morning and found him sitting at the table, belly sticking out, with glasses on, gazing at the newspaper in royal style. Joe said he laughed to himself, hoping he didn't end up like that. Then he realized it was aloud.

The regional quickly removed his glasses then gave out orders for the day. Guess that special eye form isn't used by everyone or it takes awhile to work, in some cases, Joe thought as he headed to school for another day of Mooing. Same thing with that weight reduction special movement, and the mental communication building…

The Bates Method is the proven source of the palming technique twisted and gotten wrong again by Kim. Dr. Bates did most of his work pre-World War II. His research published after his death, it has become popular with those seeking alternatives to corrective eyeglasses. For less than twenty dollars at any retail bookseller, you can learn the techniques yourself. It's not magic, just common sense backed up by years of clinical observation and evaluation by those truly qualified to explain. Bet they even have certificates to prove it.

At the peak of Moo in the early to mid-90s, they had approximately fifty schools. Mean duration let's say five years, conservatively, times fifty students per year equals a low-end estimate of twelve thousand five hundred people exposed to the scam. If just ten percent (1,250) of the apprentice population contributed $10,000 cash, the government estimate of the amount of unreported income and unpaid tax is woefully inadequate. Yet, the cult continues on today, marketing their Week Longs and Sae Gae Herbal trainings for ridiculous sums of money. Some people just can't pay enough, it seems.

WHEN TO MOO, WHEN NOT TO

The day before the wedding of a favorite head instructor from the south side of town, Joe and Luke, compadres of six years went out to a restaurant they took refuge in once in a while. This place was tucked away in an office complex where on the weekend and late at night, there was less probability of running into students. Under Moo doctrine, it was difficult to maintain chill with too low of belts around.

Relaxation period over, they decided to head back early enough for a good night's rest before the long day tomorrow. On the way out, a college football player hanging with his crew approached Luke and suggested in a boisterous nature they butt heads; he grabbed Luke from behind on the shoulder. Luke turned quickly and knocked his hand away, the lineman seemed surprised. "Come on man," he shouted to everyone around, "let's butt heads." He wasn't intoxicated; he just thought he was something.

Joe knew Luke would eat the big boy alive, and probably felt he had something to prove to his friend so he stepped right up to the aggressor, reached up with his left hand, arm fully extended, above his own forehead and grabbed the lineman's throat and squeezed, but not hard enough. The footballer's eyes narrowed like a German

Shepard ready to bite. With greater reach and bigger knuckles he pounded Joe twice in the left side of the head to make him let go. Joe stumbled back; they traded glancing blows as the bouncers grabbed everybody.

Joe got the worst of it, a black mark under one eye and some lumps. The lineman's ego was more bruised than his throat. None of his buddies had jumped in. They did not like the way the two Moos stuck together. Joe and Luke waited outside, and the cops show up. Filing a police report would only bring more screaming from fatter Moos and they would be interminably reminded of the incident. They decide to retreat, angry and vengeful.

Within a few minutes, Joe has learned a valuable and important lesson. Outside of the closed environment of the Moo school, there is no position, no recognition of rank, no privilege. He decides to lick his wounds and resolves to practice harder.

The next day, the black eye appears and the lumps are still painful and visible. He can not attend the wedding. Luke covers for him best he can, but that night Joe gets summoned to appear before nationals. He admits he made three mistakes; he did not handle decisively, he failed to report, and he used a fellow Moo to cover for him. This happens three days before his probation for third degree was to conclude. Of those promoted he had the least amount on the timetable.

Something a popular high school coach was known to say reverberates through Joe's mind, if you're looking for trouble, you can be sure to find it. Thing was, Joe often used this when sizing up informations for their intent, it served to defuse situations. Asking 'you looking for trouble,' would back down a smart aleck who tried to spar with him right after walking in. Higher belts would tell him that's why he is in that location, there's a lot of street wise traffic that walks in. Your job is to pound them if they get out of line.

And he did too; Joe had completely blasted his share of dingys. The supposed master black belt who jumped front snap kicked at him in the back room, he was attended to by paramedics after being hit in the head with a Tong Bong. The weight lifter, who walked in, took off his shirt and began flexing his muscles in comparison to the instructor pictures in the waiting room. He got knocked down right by the front door. There were numerous other cocky types who after a twenty minute rigorous sample workout, then watching Joe flash swords around and seeing he wasn't tired; decided to either sign up or leave, but not swing real fast after feeling what chung meant. If they did, he blasted them.

Joe was careful with informations. The goal was to sign them up, to get them on course so they too would have a chance at the glory of Moo. If they had other training that was good Joe thought, now they can see what real martial arts are like. If they got goofy, Joe stood toe to toe with them, never backed down.

But here was the key: in Moo, it's a controlled atmosphere. Students or informations, acquiesce to the black belt and the uniform. A quick flash of movement and the snap of the garment looks and sounds impressive to most. And it was Moo turf. Those that tried something got pounded. Joe would have to psych himself up in fractional seconds every time but he did it. Moo students don't punch fast or try to test their teacher. This belittles both and develops false confidence in the higher belts. The arrogant sneer, the broken Engrish, the expectation the aggressor will back down.

This time the football player turned on the juice before Joe did. And then Joe realized something else very important, more so than the first revelation. Every time he had gotten into a scrape and had to fight, he did not use Moo. He used what came naturally and won. When he used Moo and tried to apply it, he lost. Stepping in and grabbing the throat was Moo. He set himself up to get punched. He should have cold cocked the dolt the way he took out the other flexing football players. Joe's left hook never failed him. Or, more reasonably, let it be and laugh it away. No one was in any real danger until Joe felt compelled to handle due to the years of Moo improper teachings.

So what am I training people in, what am I teaching them to do? He asked himself. Joe looked at the punch techniques and self-defenses learned in Moo. After more than seven years he was Moo proficient, and higher belts had voiced their confidence in him, although a few still liked to scream at him for their own enjoyment. He and the other Moos did practice diligently and hard, they had lots of bumps and bruises but still it wasn't good enough. Sometimes the informations coming in had years of well-regarded martial art experience and questioned the Moo applications. This used to set off

Joe and the other Moos. What! How can you question? This is where all martial art comes from, they'd say. But is this true? A lot more questions than answers began to come forth.

QUESTIONS ON THE FUTURE

More new schools were planned, the future was so bright, the U.S. can handle over one thousand schools, we heard so many times straight from Kim himself. One night, as a substitution for instructor group lesson, they were shuttled over to the Farm in clusters to be interviewed in front of the Kim. He was looking for those he could exploit, those willing to give up everything for opportunity. Joe had seen a few things, the dark side of Kim and was by now feeling him out the same way Kim had been doing to everybody else for years. Kim was attuned to these vibes so he'd point out things to keep the inquiries off balance. Like Joe not opening up the door fast enough or the room smelling of window cleaner. Hey, ask the fatter belt, it was his idea. At the end of the night the champion of all Asia was visibly showing his back pain so he left Joe's group with, "If have any questions on future part, nationals will answer."

A couple of days go by and the friendly national sets up an off-site meet with Joe as was forecasted back at the Farm. A senior assistant is left to handle the school; the meeting is in a park. They talk freely. Joe has concerns about being married in Moo, given his track record so far, and not having enough business skills to understand why things are handled the way they are, it does not seem to make sense, respectfully, he says. He also relates in the past he has been wary of pimping the screaming regional as the guy goes off on people for no reason. If there was a purpose to it, Joe would understand he confides, but we were past boot camp awhile ago he adds. The meeting lasts about an hour and the national tells Joe to return to school and take care. Joe brings back some food for the assistant and himself and reflects on whether or not he was perhaps overly forward in laying his cards on the table. Nah, he won't screw me, he's a good guy, Joe remembers thinking. He spoke on the phone with Luke at his school, which was another Moo no-no; they talk for a few moments anyway.

That night, the U-shaped tube chatters loudly at 03:00. The national explains Kim has decided Joe would be better suited lending a hand as an indentured slave at the start-up printing facility. Joe unthinkingly says yes, be alright, and puts down the receiver. He just agreed to be under the full time non-stop thumb of the screaming regional. He is to start at 08:00. He turns to Luke and tells his friend of the change, "I'm fucked."

WHEN A HIGHER PRICE IS PAID-

—The more the value is realized, is what the old blue literature of Moo used to explain. After Joe was re-deployed to the printing facility, he became acutely aware of the sacrifices others had made. One newly promoted second degree had his own machine shop business inherited from his father. A modest man with wife and two small children, Bruce had worked very hard to pay off their first mortgage, rent that house out and buy an upgraded one. Comfortable, but not extravagant, Bruce and family lived well.

But then he decided to Moo. Taken in by the chance to improve his health, the hard workouts and mentoring from a caring head instructor fit the bill. The contract commitments and heavy payments kept him Mooing along.

Because of his potential cash utility to the cult he was kept away from too many ritualistic responsibilities such as broken mirror handling, salting doorways and throwing out food. He was promoted as the cult needed, as we all were. For the printing company they needed practical business sense because the screaming regional had none. They also needed a large cash infusion from like say, the sale of a house, to buy equipment and secure a building lease to make it appear they had been in business for some time in order to entice customers.

Of course Kim heavily stressed the "this is your opportunity, first chance and last, either going up or down" conversation. Bruce expected to be placed in charge of the operation, but Kim had also promised this to the fourth degree screamer, on purpose. Kim had to remain in control. The result was a disaster. Several instructors and head instructors were consigned to build out the fake company.

They worked for weeks straight on end to meet a ridiculous deadline so a new customer would give them a chance at a contract. In point of fact it was their first customer being suckered a second time after the fly by night name and address change representative of Moo. Led by the screamer, the first venture to hoodwink the brother

in-law of another regional failed when the required product quality could not be met, even though it was promised it could be. Outright lies were told to get the business. Having been rebuffed, the Moos under Kim's control and direction induce guys like Bruce to sell homes and submit the cash for their opportunity.

The venture fails, more shenanigans are tried without success for a couple years and then The Cult and the Con, the CBS News special report is broadcast. The printing company had stumbled along, treading water with constant infusions from more fools believing they too were opening the door to Utopia. When the television reports were about to air, one no-mind regional, ever wanting to be kept in the loop suggested a payoff to one of the electricians at the station to sabotage the broadcast. They coerced a student to set it up. Ten thousand dollars was needed, Kim said not to use school funds as it would attract too much attention. Besides, intake was down due to the recent publicity. So, where to get the cash?

Why, from an indirect line company, of course. It was taken from the unemployment tax reserve and other cash accounts of the printing company. The attempted sabotage was discovered; the perpetrators fired and charged criminally, the monies paid forfeited. Incredibly, the regional no-mind insisted that for another ten thousand he could have it done right. He ended up serving four years, and stood trial separately due to health reasons, demoralized Kim did not defend him as promised.

The real tragedy was Bruce and the other instructors who were scammed into investing everything they had into that company were left responsible for all debts and to the IRS. It took more years to pay that off than Kim did time. Bruce lost his house, others their careers or families for want of a phony black belt.

GO PICK UP THE ORANGE JEEP

"It's at the gas station, the garage down the block. They want $600 for the repairs to the engine but we think that's too much. It's been done since yesterday and Master wants us to handle certain thing by the Farm so we need you to help us get it back, they are over-charging us," said the big dumb national, Tom. His master considered him a hillbilly.

"Go there, ask how much it is, like you want to double-check then tell them you can only pay half. Get them to agree, then come back and we'll hand you some change, you don't have any, right?" the national finished.

Joe told himself beforehand he wasn't going to help them screw anyone over. Joe went there and said he was supposed to ask how much for the repairs and the guy starts getting nervous. Tom the hillbilly and the others had been there yesterday. It was a small independent place, a little run down, depending on word of mouth for customers. This was big money to them and no doubt the Moomoos haggled with the guy before, during and after hoping to wear him down; or they might have used their other ploy, saying just fix it, only to come back and quarrel unreasonably about the price. They chose this place to get the work done as they thought they could win.

Joe was not likely to be dispatched to handle cars as he did not follow the instructions very well. For example, it's ten o'clock on a Saturday night and he was supposed to check on a car driven by the regional screamer. Yep, drive by, it's there alright, goes home. They just wanted to keep you busy, under their thumb. It was said by the level headed national handling the schools that he thought as did most others Joe would take a bullet for anyone in the organization. But, there were some so-called higher belts at the time for which it seemed like Joe didn't want to be around too much. Yeah well, nobody's perfect.

When dealing straight up with people, you get what seems like an honest estimate, you negotiate a price for work on good faith and hope it fairs well based on your research and a little luck. If not, you work it out. Over the years the Moos selectively chose who they could manipulate to scam for them. They do it for their websites, their homes, whatever they need; which way, you want chance or not, they put to their targets.

It's unethical, deceitful and despicable to agree to and then try to snake out of what was promised. The Moos characteristically use this to even the score for the sake of preventing being taken advantage of. Landlords, car owners, anything with something they wanted they just took as it was for higher and better blah, blah. Yet they profess about honor, it's all crap. They don't know true Mu Do. Wouldn't recognize it if they got hit in the head with it.

So Joe says, "How much for the Jeep?" The guy at the garage says $600.

Joe said, "Thanks, oh, what was the work done, just curious." It was nearly a complete top end re-build plus some. Jeep parts aren't cheap and there was sizable upfront costs for the small business owner, the labor was reasonable. Joe agreed. He was going to leave and pointed to his junk, they both laughed about rebuilding that motor.

He stopped for a burger and coke and was hoping the hill-rod was gone when Joe returned but he wasn't and demanded to hear why Joe hadn't gotten the Jeep back.

"You could have left your vehicle there," said the fat national.

"They would not give me the vehicle without payment," countered Joe.

"Why not just take it?" Tom had given out a second set of keys previously.

"The Jeep was parked inside, they had it locked up," Joe said, hoping to satisfy the questioning.

"You could have said you wanted to check something, drove it out of there, that's why you take martial arts isn't it, so people don't take advantage of you. Or, you could wait for him to step out and then take it…"

For a few seconds Joe did not realize the higher belt's tactics were trying to push him down and thought he was referring to the rescue of a car Joe once had from the clutches of an unscrupulous tow truck pirate. But here, they clearly planned to defraud and wanted Joe as a front man. Joe had refused. He now saw how they really are.

Soon afterward they questioned Joe's loyalty and said he didn't really fit in; there was nothing for him to do within the cult. The national Tom and Kim said they'd make Joe disappear, and he should be careful about saying or doing anything against school as they would take care of him, that he'd wake up dead. Joe told me, I was beginning to think Kim wasn't sent to finish the work of Christ but was in fact an evil person. Duh, Joe, ya think?

Kim didn't want those around who could see through him. We just wanted to learn martial arts and be around the right type of people. Instead, we committed ourselves to a laughing stock cult with a megalomaniac at the helm and street punks for leaders. We kept wanting to believe.

Joe left the next day with twenty dollars cash, a half tank of gas, a change of clothes and some pride. He gave back their belts. And a fancy coat. To Hell with them. He slept in cars and worked in odd jobs and got real in about two months. Joe became successful in occupation shortly thereafter, earned true friends and no longer worries about goofy Moos. His position is such that friends explain if the Moos do try anything, they'll be the ones to disappear.

After the bad taste dissolved, many of us began learning real martial arts and the difference is unbelievable. Since we shit out the Moo every day is a better day and will keep being so. It took time for them to slowly ingrain us with their carefully thought out manipulation. It takes time to awaken; you face tests then it takes time to put it behind you but the process accelerates as your mind strengthens. It is not without pain.

We speak out because the Moo has to end. The places were I live have all closed; they have publicly disassociated themselves and are transforming to something better. Joe, myself and many others hope that those we showed what we thought was form or those passed knowledge onto are not too adversely affected. If we erred, then will stand up for that, it's on us. We offer our deep apologies if they will accept. We were told about all the people we'd help over our lifetime. Must realize the opposite has happened.

In the early 90s I read about the body of an ex-Moo long departed from the cult found in a wooded area near the Chicago schools. Many of us lived in fear of them for a long time. I realize now there was no involvement with that death; there is no psychic hit, there is no higher form, no all Asia championship and no schools in Guam or anywhere else except in those states with weak consumer protection laws. Kim's skill and ability is pure fabrication, its only relevance is to those who still believe in the cult's stories.

TRAINING DAY

This is compiled from multiple sources and viewpoints, names and overt details have been reserved. Five of us were newly domiciled to handle one of the outside parts, meaning Moo businesses. The former occupants were now at the Farm full time. This place was on the outskirts of the city main metro area, so interaction with any other droids was unlikely. If we ran into one of our fellow chumps we would have to watch out not to share information, lest they become jealous of our new status. Right, guys we knew for years we can't talk to anymore and we're moved quickly with little explanation just to satisfy dear leader. With one phone call, can make over one million move. So this is how he does it. And lucky for us it was also close to the Book Road commune so we could have opportunity whenever Kim was in town.

This was of course, the biggest fallacy. Kim was in town all the time, he merely alluded to going to handle other parts, traveling, checking; he was just shopping or living it up. When he did travel he was taking vacations with the cash he took from the organization. All the stories about checking out of state locations were crap.

The five of us were transferred to this very small, two bedroom plus loft townhouse with an unusable one-car garage brimming with junk as predictably happened with Moos. Rented abodes became storage lockers for the cult. You could dispose of a body in there and no one would know. The one redeeming attribute was a large communal area in the back, if only we had time to get some practice in.

One Sunday we were all at the new house, trying to finish moving in. Fall was going fast, the weather turned cooler rapidly; it was going to be a tough winter it seemed. The building out of the business was about complete after a month of intense non-stop labor. We were finally starting to ease into what we thought might be some sense of normality like a real dinner at least three times a week, regular showers and being allowed to sit on the furniture.

Due to the tight accommodations, five guys in 1200 square feet and one and a half baths, about right for that close feeling; one guy's place to sleep would be the dinning room floor adjacent to the kitchen. A bed had not yet been set up. Clothes were heaped in a pile, albeit a neat one. It was a nice pile, all his.

Kim shows up with fatter belts in tow and a little dog given to Kim as a wedding present by his wife's parents. But Kim didn't want the dog around where he was since he did not give it out, he had to control everything. His wife and kids might enjoy the dog thereby taking attention away from Kim. So we got to take care of it. We soon hated it, one more stupid thing we were charged with because a higher up didn't want to deal with. Let a freaking national take care of this opportunity.

So Kim swaggers in unannounced with idiots trailing behind; he looks around doing his mind check thing, looks at one of us and says in front of everyone to straighten up, this is your last chance. The student's role at the outside business was maintenance; to mop floors, ensure cleanliness and assist where possible, handling deliveries or receipt of goods as needed.

"Hmmm, you want to go back being worker at other job?" Kim demanded.

Joe had been a very productive main droid for years and had few mistakes, now was facing ostracism for no reason other than raising questions. This was classic Kim-cult methodology, point to one, the others fall in line.

"Which way you are? You want to be pilot, you can not be pilot, you have to go up, down, all around, you can not be pilot," Kim ridiculed the sap in front of his peers, using exaggerated body and hand movements for emphasis. This was a thinly veiled threat of physical harm, although he was becoming increasingly clumsy over the years each time he flicked the same, tired hand techniques about, attempting to keep his charges respectful. Whatever he once had, he was losing it.

Someone at some point had told Kim this clod's private dream, what he would have really wanted to do if hadn't blown off college. He began Moo to get in shape for the military, believing he could better qualify for that training. Instead he Mooed past his real opportunity. He left Moo a few days later, the Orange Jeep episode made him expendable. I wondered what kind of pilot Kim would make, so I put him in that frame in another story. Ladies and gentleman, I want to draw your attention away from the flaming debris now exiting the right side of the aircraft and instead tell you about today's in-flight movie, Chong Su the Magnificent…

Another ex-Moo writes:

Snakeskin boots, don't forget the frickin snakeskin boots everyone was wearing. Yeah, Kim and crew have really expensive shoes and very high price designer training suits on, and we have no food, junk cars and steal underwear for fun and profit.

And from another ex-Moo:

I remember that day, Kim also blessed the house, put his mark above all the external doors, to give us good luck, keep us on the right path. From this point foreword we were jinxed. There was a similar conversation with regional, reinvented as national instructor, Bob Sawinski, when the Chicago schools had crumbled. He was blamed for a lot of the news media problems, even though he had little to do with it. Those remaining still loyal would not know any different. There was no place for him to go, word was put out; so he was sent to NPG the printing company, and told this was his last chance, the traditional Kim-stratagem. That it would be good for him to give a hand at NPG, and learn what it was like to work again.

So he would come in day after day for about three weeks, working, cleaning. Then he was shipped off to Pittsburgh. At that time, schools were just opening up in that area. Another Moo was going to be opening the first location there. We were ordered to help move this compatriot and to do the shell build out of the facility, Bob was sent out there for support.

About six months later, because the joker we moved never finished the school, we were sent out again to give a hand. Turns out the transplanted candidate did not have the cash to complete it; we were then sucked dry of our credit balances to purchase supplies. Bob was also around but he wanted nothing to do with the new school, he would disappear; have something to handle, as we used to say, unless there was a higher belt around.

At this time Sawinski was working on getting his insurance license, he was going to sell insurance, he tried to sell several of us on a policy. He was still referred to as unqualified and pushed aside. Several Moos were encouraged to try insurance; this would generate legit cash to the organization and defray their own insurance cost. Kim was trying to create his own mini chaebol which of course self-destructed like every one of his other ventures. Greedy + bad karma = failure. The next thing we knew, Bob was in Washington State and put in charge of a couple of schools, his reward for remaining loyal and visiting Kim while in prison.

So here's a guy pushed aside and given no responsibilities for years, but when it best suits the needs of his cult, Kim puts the unqualified one in charge of those who he once had to buck up to.

Another ex-Moo brings it home:

While all this was going on another generation who were also promised opportunity to handle another new frontier of schools, the future for the organization (read: slaves) were building Kim's houses in Texas. Slab granite floors, Corion counter tops, custom kitchen; $4,500 chandelier and 5,000 square feet of living space plus Kim was going on at least four vacations a year for a total of about two months. Not to mention the weekly shopping spree at the Galleria. Oh and the clothes, nothing under $200 for shirts or pants. Training suit costs on average were $700.

Author's note: Are you wondering where your hard earned course, testing and birthday fees went? Kim doesn't need the money remember, he is Master, he has no concern for it, but he has to spend it to make you feel worthwhile. You can understand. Are you clear or what?

Other ex-Moos will remember this:

At certain gatherings at certain times of the year, in order to promote "more care ways," Kim would have piles of hand me downs he and his brother didn't want anymore and give them out to the crowd. Am sure some of us were or know of others raised via some public assistance and/or state aide. These handouts were insults. Yet, you were supposed to be honored by these offerings, main part once wore that, you should take special pride he gave that to you. More like he wore it once and now its good enough for you to wear, you don't need anything besides what the cult can provide.

Some never took, like Joe, saying they didn't need, that they had plenty, straight to his face. This severely pissed Kim off. He couldn't control all things all the time it seemed. Not that it's a cult or anything.

THE NEWS REPORTS

As the schools grew every more numerous, over a dozen locations in Chicago alone by the end of the 1980s, the notoriety of outrageous costs, the controlled speech and behaviors required; added to skepticism of the school's fantastic claims. Until now small scale media inquiries had been thwarted. Cable news requests or local print media forays were dismissed at the main instructor level.

"No, we don't allow filming in our school," Joe remembers telling one persistent reporter shortly before he left the organization. "If you or crew wants to try a free lesson we can arrange that. But, giving away our methods and proprietary information on school operations might allow others without students' best interests in mind, to concoct a situation where they can take advantage of people. And we don't want that to happen," he said on the fly as a three man cable crew showed up unannounced one morning.

Naturally, he reported the incident as soon as possible. Fatter belts seemed uninterested, they were more concerned about instructors on the front line getting a big head and thinking they can handle. It was about time to consider what to do with some of them; either move them out of state or shuttle them to the indentured servitude program at one of the indirect line businesses.

Not too long beforehand, after six years in the Moo, a third degree head instructor was deeded a house by his retiring parents. He agreed in principle to sell and bring the proceeds into Moo to fund a business of which he would be put in charge. Upon seeing who he would have to report to, his least favorite regional, he balked and decided to leave the organization. Six months later he asked if he could still practice in the schools. He was given the opportunity, but stripped of rank and title, demoted to fourth section and only allowed in late at night at a place far away from his previous daily handling so no students would see him, to make an example to anyone else who: (a) decided they could leave after making instructor, (b) reneged on bringing in all the cash they had, or (c) both a and b. If you choose (c) above, you may qualify for being true Moo.

After the news reports cast the Moo unfavorably, the organization sought out several such ex-members to return, gratis, in attempts to rebuild the system. They declined, as did Joe and others of this generation who wish to remain anonymous.

The local media interest would ebb and flow over the next couple years much as it had in the past. A few celebrity students like football players would generally be positive. However these types were handled special. They were worked with away from main groups, talked to with private conversations and charged steep but not outrageous prices in the way some wealthy but emotionally needy students were conned. The goal here was not to suck as much money as possible from them, as it was unlikely the professional athlete would become a black belt, they would not stick around for that long although one or two in the system did, eventually. The mission with high profile students be it a doctor, lawyer, CPA or pro sports player was to leverage their position and shape their perception of school so that when they spoke about it, the representation would be positive. Not overwhelming, just positive.

As the school name grew more visible and the regionals more ego driven as a result of being around Kim and not having Forrest to keep them in check; disaster reared its televised head. Several wealthy students had made it to near black Moo belt. They were generous with toys and money, donating heavily at Christmas or for Kim's birthday, picking up anything school or instructors might need. They brought along the best equipment and tents and trailered ATV's to the campouts, putting in extra for whatever might be needed by higher belts. These were after all, friends, their only true ones. Seems their old friends did not understand them anymore after they found Moo.

With a couple years in and a few tens of thousands of dollars invested, it was put forth to a few better minded ones that one hundred thousand dollars would secure their future. Problem was they did not have it. A conspicuous instance was one who had quit his finance related job with the family business in order to be around school more and had spent most of his personal savings. Tapped out, he approached his parents for a loan and they balked. Of course he would pay it all back with interest once he had his own school or business just as higher belts in Asia have lived for thousands of years. They remained skeptical even though they were drawn into the banquets and other events designed especially for families and friends to sample a taste of Moo-lite. The purpose of the special lessons and events was of course, to dispel questions about Moo being a cult. This didn't work; instead it drew more inquiry from those who were not overtly controlled by the Moo.

Acknowledging their son needed rescuing, but unable to reason with him, the family turned to their friends for advice and assistance. Recognizing a worthy story, unrelenting pressure from the local CBS affiliate coupled with the Moo's own arrogance, thinking they could handle the exposure and spin it to their advantage, opened the gates for the cult's dirty laundry to be spilled onto the sidewalk. The build up during sweeps month was intense. The Cult and the Con was previewed weeks in advance of its November 1989 showing. If it bleeds it leads was the mantra of the local affiliate and the senior lead investigative reporter seemed to take a personal interest.

Claims by the Moo were debunked in front of a large audience for the first time. The high costs, the supposed confidential forms, the rigid behaviors and required mannerisms; all were made to seem ridiculous as was much of the crap that went on in Moo. The apparent worship of John C. Kim, the unfounded reverence given to the pictures set within the school were highlighted and made questionable. Former students, ex-instructors and family members, some appearing in cameo with disguised identities for fear of reprisals made condemning statements against the cult of Kim.

The expose played out over a week as an exclusive report airing twice per day during prime time newscasts. It was repeated over the months ahead and over the ensuing years during the Trials, there were follow-ups. The most damage to the cult came from the Moos themselves. The reporters had asked several noted leaders in the surrounding Chicago area martial arts community about John C. Kim's claim as The Champion of All Asia from a tournament purportedly held in 1956. Never could have happened, was the consistent reply. Given the political climate in Asia during the 1950s, a tournament of such magnitude seems highly improbable.

The first large venue Judo tournament was held in Japan in 1956. Tae Kwon Do, from Korea, was tested as a future Olympic sport in the early 1960s. To claim an All Asia Championship from an earlier time is nothing more than a big fib. Singapore, towards 1970, did begin hosting no-holds-barred all Asia tournaments for a variety of martial arts.

During the broadcast of The Cult and the Con, the reporters asked the lead Moo regional stationed in the school where the investigative team focused their efforts, "Where was the tournament Kim claimed he won, where was it held?"

The four-stripe Moo answered straight into the camera as visions of uniforms in motion from the practice room were seen in the background. "Where was it held?" parroted back the regional Moo using that condescending smirk of disbelief Moos in charge use to deflect what they are hearing, e.g. what? what?

The reporter repeated the question. "Where was it held? Where was the 1956 tournament held, where did it take place?"

"Where was it held?" The Moo again mimicked back, then thoughtfully answered, using small circular hand gestures for emphasis… "In Asia, more Asia ways get in."

Cut to the conclusion. Nationwide a cry went out from all the Moos watching. That's our leadership? Along with threats made to the reporters by other more senior and fatter Moo-moos which were revealed to authorities, the cult was doomed.

Through all this, Kim was already re-established at the ten-acre compound near Houston, Texas. So he just kept hiding out there, communicating frequently with higher Moos in Chicago, telling them what to say and how to handle the media. It was on his word the reporters were told to back off or else. One would think that a bona fide master under such a line of attack would answer up. Surely the royal family should not be disgraced. This was not Kim's choice. Instead, he moved from Texas to a rented California home.

Investigators made the link as to which schools were most directly influenced by Kim. The East Coast and Florida operations were tolerably distanced from the day to day oversight of Moo central command, so the Feds concentrated on Texas and Illinois; the Ranch in Texas to hopefully spot Kim, and the Chicago schools to better understand the cult's operations, keeping them under surveillance for nearly a year. Agents were planted as students, observing times and methods of internal cult functions.

The IRS raid on a late August night in 1990 backed up by federal, local and county law enforcement resources was not a complete surprise to Moo. Remember, Kim can see into the future. He can step into a room and read five hundred minds at once. The exact timing and scope of the take-downs did though, catch the Moo off guard. The cult's nightly rotation was well understood by the cops as they waited for the cash to be transferred at the Lombard school. The Cult and the Con had aired ten months earlier.

The authorities moved in near simultaneously, advancing upon schools in Chicago, plus the Farm and the Ranch in Texas. The Moo's secret forms were useless against helicopters, ATF and FBI

SWAT teams. Infrared sensors detected large objects in the outer buildings of a neighboring property near the Houston compound. Moos hiding, was it? Nope, just hogs, hard to tell unless you get up close, even then...

The new sub-lead regional in Chicago caught with an open briefcase had a clever attorney who tried to have this evidence suppressed. The purse, as it was claimed to be, and the contents thereof, was however ruled admissible during the federal trial based on established precedent by Magistrate Judge Ashman (case 95CR214 and related dockets). This and other items the same regional had forgotten about, records left in the basement of a past residence, were key pieces as to the latitude and scope of the Moo enterprise puzzle.

Most of the Chicago schools began to fold under increasing public distain. Some owners went independent and tried their own brand or changed styles completely and found truly qualified teachers to learn from in the following years.

In early 1991 the crafty Kim moved to the high rent district of San Diego. A couple of stores were opened up locally and the three or four Seattle locations provided cash collection opportunities. Instructors who had been methodically kept back or pushed to the side were brought forward for their opportunity. Coupled with lax consumer protection laws and a new spin on the Moo mojo focusing on herbal concoctions and better handling of select wealthy students, Kim maintained his royal existence.

While living in San Diego, Kim was hiding out again, using an occasional trip to Lake Tahoe or further up the coast when he got spooked. His kids in private schools, his trophy wife with established credit at the best stores and salons, his national Moo-droids running errands and cooking his meals; the habit of sleeping in was his weakest point.

He became a master at recycling, of stories and legends, of form and of people. He shuffled instructors around, changed their positions and rank via promotions, using the time honored tradition of setting those up who had not previously given all they had. Kim opened the gates and passed new forms never before released, as those still loyal had proven they had earned. But the new forms were just the old forms, changed around or gleaned from cable TV or Kung Fu Magazine with his tweaks to the postures.

For at least two decades Kim never practiced himself. Instead, to preserve his dominion over his subjects, he would intermittently have one of his nationals or regionals go through their paces and then adjust what they had. The result was a mishmash of poses with no martial or fighting meaning. Oh sure, there was aerobic benefit from jumping around and if you believed the stories about the movements being passed down from the mountains or whatever, then you were all set. The more recent inventions of holding herb-filled beanbags in twisted postures, hoping to absorb magical properties, are perhaps the most perverted.

By 1994 the Illinois and Texas Attorney Generals had settled complaints v. Moo, the Farm and the Ranch had been sold. The Feds took special notice of the cash-based Moo enterprise. But since records were systematically destroyed, testimony by former members proved invaluable in building the case.

By the spring of 1995 the IRS had developed satisfactory evidence to bring the case before a Grand Jury. Arrest warrants were issued for Kim and key persons of The Kim Organization, see following article at the end of this chapter.

John C. Kim a.k.a. Jack Park was placed spread eagle on the floor of his ill-gotten mansion, cuffed and dragged into custody in the early morning hours of April 12, 1995. During the arrest at the home in an exclusive La Jolla neighborhood, several nationals were there and told the federal agents Kim was not around.

The lead national said to the others, "Hold your ground, they can not do anything." The nationals were posing as if for pictures. The agents dumped the lead national on the ground and cuff him. They find Kim hiding behind the furniture he did not pay for, crying. They cuff him and take him into custody, crying all the way. Kim's wife and children watch the ordeal conclude. The federal agent in charge it turns out, the one who dumped Kim's highest belt, is an accomplished Jujitsu student in addition to his federal law enforcement training.

Other Kim accomplices were rounded up at their homes in California, Texas and Illinois and brought to trial on charges of conspiring to defraud the IRS. Finally out on bail, Kim stayed at luxury hotels in Chicago and retained an expensive out of town criminal defense lawyer specializing in tax cases. The national, regional and head instructors charged alongside Kim had to rely on public defenders so as not to attract attention or take too much from the schools for support. That would be selfish.

Kim told those on trial with him and those still loyal handling the few remaining schools he had looked into the future and saw all charges would be dismissed. But, he said even if something was to come towards schools, he would step up and handle, he would turn the judge's mind to mush. He, JCK, would gladly go to jail if necessary before any instructor. And not to worry, as has been passed down for centuries Chung Moo would step in and handle taking care of all instructors, their wives and children. All over the world, with one phone call, school is ready to handle.

Throughout the summer of 1995, a deadly heat wave moved through the Midwest. Thousands of deaths were attributed directly to the horrible weather. Over four hundred and fifty people died in Chicago in July alone, the total through August would reach over six hundred and fifty. Tabloids ran headlines describing Satan's face seen above the Chicago lakefront. Sketches allegedly made from eye witness accounts depicted an eerie similarity to Kim. By now Joe had left the area, moved to another state. A friend still in town described the weather's effects and the drawings to him some months afterward. They shook their heads, wondering how far was it from the truth.

Amazing still is how the national instructors who were at the house and watched their master cry and be manhandled just as they were and put in jail, continued to nod and bow and thank and believe in the grandhamster. Such is the hold of this cult. Easy to make is easy to break, we used to be told early on. After so many years, it was impossible for these guys to see their way clear; they stayed in the cult having nothing else in their lives.

During the trial which lasted from September to early December 1996, Kim's lawyer, at his direction, painted a picture of the nationals and regionals misusing their positions and licensing agreements, that Kim was merely a pawn, not the instigator. Kim turned his back on his cult when they needed him most, just as he had planned all along.

In less than two weeks, including Thanksgiving holiday, the guilty verdict was reached. Pending sentencing, the judge ordered Kim to surrender his passports. He was suspected of having at least two due to his alias Jack Park and from information provided during the trial from several of his devoted followers who finally realized Kim was screwing them.

This was one of the few instances when Kim spoke before the court, claiming his wife had misplaced his passport but he was sure he could locate it, if he would be allowed a couple of days to look for it. The gavel swung down nearly before Kim finished his purposefully used broken English sentence.

"Remand," ordered the judge. His bail revoked, grandhamster Kim would be caged until sentencing.

THE TAX CASE

For nearly a decade the Moo vacation spot was San Padre Island off the south Texas coast. Every few years on the norm, instructors would get in lessons on the beach near a rented villa. Kim would have the higher belts enjoy watching him relax. On the odd occasion to keep the interest level peaked, Kim would order instructors to dig pits in the sand and they would bury each other up to the neck for half an hour or so. Kim would lecture about how this ancient, never before released form was the ultimate for curing arthritis or if practiced correctly, the way he would show to qualified ones, how to prevent other diseases. The warm sand infusing magical earth heat into the bodies of the select few lucky enough to be close to Kim.

One form that did seem worthwhile for a time at least, was the 'big log' form. There was some cool sounding name for it like Suk Sul Bong Bope whatever, but this isn't important. What is important is it was nicked from other training methods, not necessarily martial arts; as all things are in Moo. Catch an early morning Fit TV or similar program and you'll find the source for secret forms. Check old martial arts flicks, the import kind found in local Asian specialty market stores and you'll be on the right track to royal learning.

When this particular form was passed to main instructors at the weekly group some three years hence, a landscape timber would be held at length across the front of the body and to the side. By grasping the big log and walking slowly, carefully, for twenty paces or so and balancing a glass of water at the end and not spilling any, body strength would build quickly. Back and forth across the room the instructors would take turns. Very soon thereafter one was supposed to get into Tong Nong for at least twenty minutes or the body would become rigid. Important safety note: do not practice this first thing in the day as body will become rigid. This was as seen on TV. It was a good ploy to get everybody on vacation at the time worn out, to feel like they did something. The emphasis was that the Kim was checking you, that's what made it special.

It was expressly ingrained in everyone that once you leave Moo, the forms you think you know can have a detrimental effect because you have lost the connection to real understanding, that without Master's explanations, the forms will be harmful. Just as Kim was said to be a Chum Sa or spiritual guide, he could help you to reach the next life. You could do it on your own, but you probably would not make it and even if you did, you would not have the position in the next life as great as the one he could provide.

This is completely contradictory to real martial arts, the ones the Moos put down, the ones the Moos say they looked at but never really did, instead they choose Moo. In Tai Chi for example, the most powerful stances and practices are shown in the very beginning. There is no strain into forced postures. It is the opposite. The student learns and develops what has been taught, the teacher explains more and the student continues to grow. The student keeps what he keeps, he knows what he has. There is no hocus-pocus, no mysticism, only physics. If the student no longer learns from that teacher he will not be damaged by practicing wrong for he or she has already been taught correctly. Real masters are humble and quiet; they don't need to talk about their greatness to convince anyone of anything. Again, this is the opposite of Moo.

Aside from time spent listening about the future of Moo and the significance of the presence of Kim exponentially talked up as the Second Coming, instructors were mostly deployed as servants, butlers and chaperones for Kim's family. The entourage stroking his ego when shopping at The Galleria on the way south or along the tourist shops on the island.

During an off year when Kim had a relatively new crew of dupes to be schooled in beach etiquette, a lesson of abnormal magnitude occurred. It had been years since Tong Nong or any real form had been reviewed. In a replay of the campout lesson some ten years earlier, instructors went through their paces in the sand in front of Kim. Tomorrow they would head back to their home schools after a week of running errands, cleaning and handling. This was their long awaited lesson as promised.

The tradition of not teaching and making everyone wait then saying, faster ways getting in, you understand main point, you can catch up later; is a Moo hallmark. This would become painfully obvious to instructors attending the future Week Longs as they would be finally taught something during the last few hours before they had to head back to the airport. Oh, have to leave soon? (after a week of standing around) well, we were going to get in form, but…

This day on the island, up since dawn and sent out and about so as not to find the Kim sleeping in, by lesson's end scheduled far into the day all were exhausted as the late winter Sun began to set. The lesson concludes and Kim is silhouetted as instructors began to line up to ritually shake hands and be mentally checked one by one by the Kim.

What Luke, the Chicago veteran and Joe's friend, saw at the conclusion filled him with dread. A devil's face inside the outline of Master Kim, no flesh only bones; a repeat of something he had seen years earlier at the Farm at the end of the very first Suk Chung lesson, the day he fell off the foot bridge. This time the image was so clear, so vivid it was unmistakable a demon was teaching Chung Moo and always had been. Unsure what to do, there was no time to rationalize, only to step forward and shake hands with the devil.

"Hmmm," Kim said pointedly, "Luke can see now, step through," and he motioned Luke to proceed. None of the dozen-plus other instructors there had seen anything unusual; they were too internally focused and did not take exception at Kim's remarks. This was Moo perfect. Blind devotion breeds exceptional ambivalence. If a comment wasn't meant for you, your case concerning, you completely tuned it out. Everything in Moo is compartmentalized, by rank, by time in, by course, by outside position; need to know or need to see.

Long ago it seemed now, Luke remembered just before Joe was to step back from school, Joe had confided to Luke he had a strange experience; a repeat of something a year or two earlier. When late at night pictures of Kim in the white jump suit seemed to move in the frames just out of peripheral vision. It startled and shook Joe. The other time was late one night he was cleaning the office in preparation for the nail day chore of cleaning certificates, he saw Kim's picture in the certificate reveal horns protruding from inside the curly permed hairdo, with a slight smile.

Luke paid close attention when his good friend related his observations and fear. They were both dedicated Moos, unquestionably. Main instructors, been through scrapes, defections of buds, numerous hard lessons and screamings over the years. This was a different enemy. After Joe finished telling his account that night back at the commune, Luke confided that during the Suk Chung lesson at the Farm he had seen Kim's face melt into a devil-like form, back-lighted from behind by the setting Sun as instructors were leaving that day.

"I wondered why you were so spooked then, Joe said. "I thought it was because of the lesson, but I should have known it was something bigger." They both tried to laugh it off and went out for a rare beer. One of the last few good times they'd enjoy at St. James. Joe and Luke both agreed it was just their minds playing tricks, they hoped the stories of going crazy when reach certain point weren't going to affect them. As they understood it, to reach a level of real knowledge, there were "certain things had to go through" as a test to determine the worthy. Many instructors had experienced strange phenomena as they progressed in Moo; hearing bizarre sounds during late night practices or having unnatural apparitions appear before them.

Joe and Luke decided not to speak of their encounters again. Fast forward a couple months, Joe leaves, Luke is shipped off to Texas and makes regional instructor handling all the schools in a major city. The lesson at San Padre, where Luke again sees Kim the demon, is five years in the future.

A year or so after the visualization at the beach, a series of events are put in motion that will shape the rest of Moo history. National instructors in Texas and California, where Kim was hiding from the media, were placing increasing amounts of pressure on the schools in all regions to bring in ever more cash. Kim wanted an expensive home in Pebble Beach, California and the Moos were going to get it for him or they were not qualified. Responding as good Moos, over sixty grand is turned over to Moo headquarters from one city alone for just one week leading up to Kim's birthday. Attendance, course signings and belt development is strong in Texas. Well beyond what Kim and the nationals can control.

A large monthly deposit of cash was to be transferred in persona between Texas and the visiting senior regional who would bring it to Kim. After tender, a significant portion is supposedly missing and Texas is suspected of holding back. Luke is called on the carpet repeatedly but remains steadfast, we did not mistake, there is no reason for the missing cash, we did not miscount or need to use the missing thousand dollars.

Kim intervenes, promises Luke a national instructor title with direct reports to include the senior regional with sticky fingers. Suspicious of Kim's intent and the vision from the beach still nagging his memory, Luke decides to not take the promotion as he does not trust the regionals, a big insult to Kim, and makes plans to leave the organization.

Expanding his own learning, Luke opens the gates and brings in teachers from a choice of organizations for seminars, incorporates tactics from ex-military Special Forces instructors into the curriculum, and develops multiple levels of sparring programs with new equipment. The students love the results. Luke's school continues to grow, he builds alliances.

The Moo nationals and senior most regionals, including those who skillfully handled the television and newspaper reports in Chicago, begin calling Luke at home. "Luke better be careful, something might happen," they tell his wife when he is not there. With a young child to protect, Luke's wife leaves him and the Moo behind. Subjected to years of manipulation and now threats, Luke puts his exit plan into action and takes down all the Kim related paraphernalia; the pictures, certificates, literature and stuffs it into boxes. "You want your crap, come and get it," he calls to Moo. They never do. Instead they send a series of droids.

The first was Bill, the brother of Kim's second in command national hillbilly. This guy had been kicked out of schools several times over the years but was brought back in and given inflated titles without any real qualifications. His addictions were controlled substances; cocaine was allegedly one favorite. Moo and the semblance of belonging the cult provided was the other. He snakes his way into school just after opening hoping to surprise Luke and the other instructors who were already practicing. His mission: to terrorize the rogue school and earn his place again with the Moos. He fails.

Bill is recognized immediately, and runs from the school, clutching something in his pockets. Luke and the instructors held broadswords. Real ones, not like the Moo trinkets stuffed into boxes.

Another month goes by when again before school is about to open for the day, an improved version arrives. He walks straight into the practice room with his shoes on. He is well over six feet and two hundred and fifty pounds. It is discovered as more Moo schools leave the system this guy is from out of state, sent by the nationals to handle Luke. When asked what he wanted and who he was, the enlisted mercenary tried to punch Luke in the face then kick him. He missed. The intruder ends up in the intensive care unit after his introductory beating and face opening. One of the cops and one of the paramedics dispatched to the scene are students in Luke's school. The intruder is checked up on in the hospital, but he is not to be found, his room empty, some clothes left behind.

Desperate to teach Luke a lesson, the Moos convince a head instructor from another state it's time for his opportunity if he can pre-pay the lease on a giant empty location right down the street from Luke's fully independently owned and operated martial arts studio, which continues to flourish.

The new mega Moo store dies after six months, they could not afford the rent, and the assistants sent for support are inept. The migratory head instructor-owner finds himself heavily in debt in the 1500 year-old tradition that is Moo. He leaves the cult shortly thereafter.

So the Moo, at the direction of the Kim, try a different approach. A few more months go by and Luke receives a visit from the IRS. The Feds have been probing every Moo school since the news reports in Chicago. They had been given, mysteriously, information about a couple of newly independent schools in Texas. It was the Fed's remaining lead and the time limitations for completing their investigation based on data collected in Illinois with cooperation from the Attorney General there, were going to expire soon. They were pressing to make a case.

Upon the advice of counsel, who happened to be a student with good connections in the legal profession, Luke cooperates with the IRS. Along with several other senior ex-Moos he helped the federal authorities make contact with, Luke testifies against Kim. If not for the tenacity and rejuvenation of character found by these schools leaving Moo and standing up to Kim, the Tax Case would never have happened. The slam of the penitentiary doors on Kim's evil was however, only temporary.

THE KIM ORGANIZATION CONVICTED ON TAX FRAUD CONSPIRACY
BY SPECIAL AGENT BARRY UNTINEN,
IRS CRIMINAL INVESTIGATION DIVISION

John C. Kim, a martial arts master, and an organization referred to as the "Kim Organization," owned, controlled, and operated martial arts schools located in Illinois, California, Massachusetts, Minnesota, and Texas. These schools had various names, including John C. Kim Style School of Chung Moo Quan, John C. Kim Style School of Chung Moo Doe, School of Chung Moo Quan, and School of Chung Moo Doe. John C. Kim was the head of the organization and controlled the operation of the schools through a hierarchy of trusted individuals.

These individuals held the titles of National Instructors, Regional Head Instructors, or Assistant Regional Head Instructors. They included Thomas White, Kenneth Krisciunas, John Liska, Thomas Martin Hnat, Frank Kucia, Joselito Jakosalem, Sante Furio, Nicholas Gallo, Thomas McGee, Scott Gigliotti, Thomas Condon, Michael McKay, and Robert Sawinski. At various times during 1977 to 1995, these individuals operated more than 30 martial arts schools nationwide, including more than a dozen in Illinois and others in Minnesota, Texas, California, and Massachusetts.

On April 11, 1995, a Grand Jury returned an indictment in the Northern District of Illinois charging these 14 individuals with engaging in a massive tax fraud conspiracy that lasted as long as 20 years. According to the indictment, beginning in the early 1970's, these individuals began to defraud the United States government by conspiring to obstruct the Internal Revenue Service in the exercise of its lawful functions in violation of Title 18 USC §371 (Conspiracy to Defraud the IRS). The indictment alleged and evidence presented at trial proved that the defendants skimmed large amounts of cash obtained from the operation of these schools and concealed a portion of the cash from the Internal Revenue Service.

In particular, the defendants charged large amounts of money for courses at the schools, and in some instances they charged over $18,000 for a single course. They directed their students to pay for the courses in cash. Only a portion of the cash paid by students was deposited into bank accounts for the schools and was reported to the Internal Revenue Service. The rest of the cash was passed on to Kim and other co-conspirators to pay their expenses, including the purchase of a ranch in Texas, a house in California, a Farm in Illinois, and to start up and fund various other businesses.

As a result of the investigation, 6 of the 14 individuals indicted pled guilty, 5 defendants were found guilty at trial, and 3 defendants pled guilty to superseding informations. The case was one of the largest federal tax conspiracy trials ever held in the Northern District of Illinois.

John C. Kim, founder and owner of the schools, was convicted at trial. Kim, 63, born in Korea and a former resident of Naperville, Illinois; Houston, Texas; and most recently LaJolla, California, was portrayed at trial as the instigator and mastermind of the tax fraud conspiracy. Witnesses testified that Kim came to the United States with the goal of making himself one of the world's richest men and that he justified his failure to pay appropriate taxes by stating that the American government routinely wasted tax revenues, citing as examples the government's funding of social programs and foreign aid to countries such as South Korea, which were misused.

Upon conviction, U.S. District Judge James Holderman granted the government's request to revoke Kim's bond. John C. Kim was sentenced in July 1997 to 60 months in prison and fined $17,500 for violation of Title 18 USC §371. Others convicted at trial were: Frank Kucia of Encinitas, California; Joselito Jakosalem of Maple Grove, Minnesota; Thomas Condon of Largo, Florida; and Michael McKay of Pittsburgh, Pennsylvania.

A mistrial was declared in the case against Thomas White of Oakland, California and Robert Sawinski of Bellevue, Washington. Defendants who pled guilty before trial were Thomas Martin Hnat of McDonald, Pennsylvania; Kenneth Krisciunas of Bellevue, Washington; Nicholas Gallo of Shoreward, Illinois; Thomas McGee of Seminole, Florida; Sante Furio of Encinitas, California, and Scott Gigliotti of Richardson, Texas. One remaining defendant, John Liska, was ordered to stand trial separately.

Defendants Thomas McGee, Sante Furio, Kenneth Krisciunas, Scott Gigliotti, Thomas Condon, and Thomas Hnat were each sentenced to 60 months in prison and fined $2,500.

Defendants Nicholas Gallo and Michael McKay were each sentenced to 60 months in prison and fined $2,000. Defendants Joselito Jakosalem and Frank Kucia were each sentenced to 57 months in prison and fined $2,500.

Defendants Robert Sawinski and Thomas White pled guilty to superseding informations, and both were sentenced to one year in prison and fined $500. Defendant John Liska also pled guilty to a superseding information and was sentenced to 48 months in prison.

Published in The International Association of Asian Crime Investigators Spring 1999 issue (Article Publicly Available on the U.S. Treasury Website)

PART VIII

ANTI MOO

"All that is necessary for the triumph of evil is for good men to do nothing"

—Edmund Burke

PART VIII — ANTI MOO

THE PSYCHIC HIT

It was believed Kim possessed great mental powers, able to generate a projection of his mind, by putting concentration in or towards things, people or places across great geographic distances. It was said he watched instructors and schools from afar. When a new place opened or a place moved, mind was put in, or taken out as required.

Back about 1980, a first degree named Martin (the Martian, kudos to whoever coined it) was finishing Moogwa at the Worth, Illinois school when he passed out. Those first learning this movement can understand it should be executed in a manner so that one does not constrict blood flow to the head, make the neck relaxed. This occurrence was often cited when the form was passed, don't do this or you'll end up like one instructor who almost didn't make it.

Well, what also happened was not readily told, depends on how many lower belts were around. But the event was related consistently and often enough it was thought to be true. After Martian collapsed and Dan, the highest belt in the school was unable to revive him; Dan called head instructoids, who called Kim who was said to be out of state.

After direct instructions via telephone from Kim to Dan on what techniques to use, what points to touch and how failed; Kim realized he had no choice, he sent his mind to revive Martian. This of course succeeded and Martian recovered, literally brought back from the beyond. It was said without the intervention he would not have survived or would have been damaged.

This event convinced Martian he had found the true art he sought. It was common practice for Moos to say they were accomplished in other types when in fact they were not. Several had met Forrest at the original Westmont place and were convinced to sign up.

Most of the inner circle at the time of the Tax Trial was the run of the mill slughead off the street. This was the result of another Moo belief; that of transforming the lowest stature in our culture into the highest titles, one of mind and body and (insert current cult dogma here). The Moo's symbol placed upon every artifact and trinket in a place, the upside down king inscribed by Kim himself reflects this ideology; that every position in society is below a Moo, for which they worship Kim.

Marty however, was one of the very few within the Moo who had really trained in another style before joining. Jerry, still a current national, was another so they say. But, this is probably just more hyperbole to make it sound good. The young Martian was a brown belt in Kung Fu where his master had told him to begin training with a young bull on his shoulders and jump over a hedge. Each day the bull will grow, as will the hedge and each day as you train you will get stronger. When Marty explained this to Forrest during a walk-in introductory beating, Martian like many of us was quickly introduced to what chung meant.

Moos by their conditioning threaten those who they believe would turn against them or divulge their underhandedness. Their malicious, stupid attacks on those who leave the Moo are well documented. The Psychic Hit was possibly the most compelling example. How could one stand against it? Look at what happened to the likes of Bruce Lee and one seventh degree in Asia who was stopped as he didn't think Moo form should be passed to westerners. Insiders know Kim possesses abilities that are difficult to understand which generates the fear he uses to manipulate the willing. Stories of higher belts coming over to handle were propagated along with Kim insinuating he'd take care of those who he said hurt his Moo. Undoubtedly, prolonged involvement with this paranoia caused many higher belts to act even more irrationally in support of Moo doctrine than they would otherwise in pre-Moo lives.

Colleagues had relayed the build-up to the CBS News report during sweeps month. Having been out of touch for awhile, a way to monitor the broadcast was set up. When the news anchor finally got to "…And now the special report on Chung Moo…" the screen went completely static as if we'd lost channel or the coordinates changed. It took a few moments to get back on and we picked up at "…It was if a bolt of lightening had hit the transmitter, and now our report." The news anchor seemed visibly shaken.

Well of course, it was the astral energy shot to the Sears Tower from out of a clear sky. What else could it possibly be? Many thought the same and were fearful. All the prophecies were true. God save us now, the Kim would be coming after everyone who had ever deceived him.

It was not until discussions on Martial Arts Table Talk circa early 2002, a popular Web forum before the Moo spammed it to death, that the question was put out for comment about the interruption of the broadcast. A respondent explained how an electrical engineer backstage had been given ten thousand dollars by an inner Moo to throw switches and attempt to prevent the report from being aired. The objective by the Moo cult was to thwart completely the broadcast; however the interruption lasted only a few seconds after a back-up system kicked on. It was also indicated that further payoffs of greater amounts were given to create as much chaos as possible but this did not happen. The accessory to Moo electrician was fired. This event directly corroborated by former cult members.

All that money, from the students and instructors and families, all their very hard earnings were wasted in a whim for a megalomaniac's desire to stay in power. For all their hype about caring for people, it meant nothing to them to consider this underhanded course of action. A reasonable person might allege all the inner circle were completely under the influence of Kim or they knew the real deal and supported it for their own vested interests.

This event clearly demonstrates the deceitful and insidious character of the Moo. Only those who completely refute the Moo are credible, in this opinion, as otherwise they continue to support the same group who still run the show and reap benefit from the organization. And, they still profess to teach true martial arts descended from royalty, with no bona-fide evidence to support their claims. Who says it's not a cult?

THE JUMP SIDE KICK EXPLAINED

From the one meter resolution view of the aerial photos in the links provided at the end of this article, north is at the top and west is to the left in ordinary frame. The building above the modern water tower for the complex is building number one, which is the background building in the infamous photo fraud displayed proudly in the front windows of the Moo schools. Proceed clockwise to building number, oddly enough, four.

In these photos, taken in April of the year; note the shadows from the Sun's angle. Submit that Kim's hoax was concocted in the middle to late summer as a higher zenith is obvious in the purported building jump photos. The flying fraud picture would have been taken at approximately eight to nine p.m. long after workers on the new site have gone home.

Observe the roof top heating, ventilation and air-conditioning (HVAC) unit on building number four. Now examine the one-quarter meter view. The camera would be along the eastern or right-side edge of building number four; the photographer propped up with his back to the eastern edge, and points the lens northwest (to the top-left) with building number one framed squarely in the backdrop. The old water tower shown above the St. Benedicts Abbey in Kim's 1970s picture is long gone; the newer tower for the apartments is now in the courtyard. With the setting Sun it's a true Moo moment. Using a filter provides enough graininess and coupled with the difference in background focus makes for a cosmic event.

Jumping Over the Sun is nicked from Gol Gu Sa, also known as Sun Mu Do, a Korean martial art rather obscure until more recent times, which for some reason perhaps known only to himself, Kim tried to mimic. They wait until close to sundown then shoot their scam. Forrest, as chief maintenance engineer has the access; Kim as his flunky and token Oriental has the cool looking black suit. Which, depending on the website from the current Oom Yung Doe schools you look at, has the belt tip on his right side turned over to white in the negative or it shows black. Not that there was ever any doctoring of the original photo at any time.

Kim, running north to south along the west side of building number four; jumps up from the roof behind the HVAC to make it appear he's clearing the molding of the unit. They pass it off as the corner of the roof upon reviewing the best possible slant like they did with their takes in the field of the staged vault and other preliminaries. The vault picture never makes it into official Moo publications for obvious reasons. Building number one in the background is straight in line with the corner of the HVAC unit on building four.

Remember, they practiced setting this up, using Kim's often

mentioned Hollywood experiences of consulting for the Billy Jack movies. Of course this is satire, referring to yet another lie put forth by the Moo at Kim's direction. It was the legitimate Grand Master Bang Soo Han, not Kim, who was instrumental in Billy Jack.

Over time, Kim changed his jump kick fairytale just enough to deflect anything more than mild curiosity. At first it was said to be five stories high, but people might go look and see, so he changed the yarn to eight stories deleting the use of the property name knowing it would be hard to prove. After a few years they made the account as an eleven story jump after newer buildings were constructed at Four Lakes thus it would remain difficult to pin down. One thing about the Moo, they are adaptive little cult creatures, ever twisting their canon to meet the demands of the market. After the newspaper and television reports of the late 1980s, the Moo stopped advertising having schools in major foreign cities, or of the instructors being registered to Asian governments, instead changing their claims to internationally recognized training.

After the well-publicized debunking of the aforementioned lies, Kim invented the fable about performing the floating jump in Asia from an eleven story building before he came to the U.S. The location in Asia is never detailed, nor is the structure. The breeding of true Moo Doe shows when you ask any Moo about their legacy and they don't know any details, they can only parrot back the fairytale. Same with the background on the 1956 championship; where was it held? In Asia, more Asia ways get in; is the best they know.

Now they say Four Lakes isn't even in Lisle, Illinois; it never existed. Just like there was never a federal Tax Case. Then they come clean and say alright, there was a Tax Case; and trials for consumer fraud and no, Moo is not in any other countries. But still, we didn't do anything wrong; just ask our leader. See, we're not a cult, we are told everything we need to know. And besides, he now believes he can jump from thirty-two stories. Supreme Grand Master Kim said so to national instructors in Seattle just a couple years ago, and they told us, so there.

JUMP SIDE KICK REFERENCES

Four Lakes Links: (from Microsoft Terra-server and the U.S. Geological Survey)

http://tinyurl.com/4mtky	One meter resolution of Four Lakes complex
http://tinyurl.com/4a4bf	One-quarter meter resolution of Four Lakes complex
www.oomyungdoe.com	Central page, look for roof top jump picture

MOO HOME SALES

This ploy is universally brought into play by Kim but not advertised openly. It started with Forrest and the Vess street house. Let's review. Forrest was the main building engineer for the Four Lakes complex. A big deal back then, large compound, good position, lots of expansion, lots to do. After work one day, Forrest pours a beer on the chubby stubborn foreign-looking guy who was insisting to scrub the floors under his feet, but then feels sorry for the immigrant and gives him a job as a janitor. Forrest was taking Karate and asks Kim if he knows any because all stupid 'Mericans think all Asians know some kind of martial art.

Together they stage some photos and Forrest goes along with the gag of calling him "my Master" until he gets screwed over and demoted, not long after the Vess street house was sold to help pay for the indirect line businesses. His first wife and son are ordered out after she questions the sale. Several others were used for their family homes in hope of securing position for their opportunity in serving Kim.

The Farm was first purchased by higher belts newly promoted due to family wealth; whose bank accounts could be used to shuttle funds, the offspring now fully ingrained in the cult and could be trusted to sign land deeds in the traditional gift of strife for life-style of Moo Doe, soon to be renamed the Chung Doe line of martial arts.

When the Illinois Attorney General wanted to press liens against the property as a source of ensuring restitution to those bilked under the illegal contract schemes used by the Moo, Kim had his attorneys file delaying motions until half of the named defendants were sent out of state for their opportunity. Thus explaining the real culprits were not around anymore, they mishandled. Case number 89CH10044, originally filed in November 1989, was ultimately settled in July 1994 with the key outcome of Kim having language inserted into the consent decree allowing him to cancel the licensing agreement of any school owners who in the future were found to break the law. He used his powers to look into the future, deciding to craft an escape clause for the federal trial he did not know was looming ahead, thinking if something did come his way again, he could simply lay blame on the underlings.

Besides, with one phone call, fifty are ready to replace any one of them. The staff of lawyers at the Attorney General must have been smiling when they signed the documents stating no further investigation was underway or contemplated by their office. It wasn't. By then the IRS was well engaged, the federal grand jury already selected.

In the interim, not wanting to lose the investment of ego and status gained by the Farm in the eyes of the cult, Kim shrewdly convinced a still loyal member, an up and comer also with family wealth, to take possession by a straw man sale but at inflated prices. The scam would have worked, Kim would have convinced this trusting soul to hand back the land and buildings, using the centuries old tradition of guilt. "After all we've done for you, more correct ways is you should hand back…" is the way Kim would say it. It would have played out just as it had many times over, in Minnesota, in Texas and in California; except this fellow woke up and kept the transaction for his own efforts, he saw through the con.

The Moo reaction was to use a file video tape of the loyal subject from a few months earlier. Filmed after a special lesson, driven for hours to near exhaustion, the instructor's physical conditioning seemed substandard, but it was a set up; designed as a security to use as blackmail should any new generation associates decide to leave. The second half of the tape shows a national in fresh uniform and newly rested, gliding through bits and pieces of the same movements shown by the now allegedly unqualified confused one who had seen the deception and left the cult behind.

The remaining cult members from around the country were shown the tape. Students were told they should only learn from qualified Moos. And main Moos who until then, told they were qualified now told to watch out, better pay franchise fees on time and attend all required seminars or you too might be the next one shown in an unflattering video.

The results backfired, as a dozen more independently owned and operated Moo Doe schools left the system, searching for real teachers and credible learning. None have ever returned to the fold.

As for the Farm real estate, it was sold, providing a good return for the now ex-Moo. This is how the process works; the cult finds out you have a house. The Moo wants to take it from you. There are two possible outcomes. Either Kim gets the cash or you do.

TRUE IS THICKER THAN BLOOD

It was said that after Kim passed a certain test, he was bestowed the title of master by Grand Master, who had not yet been given the name of Wang Po at the time this story was made up for us. Until this point in the fictional timeline in the made up history of true Moo Doe, all the other masters prior to the so-called eighth generation master, Kim (or is his name really Park), all the previous masters were Chinese. Kim was said to be the first Korean to hold this belt. This was significant due to the long history of prejudice and hatred between these two races. That a Korean had learned from a Chinese master and was judged to be more qualified than any other contestant for the position was truly history in the making (up).

Upon announcing his decision, the unnamed grand master said Kim has earned his place in Moo Doe legacy despite all the disadvantages the system held against a Korean. True is thicker than blood, were said to be the words uttered by the unknown grand master. The takeaway for us was that no matter what, you can earn if you try hard enough; a valuable lesson. Don't listen to others telling you what you can or can't do, you just have to be true and you can make it, you can reach certain point with Moo Duh-Oh by your side.

When Christmas comes around and you have to decide between relatives and Moo, you choose Moo because you're so true. Don't provide gifts to your family, give the cash to Moo. On anniversaries, birthdays or special occasions such as graduations or weddings, don't concern yourself with any frivolous trifles for anyone outside your real kindred clan, the one that has been patiently waiting for you to turn true.

Instead, give the cash and spend hours on the card or note to Kim. Spend five minutes on the birthday card to the wife but spend hours making sure nothing is needed by Kim before you go out and treat your life partner to a Value Meal. You need to remain true. Ask your higher handlers about how much sex to have, how to raise your kids, how to handle your business. You'll do fine and end up like all the others. Kim took their money, homes and women. You'll be fine with it because you've got true Moo Duh-Oh.

At least until you finally figure out OYD is a cult and then you can use all your pent up reason to live life reasonably normal. However, being true, you'll want to visit oomyungdoe_discuss@yahoo/groups and catch up on the progress your still-trapped brothers and sisters have made in their cult world, living the good life.

You'll help them best you can, provide them a source of reason (you've got extra now) and if called upon can explain that no matter how much prejudice and hatred they have to go through to earn the position of not having a fake master, it is worth it, once you see that *true is thicker than blood* was just one more control tactic rendered ineffective by Anti-Moo.

THE BEST MONEY MAKING SCHEME EVER

Open a fake martial arts school with phony but real sounding names like Chung Moo Quan, Chung Moo Doe, Ying Yang Doe, or Oom Yung Doe. Suburban strip mall rent is cheap, and return on invested capital is huge. The working capital; furniture, rugs, paint and decorative weapons needed for start up is only required once. Get used or discarded supplies to begin with. Afterward the new members pay in as they go.

Get a Korean to be front man, any Korean will do since they all look alike, and have him proclaim to be the champion of all Asia and holder of a direct line of martial arts knowledge kept hidden for 1500 years. Heck, you could say he's the reincarnation of Master Ba Gua himself, the market for made up martial arts is that good here.

Charge high prices and use pressure tactics along with strenuous exercise. Mix in some Pilates and U.S. Marine Boot Camp tactics. Get a few uneducated thugs and a couple of average Joes for your first round of future franchise owners. It'll help balance the inductees once things get rolling. You'll see.

Paint the front windows vibrant colors in authentic looking characters. What it says is not important, those coming in don't care, those that can read it will just stay away. You will get much more money from the first group anyway, so don't worry.

Make the inside look authentic too. Checkout decorating idea books from China or Korea. Use some bamboo, but be sure to include the American flag prominently in the scheme to play upon visitor's sentiments in the most cash-seductive approach possible.

When showing what folks will learn for the outrageous prices you'll charge, flash some techniques from hard-to-find books or magazines or movies. It doesn't have to be real; it just has to be real fast. And make the first month a little high but not much. Once you get the sucker's interest you can charge whatever you want 'cause he'll want it that bad. $15,000 a year is about right.

To get that kind of dough forked over largely upfront, you point to people's flaws and acknowledge you know they want to be better, and that you can plainly see they really don't know what's best for them. Luckily, you add, they found you and you can help them achieve their goals but, they have to want to work for it. That's right, appeal straight to their Anglo-Protestant work ethic you hate so much. This is their chance to make something of their lives; your way is the best way you tell them.

Look for those without many friends, the insecure ones with good paying jobs or family wealth or the older ones that just want to be around. So long as they pay cash and can keep paying cash it's all fine; when they stop paying, you cut them out. Stay away from cops or attorneys as they ask too many questions. In any case the plan is to find out what they want and then tell them you've got it. It doesn't matter what it is, just tell them you can help, but (here's the hook) they have got to pay. Once they pay, they'll keep paying, because they want to get it. Oh, and here's the beauty of this system. You can change "it" when ever you want! You can just make "it" up! It's that simple.

Once you have a few recruits that start to make progress in your contrived ranking system (explained below) they'll want to be your friends and will bring in cash by the boat load just to be around. You won't be able to count it all. You'll have to throw it away on frivolous watches and fur coats and big houses.

You'll say it's all for their benefit and they'll believe you. Why? Because you are their friend and know what's best for them. And, don't forget to emphasize there is 1500 years of knowledge behind what you say. You can say 2,000 years or 500 years but our surveys to date show 1500 produces the best results. More contracts are signed with the 1500 years tag than with any other number.

Don't be afraid to be hard on them and make up shit for them to believe in. Tell stories of how your astonishing forms were developed and how all other martial arts suck. You must emphasize this at length. After a few months start to increase the frequency and lengths of stories you tell as well as having them do more chores around your place; calling it a school is a nice personal sales touch. Get them to spend as much time as possible thinking about the school and how they can, in any way, bring in more cash.

This is critical to ensuring your pigeons start to home in on everything you tell them. Your continuing cash flows depend on it. Be hard on them and make it difficult to live normally. Harass them at all hours and on weekends. You have to make them earn, understand?

Make up a ranking system, use shoe polish to color in their worthless belts, they'll never know the difference and keep opening as many new places as possible. As soon as you've got someone gullible enough to think he knows something and has been sucked dry of cash he's ready. He's got no place else to go. The bridge is burnt, he has to go forward.

If that place does fail, well it's his fault anyway, certainly not yours. He misunderstood. Besides, you'll have dozens of replacement idiots jumping to step in at anytime, think of how much they've put in so far! Now is their opportunity! Believe us it can't miss!

At some point, the system will have to be re-aligned with current market conditions as in any business. You might do some jail time. So what? Look at all those executives who had regulatory issues. Our program is just like that.

But don't worry, after a brief all-expenses-paid stint at club-Fed you'll regroup quickly from our plan's trademarked can-in-the-backyard savings program and you'll be back in fraud in no time! In any states not having limits on personal service contracts, that is.

So for a limited time, for the first time in history, this authentic, proven system recognized internationally as the best money-making scheme ever is available to you.

Contact www.oomyungdoe.com and ask about franchise opportunities today!

AN INSTRUCTOR'S LETTER AND THE GREAT EXODUS

After Kim and the majestic ones went away to continue their training and write essays for future generations, as students were told about the prison terms, his immediate influence on the group lessoned. He still controlled the organization via his wife and a few remaining henchmen who had until now been pushed aside. These guys would most likely have left the cult after being ignored and passed over for so long, but now was their opportunity to step up and handle. Add promotion and stripes, stir well, bake with story until thanked and bowed = new national instructor.

One of the regionals made a scapegoat by the cult for the problems caused after the CBS television news expose in Chicago tried to repent and come clean during the Tax Trial. He finally woke up and turned against Kim, providing additional information to investigators, but he was not granted any leniency and was sentenced to the maximum along with the others.

His wife, left alone and despondent, wrote her story of the manipulation and abuse handed out by Kim over the past seven years. Supposedly she had a certain physical condition, everyone was led to believe, that only Kim could fix. But, it had to be handled in private, behind closed doors and she was not to ever tell her husband about the treatment. Of course, she was being used by Kim in the worst way. And her ever loyal regional instructor mate was blind to the truth until he was incarcerated.

She wrote her story, addressed to Kim's wife since after eighteen years in the strictly controlled Moo upbringing she wanted to be correct and explain directly to the one she felt was most cheated. The letter was also sent to all the schools to expose Kim as the deceitful cult leader he is. As instructors and their families read the contents of the seven page neatly handwritten confession, they could not come to terms with the truth slapping them in the face. They were living a lie.

The Moo tried damage control on a grand scale. Telling schools not to read the letter, even sending Kim's most trusted emissaries across the country to raid mailboxes and retrieve any late arriving correspondence. But it was in vain; the best the Moo could do was to use the she went crazy, she's upset because of her husband's problems excuse. The orthodox Moo hyperbole with a new twist since this story wasn't selling well within the herd. They said the excommunicated regional's spouse had threatened harm against Kim's younger children who still lived with Kim's wife at the San Diego compound. But no one bought it.

As one former higher ranked Moo put it: There was so much information from over the years; dates, places, times, who was at gatherings. I was there when these things were happening, I just never knew, none of us knew. There was so much in the letter it had to be true. I stayed in the office for hours, unable to move, I was stunned. I could not face the students. Then when the nationals tried to cover it up, I realized everything they had told me was a lie, about the Tax Case, the trials, the international organization; even though our schools were not affected, I knew these were not the type of people I wanted to be around.

The cult, despite all the promises to those continuing to pour money into the system for their opportunity, declined from over fifty schools to less than twenty as a result of the media exposure, the Tax Case and the regional wife's letter. More attrition followed as the cult demanded a higher percentage of the take from each school's operation as Kim's prison time ended; up to one third off the top, up front on any new courses signed; in cash of course. Not that this was a parole violation or anything. As a condition of release he was also required to re-affirm his citizenship oath and pledge to obey the laws of the United States. Guess he crossed his fingers behind his back, again.

COVERING THE ROYAL ASS

Every time Kim moved like say from Chicago to Houston or Houston to San Diego or traveled on any vacation or other excursion; the royal cushion had to be placed in its special container, packed along with the travel essentials and be one of the first items brought into a temporary place of rest along the way or at the new official residence.

The royal cushion was only to be used by Kim and could only be handled by specially designated persons, typically a national who had undergone the appropriate screening and who was trusted enough to take care of the cushion in the approved royal style, as had been passed down through the centuries. During the logistical process of relocation, the royal cushion's whereabouts were never unknown and was never very far away should it be needed, like the nuclear launch codes contained within the Football kept in guarded condition nearby of the President at all times. The purpose of the cushion was manifold. Besides providing support to the royal ass, it also protected the royal sphincter and served as the control icon superb as the nationals catered not only to the royal butt but also to its own independent needs. The question from Kim, "Hmmm, where is cushion?" would send the entire entourage scrambling.

The other item of interest and one which demanded equal attention in the relocations was the royal toilet seat. Whether hotel, transitory rented house or custom built site; the royal seat had to be in place before his majesty the Kim would set foot inside the porcelain throne room. "Hmmm, seat is taken care of?" he would demand.

"Yes, be alright to say everything is set, the seat and cushion both made the trip fine and are now ready," would be highest belt's reply, unless he wanted to lose a stripe.

This modus operandi was repeated during the intrastate moves within Texas and during the hideout trips from the Feds to Lake Tahoe or Monterey, California. So the team became quite the experts at all logistical applications of toilet seat and cushion concerns, no matter what, they were there to ensure Kim's ass was covered.

This practice of engaging the royal entourage in seat and cushion management techniques is no doubt just a tiny bit of the knowledge handed down over eight generations of true Moo Doe. Later on, once higher toilet seat form gets in; you'll be able to install a new ass-platform just about anywhere for your master in no time flat, just as it has been done in over one hundred countries for centuries.

E-MOO DIRECT

The top three Internet uses according to the Pew Research firm are: e-mail, online banking and searches. Under searches, thirty-five million Americans last year looked for religious or spiritual content according to The Economist Magazine. People using modern resources to improve their lives are a tremendous positive accolade of the times we live in.

However, some notable groups are not maximizing their full potential as drivers in the accelerating shifts taking place in communicative and learning preferences within advanced cultural behavior. Take the Moo for example. Those thirty-five million are a big target market and one for which the Moo could effectively re-position itself and reap untold miraculous new profits if managed properly.

We recommend a Web-based interactive platform tailored to all potential Moos or Moos who have not yet reached their cash zenith; in order to extract as much as possible from people while using as little energy as possible, much like the current demo lessons given by fat Moo-droids. Clearly new age efficiency, worthy of irrational exuberance and a few recycled arm patches for the Moos nouveau.

Moo-sultants, Inc. will conduct a complete on-line search for your body type and banking characteristics and develop a one of a kind program of semi-authentic herbs ordered directly over the Internet with specially personalized downloads of topical Moo-related dogma for your home use.

You have only one life, one body. How many steaks can you eat at one time? How many searches can you do at once? You want to make sure you get only the best for you and your family. You can do what you want but, why wait? Now is the time to be a member of e-Moo Direct!

For hundreds of days, the Moo has been quietly developing knowledge never released before to the public which is only now available on-line with a pre-approved credit card or preferably, cash pre-payment. Pay Pal is not available at this time, but you might able to handle around school or certain other thing; like let us consume your business assets. We'll put you on a waiting list and may be later you will qualify.

For $5,000 you get the base e-Moo introductory format, providing all-hours access to virtual teachings from the grandhamster himself, much like the real thing as he does in essence, appear in human form; and endless hours of droning sermons from assorted head testicles. The sound tracks can be downloaded in MP3 format for an additional royalty fee of $500. Now you can take Moo with you wherever you go! It's a gift of lies for life. It's perfect for the holidays!

And, for just an extra $1,000 per month, you can view the nationals Bob & Jerry's cartoon antics in the comfort of your own home dojo. With Moo-herbs delivered direct to your door, you're set! There is nothing to worry about, all taxes paid up front. If the Feds show up again you're given pre-written instructions on how to cry they lie, he lie; in true Moo form just like grandhamster did in front of the Dirkson federal building in Chicago. Now, you too can be just like the grandhamster!

But wait, if you don't want to miss out on the truly miraculous opportunity awaiting you via our premium service, e-Moo Direct, you'll need to be a member of Black Moo Belt e-versity, BMB e-U on-line, where for just $15,000 you can access the full range of Moo-tutorials at anytime! Simply acknowledge the "be alright to ask" prompts at sign-on under terms and conditions and you're set; once you make down payment, naturally.

You have to earn, understand? If you want to be a part of e-Moo or e-Moo Direct or not, it's up to you. Make sure you make the right choice from the on-screen selection; check "Yes" next to "I want to believe." Make sure to order a special meditation pillow when you enroll.

Some of you will insist that you have to learn the old way, in persona with a live instructor teaching you time honored and verifiable practices that truly build your body and your mind to your best abilities. For these folks, the Moo centers, e-Moo and e-Moo Direct (all Trademarked so don't try anything) is clearly not the way to go. Hopefully you already figured this out.

A TALE OF TWO MOOS

It was the best of times; it was the worst of times... Jack and Gary were both in their early twenties, in a wondrous time of technological and social change. They had good paying jobs, dated as they wished and liked the feeling of being in condition; and learning more about real martial arts.

Both were on course and on their way to Moo-dumb. They passed fourth section and went out to discuss the future. About a year and a half later they both made first degree and looked back at their accomplishments and to the future at the same time. They set their minds. Their circle of friends had expanded over the years, although now it was exclusively all Moos, all the time. They lived with Moos, trained with Moos, hung out with Moos, and lived the Moo life as only Moos know how. Overall, it wasn't bad until the real bullshit dug in.

Jack looked at the changes in his life and thought he wasn't as far enough along as he had hoped. The black belt was nice, but he had to change jobs several times to keep up with school demands and couldn't complete the college courses he thought he'd need to advance professionally. He had no money saved and although he seemed to be in a little better physical condition compared to other peers not in Moo, he determined that overall, he was behind. Jack saw the dark side. He thought Moo was controlling his life, and that Kim wasn't the guy he said he was, and all the secrecy involved with the organization's finances signaled something amiss.

Gary however, saw the bright side. He had sold everything he owned and dedicated himself totally to the Moo. He was true Moo, blindly so. Gary held out that higher belts would be there as they have for centuries, pulling up lower belts so they can have a better life. Look at all the friends, our knowledge, and our comfort of being set, Gary thought. He didn't understand how Jack could be confused now. He decided to seek help on behalf of his old friend and sought out the wisdom of higher Moos.

Jack was blind-sided. After several in-depth conversations, he decided to move on, to draw a line and put this part of his life behind him while trying to retain whatever small amount of positive he had gained during the last three years. His friend Gary would have to understand.

Jack went back to college, and with extra effort caught up in the professional business arena. He moved, got married, started a family yet still retained an interest in martial arts. He earned black sash in a genuine school of Kung Fu, although the rank was not important to him. He liked the real self-defense practice and being associated with those who also honored authentic traditions. Ten more years went by. And with Jack's children leaving high school, he thought often about his old friend Gary.

Was Gary set for retirement as Jack was with his investments? No doubt Gary's kids would be going to college by now too. Was Gary qualified to leap from buildings or had he traveled to the international Moo schools as they once both yearned to do? There was so much to catch up on!

How would Dickens or Bobcat Goldwaith put this, I wonder? Gary pretty much puked out. Did five years federal jail time, is barred from holding public office, most government jobs, can't vote, has a bad back, no friends, very little money and is a destitute failure. Got Moo?

THE THIRTEEN CHAPTERS

As the 1990's came to a close, an outstanding easy was written and posted on the Internet, detailing a wide array of the Moo cult's inner workings, beliefs and group behaviors. Entitled True Disclosures, The Thirteen Chapters; these fifty-plus pages are well written and intelligently constructed with such clarity and insight into this group that it was obviously written by a known member who achieved a fairly high rank after some years in. However, this work was published anonymously, believed to have taken place in one of the eastern segments of the Moo organization, outside of where Joe and friends Mooed, and encompassing a latter time span. The parallels, though, are striking.

The similarities and continuation of Moo social activities described therein are like the old joke; didn't we go to different high schools together? A few of the guys Joe knew back in the day journeyed to the East and are mentioned in The Thirteen Chapters. It was sad, Joe explained, to see decent folks he used to know and respect continue to be entrapped in the cult. We can only hope they see their way clear and also rebuild their lives.

COGNITIVE DISSONANCE

This concept was brought out by a fellow Kung Fu brother with good insight into the Moo's depth of manipulation. It goes like this: As a Moo, you do not want to discover or face the realization yours is not the best; that Moo is nowhere near anything they've claimed, it's not what they've told you. You do not even want to hear it. You are unable to process any facts counter to your Moo-established beliefs. Your cognition is in a state of dissonance. You seek harmony, consonance.

However, because Kim or is it really Park, someone you revere, broke your trust, you are having difficulty coming to terms with it. As in the legacy of True Mu, it is not what he said. As in the origin and history of Moo and its forms are not what they sold to you; as in explanations about the Tax Case, or the Wang Po fabrication, or no international schools. Or as in you're a school debtor, not a school owner. Lies? Maybe just misunderstandings.

Since Kim broke your trust and you still want to believe after all the sweat equity you've invested, you change your beliefs so Kim and the Moo cult you're in appears not so bad, palatable at least.

Your new beliefs are: Taxes and the government are bad. All other martial arts are conspiring against Moo. Moo is our real, true name, recognized throughout history. If we extend the logic without benefit of having to call Moo HQ every day, we begin to realize, perhaps, we don't have to make that one-third off the top cash payment from new courses to Kim anymore. We can keep what we earned.

DISCOUNTS FOR MOO MEMBERS ONLY

One of the perks of higher Moo rank was the expected travel and greater responsibilities of handling more schools. We use 'expected' here because in reality you simply become a new class of gopher for Kim.

For all the references and leading on about the grandeur of higher positions, some Moos who traveled were still looking to run a scam. Back in the day, boarding passes for airlines were printed on nondescript paper. Ticket and gate agents used different color pens to indicate cross checking against manifest lists.

For most of the 1990s commercial flights were half full and security pale in comparison to today. So it was no big deal to a national Moo to travel in the luxury so deserved by taking phony blank boarding passes printed up to look like an authentic form, mark it up with a colored pen du jour of that airline and slip on board free. Sometimes authentic looking stamps would be constructed to mimic the real ones used by the carriers.

It's the real nature of the royal manner of Moo. Everything else is made up, a fake. Why not fabricate passage to travel to handle more Moo enterprise? Besides, airlines overcharge for the service, the seats are all paid for by the government, we're just making the score even.

Dozens of such trips between major cities cross-country were made by Moo fraud-structors. Until, one national got careless and was caught at a large hub by airline personnel, suspicious of the extra passenger with the not-quite-so authentic boarding pass. The Moos had used the scam one too many times.

The evidence was a briefcase full of fake boarding passes. Banned by the airlines, the traveling nationals were black listed. The result was greater independence for the schools as the nationals were not about to drive thousand of miles or spend the money to fly under assumed names, except for once or twice per year when it was mission critical. The frequent flyer program, approved of and participated in by the Kim, was over.

So now the ranking belts stationed in semi-autonomous regions would fly to Kim several times a year at their expense to bring the money to him, hundreds of thousands of dollars tax free annually. This continued while he was in prison. Kim's wife spent lavishly on private schools, living expenses at the opulent mini-mansion and caring for three of his four children plus of course, a good deal of shopping.

During a trip to San Diego a few years prior to the federal investigations, the inner circle was found hard at work digging at various places in the small backyard of the compound. Kim had buried cash and his sacred scroll proclaiming his achievements of 1956 in a metal can but had forgotten where. Just as he forgot what form he passed, how much and to whom. This is why form in one state looks so different than the form in another, after it was passed it was ignored so long as the cash kept coming in. It's brilliant in a way. Any questions? It's your fault, you misunderstood, you didn't handle.

Finally, someone happened to remember the location, and pointed out the spot. After it was retrieved, by digging into the hillside from below so as not to tear up too much lawn and leave more obvious signs of nefarious activity; the stash was retrieved and the contents presented directly to Kim by the most trusted national, one who could barely read English let alone an authentic Asian government document, as it was held out to be to the others.

All the future holdings for instructor's families were in that can. And Kim spent it in royal style, buying his next house; which was ultimately forfeited to pay for attorneys from the Tax Trial.

DUDE, WHERE'S MY MOO?

Within the past few years, the Cult has changed their promotional marketing yet again. Now with the International Level Training, students as low as second section are moving like they are already first and second degree instructors from years past. Well that's certainly good news to any current level second and third degree black Moo belt (bmb). There was no need to earn their way to where they're at now what with the new shortcut method. Students with six months in the Cult will have the same knowledge as those with three years.

So you see there's really no reason to sign up at one of the few remaining OYD cash collection and cult induction centers. Why? It's obvious, clearly stated by the Moo-idiots themselves. Wait another few short years, more new and improved higher forms will be made up and even before first section you can move like fourth or fifth bmbs of today. Not satisfied, want even higher development? Wait about four years and then you'll be promoted to national Moodroid seventh degree just for showing up with coffee.

For centuries as time moves forward, the true-mu development curve compresses. More achievement is reached with ever-increasing inputs of cash in shorter and shorter periods. It used to take ten years to reach fourth degree, albeit it was a bmb, but it was still much better that what is taught today. With these new programs, even greater results than those currently advertised are achieved by pure thought. Cash is the only requirement; you just have to bring down. In the end, there's nothing to think about.

Although not likely, if you try hard enough, if you earn, you may be able to reach the level of self-proclaimed doctor Kim himself and be able to demonstrate the level of skill and ability of thinking yourself off a thirty-two story building. Whereas in years past we thought it was just five stories. See how much you don't understand?

WHO AM I? – BY ANGRY WHITE GHOST

I am every instructor who signed on believing in True, Right and Correct. I am every instructor who believed in building a better life for himself. I am every instructor who wanted a family of instructors, who believed in the same principles. I am every instructor who wanted to believe in Kim. I am every instructor who carried cash for Kim in the specially marked envelopes, stuffed in his sock. I am every instructor who lived on ramen and rice. I am every instructor who bowed to the east when beginning, bowed to the west when ending practice.

I am every instructor who at midnight on New Years Eve, drank a clean glass of water and then mentally thanked Kim. I am every instructor who cleared his mind and salted his school to start a new year. I am every instructor who left his family and friends behind for a promise of a better life. I am every instructor who gathered up his hair clippings and flushed them down the toilet after a hair cut. I am every instructor who forced himself to choke down kimchee and bugolgi. I am every instructor who gave up a dream of being a dentist, a pilot, or a doctor to have a chance to be around Kim. I am every instructor who believed mirrors were the gateway to different dimensions, and if you broke one you needed to cover it in dog poo and throw it into moving water. I am every instructor who maxed out his credit card making sure a higher belt was comfortable.

I am every instructor who believed that Kim could have been a major general during the Korean War. I am every instructor who believed that as a child, Kim was sent to the mountains to train. I am every instructor who believed that Forrest was wrong for pouring beer on Kim's head when they were just janitors at Four Lakes Village. I am every instructor who handed in a birthday card with "care feelings" scribbled on it. I am every instructor who gave up his only vacation time only to drive all night, and listen to endless drivel conversations at a camp out.

I am every instructor who "yesssed" and "be alrighted" to the point where it became a joke. I am every instructor who believed Kim could speak eight languages. I am every instructor who talked himself into believing that Ben Hurr was fun. I am every instructor who said and did all the right things, so he could be close to Kim. I am every instructor who believed Kim when he said he was here to finish and cleanup what Jesus had started. I am every instructor who believed there were schools in Asia, Guam, Australia, Hawaii, Seoul, Pusan, Canada. I am every instructor whose wife or girlfriend was violated by Kim. I am every instructor who believed in Wang Po. I am every instructor who went to prison for Kim.

I am you, 18 years ago.

EPILOGUE

"In a time of unusual deceit, telling the truth is a revolutionary act"
—George Orwell

Of paramount importance in understanding these sagas is that each of us was manipulated per our own personal plan, our certain case concerning, as Kim would put it; in fulfilling our royal role as form flasher, course talker, cash collector, lesson leader, construction or maintenance droid, butler boy or kitchen girl. The path to higher Moo cult belt for a factory worker is different than it is for a business owner, or attorney or mechanic; as is different for a college teacher or a fireman. From all walks of life, the symbol of the king turned upside down is in truth good people turned to supporting the evil of the Kim. Perplexed by whatever we thought was missing in our lives and believing, hoping, wishing the Moo would be the answer.

Just as informations today, as we were then, are brought into the mainstream Moo cult belief system; how much we paid in and the related challenges put before us to reach certain point was or is the result of a sociopathic algorithm designed, built and operated by Kim. It captures each mark's personal traits, family holdings and likelihood of turning against him. Each and every Moo cult member, then or now is strung along to the maximum extent possible in whatever way he or she can ultimately best serve Kim.

From its heyday of around fifty schools in the early to middle 1990's, this organization still exists today with more than a dozen remaining cash collection stations scattered in Washington, Massachusetts, Pennsylvania, California, plus a few remaining outposts in the Midwest. These states have lax consumer protection laws and prior to the Internet, were under most folk's radar. New legislation in Washington State limits the amount karate studios can charge there for instruction. The new limit enacted of $3,600 per year, will seriously affect the Moo's cash collection activities. Many students pay two or three times that annually. The hook is the same, "It's up to you, how much do you want to learn?"

Oom Yung Doe or whatever name it will use in the future is and will be a cult. It continues to exist because people continue to want to believe. Kim will in all likelihood keep his gypsy complements of royal subjects moving into new territories to exploit fresh victims for the rest of his life. Moos are parasites, existing off the labors of others. Their legacy will be of deceit, failure and misery, all the while never accepting responsibility for their deeds. It will always be someone else's fault, someone else's problem, as it has been for centuries. "No, he lie, they lie; they might say they learned from me, but they did not," are the true words of John C. Kim.

After reconnecting with old friends post-Moo, Joe asked a former senior ex-Moo, "What was the most amazing thing Kim ever taught or demonstrated that you personally witnessed?"

"Well," began Joe's friend, "there was this one time he showed breathing through his back, that was kind of cool." During twenty years, it wasn't martial arts skill, or physical talent and ability; it was selling the illusion of a higher capability described as the capstone of Moo learning. Another former inner circle member of Moo once directly asked Kim during a private audience about the lineage of the preceding masters of the supposed Chung Doe line of martial arts. Who had taught Wang Po, whose name was only recently revealed at the time, as the master who taught Kim? Kim bristled angrily with a terse reply, "What human being you think can teach me, I talk straight to above power. I decide which way."

Who is John C. Kim? His real name we may never know. Jack Park was one alias used of a Korean child who died at a very young age. Kim obtained false passports and other identification using the stolen social security number, his lawyers arguing the government bureaucracy had once again made a mistake. The year after leaving prison, Kim changed his name to Won Chin Kim according to Cook County, Illinois records. Released from federal custody in 2001, Kim was granted early termination of his three year supervised release in 2003 by his affirmations to the court.

A changed man? Hardly. He lives offensively beyond his stated income in posh San Diego County while his followers continue to pledge their personal assets and family wealth supporting the Kim

Family Trust in return for a few new Moo patches or a new Moo belt from time to time. He continues to profess grossly inflated claims of power and authority with no evidence or witness to testify to his ability. Kim considers himself above all others, using charismatic parables of self-created wisdom to explain to the captive faithful how he was sent to make things right after God and Jesus Christ, in Kim's words, failed to help mankind.

Research into what might have been his original training in martial arts reveals a faint association to well regarded masters from Korea, a few of whom have been in the United States for at least as long as Kim has. But Kim or is it really Park, keeps his operations far removed from what could have been his peer group lest he be found out as a phony. The Moos never interact in any way with true martial artists. The consensus of several of the contributors here believe John C. Kim was a beginning level student at an area in Pusan, South Korea and to his twisted credit was able to copy fragments of more than a few systems over the years subsequently concocting his own royal heritage.

The bona fide masters of Korean martial arts give great honor and credit to those from whom they learned. Kim can not. He was no doubt considered a bad seed by the real masters in Asia, so it would have been much too difficult for him to progress legitimately. During the political upheaval in South Korea during the early 1970s and by his sister marrying a U.S. Serviceman, Kim was handed his ticket to glory.

Of all the lies, false promises and manipulative crap Kim has spewed on people over four decades, the worst has to be, first you have to earn. Who is he to say who should earn or not. And what are they earning?

Instructor Jeff earned his first black Moo belt in the early 1980s and helped build the Farm in Illinois and the Ranch in Texas and stayed ever loyal through the FBI raids. He died of a brain tumor while Kim stood by and did nothing. The stress of serving Kim, nonstop for years; the confusion, the false truths and promises never realized of better mind, better body, but first you have to earn, took the ultimate toll on Jeff. Kim said he could have cured him, as he always says, but it would attract too much attention. Same reason Kim does not float around in public anymore.

Instructor Jane was the wife of a national instructor turned felon and was herself a full fledged black Moo belt, one of the very few women to ever reach such a rank in the Moo without marrying and receiving the title as a mere position. She died of cancer after years of caring for the Kim family and being a close confidant for the many failed businesses Kim used as fronts for money processing. Again Kim stood by and did nothing, not so much as a card to her family. Kim could not afford being linked.

He said he could, but would not cure her as it would be taking advantage of his power. The guy who claimed he was sent to Earth to finish the work of Jesus saying verily, after all your work you are not worthy. Jane held title documents to property the Moos needed to sell in order to pay Kim's attorney's fees. Her only visits in the hospital from Moos were to obtain her signature on the land deed. Her husband never went, he was too busy handling.

Instructor John was an electrical engineer with a solid reputation and ethic. He had worked at Cape Canaveral and for GTE and had traveled around the world. He sought better health and thought martial arts would help. He was older than most students starting out and eventually made sixth section then black Moo belt honorary for his work at the Farm and the herbal products businesses.

He died in the pool in Kim's backyard at the Farm, due to an epileptic seizure. John developed progressively worse seizures the more he was around Kim who convinced him he was better off without medication; that a cure was not only possible, but Moo had one used for centuries, but first he would have to earn. Kim had his Moos handle the situation while he fled, not willing to be linked or lend assistance in any way.

The Moo leaders are liars and cowards. There are no international schools, there are no linked generations of Moo masters of which they are the lineage holder, and there is no Asian organization even remotely associated with Kim or his cronies. Some of his followers woke up, some moved on, the rest still believe and continue to sell the lies.

The exorbitant prices to capture commitment, the segmentation through courses to establish a caste society, the misuse of the belt system to bestow false position and rank over qualifications, the fabricated histories, phony certifications to generate beliefs of authenticity, the expectations that members progress in rank by parroting the cult's dogma as a measure of value. All these tricks will be used by the cult as they have in the past to capture the imagination and the wallets of potential believers.

Anything anyone ever accomplished in Moo be it rank, improved short term physical or the memorization of steps; was in spite of Moo, not because of it. The sum of the detriments; the false martial teaching, the impractical and damaging stresses put into the body, the alterations of personality; are not fully realized until long after you stop agreeing to Moo.

When first leaving the cult, you will struggle to find the real you. Different than when you started, there are holes drilled into your psyche, the abscesses leaching cult mannerisms. You still relate to an environment where others should bow to you, that you know something better, you just haven't figured it out yet. The reality is you've been kept in a psychological closet for years and are now thrust back into society as if for the first time. Moo-ness has a strange way of manifesting itself inside us until we face it head on. Unless one confronts Moo-ness it will continue to permeate all that we do.

If you do not think you were in a cult, there is more work to be done. Retaining anything Moo be it artifacts, pictures, words, phrases, symbols; any of it is a detriment to cleansing. There is no good in Moo. Not the movements, not the system, not any of it. This takes further reflection and inspection to realize. If you proceed with real martial arts training, what you will very much need to be wary of is any new authentic learning will be polluted by the Moo experience in ways you can not perceive. The new forms gained are at risk of becoming Moo-ified, slowly at first but eventually becoming useless because the Moo piece of dirt was dissolved into the clean glass of self you thought was rinsed pure before you re-filled it. Because you could not detect the remaining Moo, the replenishment was tainted. Remember, the invisible is much more powerful. And, your new mentors may not want to deal with your past.

It will be even more difficult to erase the Moo-think. Mental processes, behaviors, habits, how one filters external information, how you communicate to others; have been through the Moo meat grinder in ways we could not realize because by the time our deeper personas went through it, we gave up questioning.

Naturally, there are disagreements about the specific reasons why people join cults and much controversy over explaining complex behaviors in group dynamics. Dr. Michael Langone, executive director for the International Cultic Studies Association, specializes in research about cultic groups and psychological manipulation. In the Psychiatric Times July 1996 edition he discussed three models, summarized here:

1. Deliberative model, favored by sociologists and religious scholars—people join cults because of what they think about a group.

2. Psychodynamic model, favored by mental health professionals without direct experience with cult members—says people join a cult because of what the group does for them, it fulfills unconscious psychological needs.

3. Thought Reform model—favored by mental health professionals who have worked with cult members says people join because of a systematic program of psychological manipulation that exploits rather fulfills, needs.

The Moo cunningly employs significant aspects of the models presented. You think you are learning eight martial arts from instructors approved by the champion of all Asia because that's what they advertise. You think you are doing something good as you start to practice, as the cult reinforces that Moo is the best way for you and makes you feel part of an elite group. Then the Moo uses subtle, patient manipulation to entrap you until willingly you sell your core beliefs and give them huge sums of money for "opportunity." You have given so much; you must have faith in it. Don't doubt yourself, don't fight it, give in to Moo.

It might be some time before you are able to identify that Moo was a sink, not a source of knowledge and vitality. Until then you push nearly everyone away, not wanting to be further drained. Reasoning becomes crystallized and rigid because that is your Moo comfort zone. You might even cling on to your Moo form, thinking the movements are the good; it's the odd behaviors and distasteful reputation, the political bullshit you want to discard. No, no it can't all be a lie you keep telling yourself. But it is. Rethink. There is no champion of all Asia, there are no international schools, there is no 1500 year-old Oom Yung Doe or Chung Doe Line, and Kim can not float nor fly from buildings no matter how the story is told.

Go back to a time before you were Moo and ask how did I think, how did I act towards others, how did I handle myself. You'll find numerous good qualities and attributes from which to begin healing. The things Moo pointed to us as our weaknesses were in fact our strengths.

At some point you will turn your back on the Kims in the world regardless of whatever form they use, better for the experience yet obligated to explain to others: Do not Moo, and here's why.

Joe Smith

MOO CULT TERMS, USAGE AND MEANINGS

Above power – also called *higher power*, attempting to replace reverence within us for God, this was the force Kim claimed he tapped into as the source of his knowledge and abilities by his alleged true understanding of how the universe works.

Anything needed? – requisite inquiry each time you see a higher rank.

Asia – the place where the mythical headquarters of CMQ existed, *more Asia ways*.

Be alright (to ask or to say) – proper manner for asking a question, or affirming you agree.

Be alright (to mention) – replaced by *say*, as mentioning by lower belts gives the impression they know something.

Better mind, better body – because Moos are better. See *see how much you don't understand*.

Bongu – shit, excrement; anything foul smelling; a hard time from your soon to be ex-boss at your day job.

Break the line towards – the cardinal sin in the Moo organization. Means to disrespect another Moo, also used as *break the line towards nature*, meaning there were some things we should not do or as a spoof by instructors describing a severe case of indigestion.

Call this weekend – to check if anything needed.

Care feeling – the reason you sell your car, empty your bank account and pay for everyone else's food.

Certain (other) part – cash or payment; unless if used as *certain other part*, which means not important.

Chance – *have a*, or *give a chance*, despite your failures and misgivings and lack of trust, you can still make higher belt.

Chance to be around – official notice you were expected to serve higher belts that weekend.

Check, re-check, checking – making it look like you know what you are doing, occupying time.

Chung Doe – the made up imaginary martial arts fabricated after Chung Moo Quan was blown apart. The Chung Doe Line was the new claimed ancestry of Kim that was always there, just he never told anyone before because they would not understand.

Chung Moo Doe – abbreviated as CMD to give it cache, this new and improved marketing was the mainstream as the Tax Case unfolded.

Chung Moo Quan – abbreviated as CMQ, the 1500 year-old fable about a line of royal martial arts.

Clear – able to understand that Moo is the best thing for you.

Clear minded ways – what you are after you sign course, but only until you need to sign up for another one.

Coming up time – the transition between white belt to full instructor.

Concentration – a mystical power you will develop by being on course.

Concerning – something related to the next thing you were going to sell to give your money to Moo.

Confused – what you would be called if you didn't sell the thing *concerning*, above.

Connect by – related to or as a result of.

Conversation – lengthy drawn out tautology designed to get you to bring in cash.

Correct – used to define a student's potential worth to the cult; e.g. *he is more correct ways*. The over-riding goal in Moo was you wanted to be correct. See *mistake* below.

Course (part) – an agreement in nebulous terms describing your obligations to bring in as much cash as possible, preferably in fresh hundred-dollar bills, in return for feeling good about yourself, *your certain case concerning*, during your next test. *Handle course part* meant you paid on time.

Crazy lady – specific label given out by John C. Kim towards a CBS Chicago reporter, with indirect instructions to his flock that someone should step up and *handle* her.

Deeper meaning – pay attention, this is important. No really, this time it really is.

Different (kind of, little bit, pretty) – used when describing the attributes of Moo.

Dingy – anyone from another style of martial arts.

Direction – a course of action dictated to you by a higher Moo.

Doe Chi – drunk on one's own thoughts. A descriptor Kim made up to describe those who left in later years to start their own schools without paying any more money or attention to him.

Donk – crap or something you didn't want or didn't expect; what your Moo roommates left for you in the middle of the living room still on the plate from the night before; it was food, once.

Don't think too much about – listen to it, but don't count it as credible.

Earn – as in *this life you have to earn*. We all thought earning a Moo black belt meant something at one point. See *confused*.

Eigo (eye-go) – colloquial Korean expression of surprise, dismay or just to make it sound like you had something to say to be able to join in deeper intellectual discussions of Moo cult activity. Used extensively early on when everyone wanted to imitate the Kim in hopes of being *correct*.

Envelope part – cash, notated in code on the outside, stuffed in your socks or inside shirt sleeve. After a time instructors on *rotation* would try to outdo their counterparts and devise new methods for concealment.

Female mind – never fully explained, just as if it was not supposed to be.

Form – basic hard-style martial arts movements linked with ballroom dancing steps in intricate choreography and supported by grandiose tales of history and hollow legends.

Friend – what your wife was called before she become more involved with Moo.

Future part – the lure of something better is just ahead, like you will have your own checking account again or there will be one thousand schools in America. When will it happen? *In future part.*

Get in – to do something or accomplish it, or if used interrogatively means your handler wants to know if you had sex recently e.g. *did you get in?* Also as a command during a lesson, *Get In!* meant to push harder on whatever silly exercise you were doing.

Getting in – multiple uses; get in some practice, have sex, or in various tenses, *I got in one time* meaning you hit someone.

Go ahead – what higher belts say when granting permission for something, as a response e.g. *Be alright to handle certain part? Uh, go ahead.*

Going out – one night per week recess time for young adult Moos.

Handle – e.g. *go ahead and handle*, means to go do (whatever).

Handling – taking care of Moo business.

Higher belt – any higher rank than you, and they probably weigh more.

Higher course – is like the course you're on now and haven't finished paying for yet but you need to get on this new course, because it's higher. See *Understand.*

Higher form – the special stuff taught only on higher course.

Higher point – the place you'll reach by being on higher course and practicing higher form.

Higher power – the entity Kim claimed to connect to until he was cut off, apparently he *mistaked.*

Hit their mind – a new hook or a new scheme needed to get more cash rolling in.

Holding – how much money was in your pocket, e.g. *how much holding have?*

Hook nose – people descended from Abraham.

How feel? – an excuse by higher Moos to probe into your subconscious.

Information – what you are until you try your first lesson in Moo.

Intergalactic walrus course – although there never was such a course offered thus far in any of the Moo-named cults, it is included here by request as the term fits the physical stature of many of today's current Moo higher ranks.

Junk dealer – a teacher or owner of another martial arts style school or facility.

Kong Su – a hard-form style of martial arts believed originating from North Korea and Manchuria.

Koondingy – buttocks, Kim liked to talk about his a lot, touching it and smiling.

Later – anything without immediate benefit to Kim or his cult.

Liberace type – male students who were believed to be gay or more feminine than others.

Light mind – anyone who did not give all, all the time, to Moo.

Light touch – the Kim using 1/10,000 of the power he claimed to have.

Lighter conversation – dialoguing chicks at a bar.

Little bit – would turn out to be as much as you had.

Location – the place where you were supposed to be, a new school before approval.

Lose your mind – turning away from worshipping John C. Kim.

Lower belt – relative term compared to your current rank status, also used to describe someone not as cool as you.

Make something happen – sign up courses, get more down payments in for the courses, generate more cash.

Make sure – in Moo terms a deliverable you are committed to seeing accomplished.

Main part – in other words if you forget everything else, remember this after three hours standing in line during a lecture. Or, it could be the big Kahuna himself if used as a proper noun.

Massage – old Moo term not used much anymore, means to put someone in the hospital due to the beating they received.

Maow – ooh, don't say this one out loud, it is the magical power women have over men. But, if you stay true, Moo will help you defeat it.

Missing (type or ways) – anyone that left the Moo cult after reaching at least a moderate rank.

Mistake – the opposite of being correct. After a few of these you didn't really care anymore, just trying to make it through the day was good enough.

Misunderstand – a classic term of denial for Moos throughout history. Somebody else always misunderstood.

More – frequently used as an enhancer, *little bit more* (whatever).

More correct ways – whatever you're doing now isn't quite good enough, but keep trying hard and you will earn. See *bongu*.

More faster ways – a hollow promise we'd be allowed to go home early after turning in the weekly cash receipts, or whatever you were doing you were not doing it fast enough.

National fat bastard – an apt descriptor of the current leadership ranks of Oom Yung Doe.

Negative (the) – used to describe the one force that could defeat every Moo every time. Once the negative gets in, it almost never gets out. But those with it do *wakeup*.

Negatives – the word "no" was not allowed in reply, therefore *I did not, there was not, not that I could see or find* (or care any less about) was used instead.

No-mind – descriptor used to define an underperforming or too independent to be controlled Moo.

Nothing there – actually there is something there, the Moo just doesn't want you to consider it, and so they tell you this instead.

Not sure – an acceptable way to indicate you'll believe or do whatever you are told.

Not qualified – a point along the food chain of Moo. *Outside ways, information, white belt, lower belt, higher belt, Do Chi, Pa Doe,* and then *not qualified.* Anybody who held a position or rank in Moo and told Kim to go back to Hell instantly became unqualified in Moo, which is a good thing.

One – a descriptor skillfully deployed within Moo to help you think only about (how many?) things at a time. Thus, you would be told to *pick up one coffee* and single mindedly do that and return like a good little Moo. You're lucky they let you outside today. See *selfish.*

One accord, one mind – words written on the Moo school walls, Biblical passages Kim twisted around.

One time – oh crap, you're in for it now, all lectures start with *one time…*

Opportunity – your one and only chance that may never ever come again.

Outside ways – anyone fortunate enough not to have been exposed to Moo.

Over-thinking – trying to make sense of Moo, it can't be done; Robbie the Robot fighting the Krel.

Pa Doe – said to be the wrong path, away from Moo

Pick up – you're buying.

Pine Sol – apparently means lemon fruit juice in Korean as the immigrant Kim purchased, then drank, a bottle of it by mistake thinking it was juice; then told everyone he survived because of his higher physical development.

Position – could be used to describe rank or status, otherwise used to describe a step in Moo *form.*

Practice – what we thought we were supposed to be doing when we were inside the Moo facilities.

Puck – much over-used verbal expression by the Kim and all his imitators describing a quick action; *puck, get in one time* was often employed during a brief showing of a technique, accompanied by the slap of the thighs with the hands or a snap of the fingers to take focus away from his crappy execution.

Put mind in – thinking about what you were doing.

Re-check – go back and do it again.

Respect line – the rank and file order of highest to lowest belts within Moo.

Retire – as in retire from your day job and *start to handle a school*.

Right ways – what you wanted to be striving for. See *correct*.

Robot – anyone who did not do exactly as they were told or did not do it well enough.

Rock-head – a *robot* with perceived less mental capabilities.

Rotation – executing high speed lane changes in defectively hazardous vehicles while transporting large amounts of black market currency to specially designated locales within the western suburbs of Chicago.

Schedule – stuff you were supposed to do that made increasingly less sense over time.

School – strip mall re-education, cash collection and cult indoctrination center.

See how much you don't understand – a rebuke of a lower belt who asked the wrong question.

Selfish ways – what you were if you didn't call in as required.

Serious ways – something important.

Set (your mind) – means to push everything else aside.

Sitting down – e.g. *sitting down handling a school* means you got to sit behind the desk, until a higher belt showed up, then you stood next to it, even though you were still *sitting down in school*.

Skill and ability – non-sequitor terminology used to defray any inquiry towards Moos.

Spending change – the fifty bucks you were handed every week for gas and lunch money.

Standing up, in or front – was supposed to describe a leadership position, in reality it meant accepting more debt. Those who *stood up* got promoted; those who *stepped back* held onto their credit ratings.

Start to move – begin practice. Or what you really wanted to do after a large plate of sesame-laden bugolgi and kimchee.

Stay on – e.g. *stay on Moo Doe ways* means do not quit your commitment to the cult.

Stepping back, in, out, over – means you were supposed to go do something; e.g. *step over towards Denny's to pick up one coffee*.

Talking about – any discussion point directed towards you.

Tell a story – means to lie, or someone, *more outside ways one*, assuredly, was lying to you. Same thing Kim did when explaining about his training and how he can teach martial arts.

Thank you – often uttered as "dank you," requisite parroting performed throughout the day. If not sure, just thank or dank along with everyone else.

That is all you need to know – obtained from the movie Jeremiah Johnson, movies were a great source of inspiration and knowledge to Mr. Kim. The Godfather and Bruce Lee movies were others. Don't believe? *Go check one time.*

The way I look – aside from his use of Revlon and Maybelline products, it was how Mr. Kim emphasized his view on things.

The way I understand – how Moos are expected to answer their thoughts about something.

Tiny bit – your personal effort or understanding.

Touch a little bit – somebody got chunged or slapped around.

True, right, correct – the core essence of what Moo was supposed to be about.

Trying hard – the path to enlightenment.

Uh – general purpose utterance, could mean o.k., no, no idea, or pass the pizza.

Understand – whatever it was, you were expected to acknowledge you heard it, not necessarily understanding it.

Waiting – a term used to fill space in a cult member's mind or daily plan. *House of Waiting* was the Wagg's Restaurant in Downers Grove where it took forever to have a meal.

Wake up – what happens when a student finally succumbs and signs up on an advanced course of Moo. In reality it's what happens when you leave the cult behind.

Walking dead – anyone who had turned their backs on the cult, former students mostly.

Well done one – slang Kim encouraged the use of to describe black people.

What – another multi-purpose Moo verbal tool, could be used as a declaration to affirm your orders were being carried out or to defray having to answer to a lower belt or as a general expression of exasperation at a lower belts' perpetual ineptitude; e.g. *what, what…*

What doing – primary utterance to check up on someone, in later years used as a spoof between instructors when a date was brought over to the apartment; *uh, what doing in there?*
What or what, certain thing – used as filler in between sentences when Kim was on a roll.
What thinking about – you've been caught daydreaming again.
Which way – what stupid people say when they really don't have the courage to ask.
White belt – anyone not inside taking lessons from Moo. Or, you must have really screwed up this time.
Wrong ways – anything detrimental to the interests of Moo.
You look like have some questions – an advanced Moo inquiry tool, leads to *conversations.*
Your case – you've been targeted as someone with special needs.
Your mind – an effective guilt trip trigger.
Your self – used to offer the illusion that higher belts do care about you.

Here's a test to see how well you would do. Try linking any of these terms to form a coherent thought and see if it makes sense; e.g. *more certain thing your case, start to handle that part*, means you have been granted authority to go ahead and do it. See how easy it is to be a Moo!

Reviews of *Herding the Moo* from Amazon.com

Inside the Cult

I was a member of the inner circle of the Chung Moo Quan organization in the late 70's and early 80's. I found *Herding the Moo* to be an accurate account of the dynamics that exist at the top levels of the John C. Kim organization. These pages reveal the inner workings of the cult that are veiled from the public eye in a very calculated way. Former cult members will easily recognize the pattern of lies, deceit, and betrayal, as well as the subtle techniques of grooming that we fell prey to as loyal followers of John C. Kim. I laughed at Joe Smith's antics which typify the ridiculous missions we were assigned. I wept when I discovered that women other than me had been sexually abused in this cult. I raged when I learned that this charismatic charlatan has continued to masquerade as a martial arts master for over 30 years. For those currently involved in Oom Yung Doe, *Herding the Moo* will provide you with information to ponder. I hope that it will generate questions. Do not hesitate to pose those questions to your instructors. For parents with children in OYD, *Herding the Moo* is an essential read.
   Kim Rieser, January 2007

Thank You Joe Smith for Telling our Story

The Moo has touched the lives of thousands. We believed without questioning. Now we question everything. Years lost, love lost, money gone, pain has followed.
   R. Johnson, May 2006

Herding the Moo

I read this book cover to cover, and then read it again. I have to say it is a very accurate account of how the cult of Oom Yung Doe, formerly Chung Moo Quan and Chung Moo Doe, operates. It clearly shows step by step how a young beginner is slowly indoctrinated and brainwashed into the cult, and how their lives decay a little at a time until they have been totally swallowed up. You can see how bank accounts are drained, and how lives are ruined, marriages destroyed; and ultimately how one's soul is blackened by the experience.

This is a good book not only for those who are in the cult of John C. Kim, but also for those who have family members, or friends involved. Every martial arts school that is anywhere near an Oom Yung Doe school should have one as well. It is a well written and well chronicled book. I found it to be an enjoyable read, and the writer's sense of humor complements the all too real events that occurred in the story.

Gian Lencioni, September 2006

Don't Become a Dupe

I spent thirteen years in this cult. The worst feeling that I have since is that I allowed myself to be compromised by the nefarious deeds of a maniacal sociopath and his under-bosses. I denied reality and distanced myself from my family because I believed. This is a must read for those who are searching for true martial arts as well as a warning for parents who are looking for an activity for their children. Stay Away from Oom Yung Doe.

Joe Smith unveils the entire charade in his service with the Moo; reality is twisted and a person's life is degraded to the point of unconditional surrender to an evil pimp. Through Joe Smith's experiences, the only way out is for someone to simultaneously embrace the truth with the conscious mind and the heart.

Chris Carreon, December 2006

ISBN 1412085144-4

9 781412 085144

Made in the USA
Lexington, KY
01 October 2011